T0326248

Late Imperial Culture

Late Imperial Culture

Edited by

ROMÁN DE LA CAMPA
E. ANN KAPLAN
MICHAEL SPRINKER

VERSO

London · New York

First published by Verso 1995
© this collection Verso 1995
© individual contributions the contributors 1995
All rights reserved

Verso
UK: 6 Meard Street, London W1V 3HR
USA: 20 Jay St, Suite 1010, Brooklyn, NY 11201

Verso is the imprint of New Left Books

ISBN: 978-1-85984-050-4

British Library Cataloguing in Publication Data
A catalogue record for this book is available from the British Library

Library of Congress Cataloging-in-Publication Data
Late imperial culture / edited by Román de la Campa, E. Ann Kaplan,
  Michael Sprinker.
      p.   cm.
  Includes bibliographical references and index.
  ISBN: 978-1-85984-050-4
  1. Imperialism in literature. 2. Decolonization in literature.
  3. Politics and literature. 4. Arts and society. 5. Nationalism
  and art. I. De la Campa, Román. II. Kaplan, E. Ann.
  III. Sprinker, Michael.
  PN56.I465L38 1995
  809'.93358—dc20   94–44394
                                                              CIP

Contents

Acknowledgements

In assembling this volume, the editors incurred numerous obligations to individuals and institutions. Several of the papers collected here were first delivered as lectures in the Humanities Institute at Stony Brook. We are grateful to Richard Kramer, Dean of Humanities and Fine Arts, Tilden Edelstein, former Provost, and Bryce Hool, Deputy Provost of the University at Stony Brook, for their financial support of the institute's activities. Two generations of the institute's staff provided indispensable material contributions and unfailing good cheer. Our profound gratitude goes to Marilyn Huether, secretary in the Humanities Institute, to Katie Clifford, Michael Hill, and Claudia Montilla, graduate assistants during 1992–93, and to Gregory Laugero, Chip Rhodes, and Shailja Sharma, graduate assistants during 1993–94.

Introduction
Michael Sprinker

'But the wars they think they're fighting were over long ago.'

Billy Bragg

The last decade has seen an extraordinary outpouring of writing on the cultural legacies of European imperialism. Edward Said's *Culture and Imperialism* (1993) – a sequel to his massively influential *Orientalism* (1978) – represents, in this sense, less the opening of a new research area than a summing up of much that has been percolating through the striated fields of the human sciences generally, and cultural studies in particular. One could point, for example, to Patrick Brantlinger's *Rule of Darkness* (1988), or to some of the Essex conferences on the sociology of literature held during the 1980s, or more recently to collections of essays and interviews by Gayatri Spivak, to articles by Benita Parry and Homi Bhabha, even to occasional pieces by Fredric Jameson and Terry Eagleton: all evidence the widely recognized need to come to terms with imperialism as a phenomenon that continues to dominate, often in occult ways, our understanding of culture both theoretically and empirically.[1] That much of this work is uneven in quality is only to be expected in a new and burgeoning field. But one aspect of it that is perhaps surprising, given all one hears these days about a 'return to history' in literary and cultural studies, is the comparative neglect of any, even provisional, periodization of imperialism itself. The consequences for understanding the real effects wrought by the European colonial empires have been far from negligible, and most often quite damaging.

1

In choosing the theme of 'late imperial culture' to encompass the essays included in the present collection, we have, in the first instance, situated them inside a determinate temporality. Most commentators in this area would probably agree that the era of formal imperialism has definitively ended, at the same time insisting that the long-term consequences of Europe's economic and political domination of the globe since the early modern period continue to haunt the contemporary world. While largely ignoring the origins of this view in the debates of the Second and Third International, recent commentators have unknowingly tended to affirm the Leninist position that imperialism has in fact consolidated its power in the wake of decolonization.[2] The essays printed here take both sides of this equation as read: imperial culture persists, even as it has moved into a new phase. To recall a famous observation from Gramsci's *Prison Notebooks*: 'The crisis consists precisely in the fact that the old is dying and the new cannot be born; in this interregnum a great variety of morbid symptoms appear.'[3] Not all the 'symptoms' examined by our authors are 'morbid,' of course, but there is a reasonable consensus among them that the cultural contradictions of Europe's imperial legacy have been acutely sharpened in the current conjuncture. Why should this be so, and what warrants can be adduced for claiming that the hour of imperial culture is determinately 'late'?

European imperialism commenced in the fifteenth century with the attempt by the Iberian monarchical states to break the combined Venetian and Muslim monopoly in the Asian luxury goods trade. The principal events in that story are well enough known not to require rehearsal here. But in much of the talk generated on this topic within cultural studies the specificity of early imperialism's historical dynamic has been all but obliterated.

When asked upon landing in Calicut, 'What brought you here?' a member of da Gama's crew is said to have replied, 'We seek Christians and Spices.'[4] This begins to explain why the Portuguese had pushed ever further down the West African coast and finally around the Cape of Good Hope during the fifteenth century, just as it partly accounts for Spain's exploratory voyages and colonization into the Western hemisphere and beyond, immediately in Portugal's wake. Proselytizing and mercantile expansion – the Iberian monarchies established their dominance over the peninsula by prosecuting the one, as they expanded their fiscal basis by vigorously pursuing the other. Omitted from the conventional narrative, however, is the complex intercalation

of domestic with international (namely, principally European) economic and political crisis that created conditions necessitating these
nations' exploitation of external resources.

Portugal's initial thrust into the Atlantic islands and North Africa
was a response to its historic deficit in grain production, as well as a
means of resolving the political contradictions induced by the decline in
seigneurial revenues characteristic of feudalism across western Europe.
The success of these early ventures then produced a powerful develop-
mental logic that propelled the entire process forward:

> Once started, the expansion fed on itself. As trade developed gold was
> needed; from the 1450s it came back in considerable quantities from
> West Africa. As sugar production expanded labour was needed; West
> Africa turned out to be a prime source of slaves and these flooded into the
> islands and metropolitan Portugal after 1443.[5]

Not a little impetus was provided by exogenous capital, first Italian
then south German, which financed shipbuilding and the outfitting of
the fleets that the Portuguese crown could scarcely afford. If the papacy
had given its imprimatur to these enterprises in the hope of extending
the boundaries of Christendom, it was Genoese, Florentine, and
Bavarian merchant bankers who recognized the value of rising pepper
prices and sought an alternative to the Levantine supply routes with
their increasingly punitive exactions. Religious conviction could thus
combine easily with commercial prospects to elicit the explanation
given by da Gama's too candid underling.

Spanish imperialism had a somewhat more complex etiology and an
even more checkered itinerary. The union of the kingdoms of Castile
and Aragon through the marriage of Isabel I to Ferdinand II yielded less
a unified nation-state than an unequal partnership of two regions that
were economically and politically at different stages of development.
The flourishing Castilian trade with northern Europe contrasted with
the declining Aragonese position in the Mediterranean. Isabel's realm
was dominated by powerful military orders who lacked any cohesive
political identity and could therefore be subordinated to the Crown
with comparative ease; Aragon, by contrast, possessed a series of
entrenched estates that acted as an insuperable barrier to royal
prerogative. The asymmetry between the two realms was to accelerate
their uneven development after the union. Castilian advance was the
necessary counterweight to Aragonese backwardness – a situation
rendered more acute when Charles V ascended the throne and set the
horizons of the Spanish state northwards. The ruinous wars then set in
train, which were to last more than a century, mortgaged Spain to its

colonial possessions, the New World's precious metals in particular. The fiscal demands of European entanglements continuously ate up the surpluses that the bullion provided, not to mention the latter's distorting effects on the national economy remarked by Braudel and Vilar. The Portuguese had found that the more their mercantilism yielded them in tribute, the more costly it was to maintain their monopoly against a variety of European and non-European rivals who were contesting their pretension to control the Indian Ocean trade. Similarly, the Spanish discovered that their American cornucopia could in the long run have ruinous effects on the domestic economy, despoiling indigenous agriculture (which was sacrificed to the lucrative export of textiles, olive oil, and wine to the colonies) and handicapping domestic manufacture by making Castilian cloth uncompetitive in international (including colonial) markets. Perry Anderson sums up the central paradox of Spanish imperialism: 'The productive potential of Castile was being undermined by the same Empire which was pumping resources into the military apparatus of the State for unprecedented adventures abroad.'[6]

Such were the origins of European imperialism. Each of the early modern states (England, the Netherlands, France) that embarked on the same course as these Iberian pioneers would find in the end that empire was at best a contradictory boon. Among the longest-lived and without doubt the most spectacularly successful of the European maritime empires, the British, very nearly perished early on when French competition (leading to prolonged military conflict) and American rebellion compelled its reorganization root and branch.[7] The Dutch hung on nearly as long as the Iberians, but as Conrad's early fiction attests, their heyday in the South Seas was already a distant memory by the late nineteenth century. After the definitive check delivered by the English in the Napoleonic Wars, French imperialism's economic value was quite marginal, even as its ideological significance from the Second Empire through the Fourth Republic seemed only to increase. The history of European imperialism thus provides a virtual textbook illustration of what Trotsky called 'combined and uneven development.'

These historical coordinates are, one would have thought, propaedeutic to any serious consideration of Europe's colonial and imperial heritage. Aijaz Ahmad's trenchant essay included here shows that this is far from the case today.[8] The 'post' in the much-bruited term 'postcolonial' no longer clearly refers, as it did in standard debates during the 1970s, to the historical fact of colonialism's formal demise.

Rather, it has come to include so many different locations (including the former imperial metropoles) and time periods (it is sometimes said to be coeval with imperialism itself) that virtually anyone, anywhere, anytime might lay claim – or have such claims made on his or her behalf – to 'postcoloniality.'[9] What meaning, then, can the designation 'late' have in the context of a discourse about imperialism that programmatically ignores elementary demands of periodization, never mind political and geographic specificity?

Patently, it cannot be equated with the prefix 'post.' As has already been observed, the culture of imperialism is not a thing of the past – or not only that. Much remains, culturally, economically, politically, from this legacy, not only in more obvious examples like Britain's Raj revival some years ago, but also in the continuing ideological sway exercised by former imperial powers in their erstwhile colonies. While the Pax Americana may have experienced some rocky moments from the 1960s to the present, US imperialism is hardly on the ropes, as the North American Free Trade Agreement (NAFTA), the revivified General Agreement on Tariffs and Trade (GATT), the 1991 Gulf War, and the continuing embargo on Cuba all illustrate. The United States's position in the world economy has steadily eroded since the demise of Bretton Woods during the first Nixon administration, while US military dominance has become, since the disintegration of the Soviet Union and the Warsaw Pact, unchallenged. This military dominance sustains a massive capacity to influence the global economy that neither a more efficient and frugal Japan nor a united Europe (still a distant prospect) can entirely overcome. Certainly, they cannot ignore it.

At the level of culture, the pervasiveness of mass-marketed US products extends apace. In the recently concluded Uruguay Round of the GATT, this cultural power was fiercely contested, as the French held out for continued protections in the entertainment industry. It is difficult to judge such resistance as more than a rearguard action, however, since North American popular culture has long since conquered air waves, movie screens, and television programming around the world. US hegemony in this sphere is evident from Bangkok and Tokyo (where Madonna's *Sex* sold out in hours) to Berlin and Paris (which latter rivals New York and Los Angeles as the premier venue for screening US-made movies). British-originated television shows typically come to the United States via the Public Broadcasting System, making a dent in minority cultural consumption; by contrast, the BBC, Channel Four, and ITV regularly recycle US series in prime time. Watching the Moscow evening news (something one can now do on C-SPAN), one realizes that only the Russian language distinguishes it from its US progenitors, so carefully have broadcast executives in the former Soviet Union aped North American style. In these not so subtle ways, the US imperium is extended over the daily lives of millions.

'Late,' then, can only mean 'old' or 'advanced.' One might be tempted to add 'moribund,' but for one prominent dimension of several of the essays collected here, which reveal contemporary cultural production's extraordinary vitality in the imperial heartlands and around the globe. The contributions by Steven Cagan, May Joseph, Marianna Torgovnick, and Robert Stam all, in different ways, testify to the rich, resilient cultural forms alive in our midst. These are unquestionably the inheritors of European imperialism's long, pathetic history of oppression and exploitation, but they are not merely – or even most importantly – its victims.

In a different register, Rob Nixon and Román de la Campa examine the complex, fraught relations between writing and revolutionary social movements. Nixon focuses on the, in many ways exemplary, career of the South African Bessie Head, particularly on her highly charged, controversial autobiography. Drawing inspiration from Borges, whom he reads against the grain of recent postmodern appropriations of the Argentinian writer's work, de la Campa examines texts on Central American revolutions by Eduardo Galeano, Julio Cortázar, and Joan Didion. He finds in them not merely a simple reflection of historical realities, but a series of highly nuanced interweavings of prior textual representations and the authors' personal encounters with revolutionary episodes in Guatemala, Nicaragua, and El Salvador.

Focusing less on specific texts and authors than on the broad sweep of issues lumped under the much-debated category of 'representation,' Ella Shohat takes up the knotty problems that emerge when one group of people presumes to speak for another. She mobilizes a welter of examples from the history of Hollywood film to indicate the dismal record of Euro-American whites in depicting non-whites and concludes her essay with several cautions concerning the limits of identity politics in redressing this historic imbalance.

Not all the essays included here focus on the contemporary scene. David Glover and Caren Kaplan take up late nineteenth-century British examples in which empire figures directly or in subterranean fashion. Was this moment, too, a late one in the history of imperialism? After 1857 (and with gathering force from the 1880s), the British Empire was in perpetual crisis, challenged by its major imperial rivals on one front, threatened by movements for national liberation on another. It might therefore be said to have entered its final phase when Bram Stoker and

Anna Leonowen were penning their texts. By the time the empire had become an established ideologeme in popular consciousness (and the word 'imperialism' itself had passed into common usage) during the last third of the nineteenth century, not only was it 'old' in the banal sense of having existed in some form for over two and one-half centuries, it was exhibiting signs of that sclerosis which, after two world wars, would leave it feeble and tottering, at the mercy of its more youthful, vigorous successor, the United States. Here again, the requirements of specific periodization impose a more differentiated, nuanced conceptualization of cultural production than is characteristically proposed in recent pronouncements about postcoloniality.

What is it about this moment in the history of Euro-American imperialism that has produced at once an explosion of writing about colony and empire and their aftermath, and an extraordinary amnesia concerning the actual record of their past? On the one hand, the discussion of the culture of empire has emanated principally from departments of literature and language, where training in and thoroughgoing knowledge of history are rarely required. The disciplinary bias of cultural studies has consequently tended to underplay or ignore altogether the complex material determinations of imperialism's history. Researchers investigate the textual realizations of conquest, colonization, and commercial hegemony as if these sprang full-blown from the heads of novelists, essayists, or even colonial administrators. From this perspective, all empires probably do exhibit striking resemblances, so that something like 'colonial discourse theory,' as it has been dubbed, begins to make sense as a research topic.[10]

On the other hand, one cannot omit to mention the quite general delegitimation of Marxism as both a political force and a theoretical resource in metropolitan Europe and the United States. The very category of imperialism itself owes much to debates within the Second and Third Internationals that were then continued in analyses of modern history linking imperialism to the development of capitalism. As Marxism has become increasingly unfashionable among metropolitan intellectuals, the discourse on colony and empire has occulted this historical relationship, rendering the dynamic of imperialism unintelligible save in idealist and ahistorical terms.

But another factor must be mentioned here as well. If we agree that the dominant imperial power now is the United States, then it must be faced that this characterization of US foreign policy has never enjoyed wide acceptance. While the modern European empires ultimately declared themselves such – even if, like Britain, they did so rather late in the day – much of the ideological labor of American intellectuals over the past century has been to obscure or deny outright the designs of US imperialism. A recent symposium conducted in *Radical History Review* is symptomatic in this regard. Entitled 'Imperialism: A Useful Category for Analysis?,' in its pages the various contributors bat back and forth the question of whether it makes historical, analytical sense to look at US history (particularly the current period) through a conceptual optic that classically has entailed 'some form of direct or monopoly control of another nation or of mechanisms of the world economy . . .'.[11] On such a narrow definition of the term, was there ever imperialism in world history? The Roman Empire exercised monopoly control over trade and territory from the Levant across North Africa and into western Europe, but it hardly imposed upon the polities of South and East Asia, even though it traded with them across the Indian Ocean. Nor did it conquer nations; rather, it subdued disparate peoples who exercised different forms of political control over the territories they inhabited. To cite another instance, neither the Portuguese nor the Spanish ever monopolized inter-continental commerce in Asian luxury goods or precious metals (the Portuguese did not even hold much in the way of territorial possessions before the nineteenth-century scramble for Africa bequeathed them large chunks of the West and East African coastal regions). Yet, for a time Portugal handled the lion's share of the pepper imported into Europe, while Spain was a major source for replenishing the continent's bullion supply that was constantly being siphoned off to pay for the spices and cloths purchased in the Mughal Empire and the Middle Kingdom. Were the Iberian states therefore not imperial in the fifteenth and sixteenth centuries?

The model of empire for skeptics about US imperialism is clear enough: Britain's economic dominance in the mid-nineteenth century, when a combination of the world's most advanced productive plant and an effective market monopoly within the sterling area vaulted Manchester, Birmingham, and the City of London into a global economic preeminence that no nation before or since has ever enjoyed. Real imperialism on this account is measured purely by its economic success, so that the Germans, the Italians, and perhaps the French after 1815 (leave aside the poor Danes and the Belgians, whose imperial pretensions were always very small beer) have to be dropped from the club of Europe's imperial powers, leaving only the Dutch and the British as qualifying members. Since the United States never possessed any formal colonies, and since its economic hegemony after Bretton Woods scarcely rivaled the scope and effectiveness of free-trading Britain a century earlier, it necessarily is exempted as well.[12]

Plainly, such a restrictive definition does not govern our title or the essays included in this volume. US imperialism has followed in the footsteps of its European forebears, assuming not a few of their burdens while attempting to outdo their economic gains for the Mother Country. What is aimed at here is a preliminary reconnaissance of the cultural terrain over which this latest, and in many ways most unusual, of the world's historical empires currently ranges. It is much too soon to say whether the United States's imperial trajectory is still on the upswing or in the early stages of a long-term decline. It is certain, however, that any sober reckoning of the current situation will demand careful comparative analysis with the record of those empires that were spawned with the birth of capitalism in early modern Europe. Ignorance on that score at this assuredly late date can only be willful.

Notes

1. Francis Barker et al., *Europe and Its Others*, vols. I and II; Proceedings of the Essex Conference on the Sociology of Literature (Colchester: University of Essex, 1985); Homi K. Bhabha, *The Location of Culture* (New York and London: Routledge, 1994); Terry Eagleton, Fredric Jameson, and Edward W. Said, *Nationalism, Colonialism, and Literature* (Minneapolis: University of Minnesota Press, 1990); Benita Parry, 'Problems in Current Theories of Colonial Discourse,' *Oxford Literary Review*, vol. 91, no. 1–2 (1987); pp. 27–58; Gayatri Chakravorty Spivak, *The Postcolonial Critic* (London and New York: Routledge, 1990) and *Outside in the Teaching Machine* (London and New York: Routledge, 1993).

2. The point is complex and deserves lengthier development than I have space for here. In brief, however, one needs to recall that Lenin (among others who participated in this debate) discriminated carefully between colonialism (a phenomenon prominent in the early, mercantile phase of European imperialism) and what he termed 'the highest stage of capitalism,' i.e., imperialism as an expression of the period of monopoly capitalism, which witnessed a close integration between industrial and finance capital in the major capitalist nation-states. That formal colonialism continued as a dynamic into this period (in the so-called 'scramble for Africa' in the late nineteenth century, for example) does not blunt the fundamental point that capitalism itself, and correlatively its imperial dimensions, entered a new phase at the end of the nineteenth and beginning of the twentieth century. That phase of imperialism, which might now legitimately be termed 'late,' is still very much with us in the era of US global hegemony (about which I shall have more to say further on in this Introduction).

3. Antonio Gramsci, *Selections from the Prison Notebooks*, edited and translated by Quintin Hoare and Geoffrey Nowell Smith (New York: International Publishers, 1971), p. 276.

4. Cited in M. N. Pearson, *The Portuguese in India*, pt. 1, vol. 1 of *The New Cambridge History of India* (Cambridge: Cambridge University Press, 1987), p. 5.

5. Ibid., p. 6.

6. Perry Anderson, *Lineages of the Absolutist State* (London: New Left Books, 1974), p. 73. I have relied heavily in this paragraph on Anderson's capsule account of the growth and demise of Spanish absolutism.

7. See C. A. Bayly, *The Imperial Meridian* (London: Longman, 1989).

8. Just as the early chapters of his much-debated book *In Theory: Classes, Nations, Literatures* (London: Verso, 1992) explain why.

9. See Arif Dirlik's terse formulation: 'A description of a diffuse group of intellectuals and their concerns and orientations [the term "postcolonial"] was to turn by the end of [the 1980s] into a description of a global condition, in which sense it has acquired the status of a new orthodoxy both in cultural criticism and in academic programs' ('The Postcolonial Aura: Third World Criticism in the Age of Global Capitalism,' *Critical Inquiry*, no. 20 [Winter 1994], p. 330). Dirlik's explanation for the apparent hegemony acquired by the term in Western academe rests upon a link between the class position of postcolonial intellectuals themselves and the new configuration of global capitalism that is at once their proximate cause and the very reality their discourse systematically occults: '. . . postcoloniality is designed to *avoid* making sense of the current crisis and, in the process, to cover up the origins of postcolonial intellectuals in a global capitalism of which they are not so much victims as beneficiaries' (ibid., p. 353). Both the *explanandum* (the massive popularity of the term 'postcolonial' among academic intellectuals) and the *explanans* (the class location of postcolonial intellectuals themselves) parallel the account given in the early chapters of Ahmad's *In Theory*.

10. On the tendency of postcolonial critics to turn the material realities of imperial domination into purely discursive constructs, see Ahmad, *In Theory* and Dirlik, 'The Postcolonial Aura.'

11. Bruce Cumings, 'Global Realm With No Limit, Global Realm With No Name,' *Radical History Review*, no. 57 (Fall 1993), p. 46. Cumings is paraphrasing the stipulations of Carl Parrini in the latter's 'The Age of Ultraimperialism,' the lead article in the symposium. Parrini takes his key term from Kautsky, of course, emphasizing inter-capitalist cooperation, rather than irremediable conflict (as Lenin had asserted against Kautsky in 1916).

12. This is slightly unfair. None of the contributors holds that US foreign policy was never imperialist; the debate concerns whether the concept continues to be a useful one and, if not, when it ceases to capture the core features of the US capitalist dynamic. One can agree with Parrini that the invocation of the term 'imperialism' for purely moralistic purposes is analytically unhelpful (although it retains considerable ideological utility in organizing domestic resistance and solidarity movements), while wondering how much sense it makes to deny that US policy towards Nicaragua during the 1980s was imperialist. The ghost of William Appleman Williams, which hovers over this entire debate, must be twitching a bit in response to the jesuitical distinctions made by some of his acolytes.

Postcolonialism: What's in a Name?
Aijaz Ahmad

When we encounter the term 'postcolonialism' these days – or, for that matter, the term 'the postcolonial' which designates certain kinds of *writers*; not to speak of the recently anointed term 'postcoloniality' as the condition of our times – we think primarily of *cultural* theory as it is enunciated in the field of literature for the most part, from which, then, it has wandered into the domain of certain deconstructive kinds of history writing. These particular deployments are, I think, not much more than a decade old, and their striking feature is that they utterly suppress the memory of some earlier debates which had also posed the question of postcolonialism, not in cultural theory but in political theory, and in relation not to literary production but to the class character and social projects of states and regimes that had arisen in Asia and Africa in the wake of decolonization. The shifts that have taken place in the modes of the deployment of this term – from its birth in the early 1970s to its resurrection in the late 1980s – can reveal a great deal about the shifts that have occurred in the political climate, hence in the politics of theory in general. I shall return to the issue of the literary theory of postcoloniality in a separate text. For the present, I want to recall an earlier debate in which I too participated – the immediate context of that debate, its contours, the very grain of its politics – which today's culturalism suppresses.

I

In the summer of 1972, some eight months after Richard Nixon had walked out to the helipad of his 'winter White House' in San Clemente to despatch Zulfikar Ali Bhutto to Pakistan so that the latter could take over as Martial Law Administrator and President of what was left of that country, *New Left Review* carried an article by Hamza Alavi, entitled 'The State in Postcolonial Societies: Pakistan and Bangladesh.'[1] The independent state of Bangladesh was then less than a year old. Those nine months of 1971 – between March 25, when the Pakistan Army began its slaughter of East Bengalis, and mid-December, when the Indian Army put an end to the process of radicalization in that region – had been, for politically committed intellectuals like ourselves, very traumatic, even though we had not suffered in any direct way. We had registered our dissent, offered our solidarity, individually and in small groups, as best we could, while regimes of cruelty unfolded. Now, some months later, the time had come to try and think our thoughts somewhat more accurately, which is to say more theoretically. The debate Alavi initiated on the nature of the postcolonial state soon assumed international dimensions. Sherry Girling responded directly in 1973, Marjorie Pompermeyer and Immanuel Wallerstein more broadly the same year.[2] John Saul published his response, focusing on the case of Tanzania, in the *Socialist Register* in 1974;[3] Colin Leys took into consideration the larger perspective of the general African experience, in *Review of African Political Economy*, in 1976; Ziemann and Lanzendörfer responded to all this, and much besides, in the *Socialist Register* of 1977. I returned to this debate, in print at least, much later, in 1985,[4] but still somewhat before the term 'postcolonial' had been appropriated in the more aggrandizing kinds of *Kulturkritik* and deconstructionist historiography.

What were the shapes of history, and the attendant theoretical impasse, that Hamza Alavi had sought to rethink? There was, first, the momentous event: the creation of Bangladesh – a re-partitioning of an already partitioned subcontinent; the first partition having come in the moment of decolonization itself, the second, roughly a quarter-century later, brought about by indigenous armies of postcolonial, sovereign states marching against indigenous populations and against each other, not in a proxy war fought in the service of imperialism but in wars of occupation and intra-national conflict in the service of the respective states themselves. There had been a great many secessionist movements throughout Asia and Africa since decolonization; the Bangladeshi one had the peculiarity not only that it had succeeded, thanks to the Indian intervention, but also that it took the *majority* of Pakistanis out of Pakistan, led by the Awami League, which had won a distinct parliamentary majority in the whole of Pakistan before the assaults began. Why had the Pakistani state preferred to let go of the majority of the population it claimed to represent, instead of relinquishing the power of its military–bureaucratic apparatus in accordance with the electoral verdict of December 1970? And why had Bhutto, representing the civilian majority in West Pakistan, obeyed the army? What was the structural imperative of the state that led to such an outcome? What sort of bourgeoisie did Pakistan have that it did not move to save the extent of its national market from the bloody adventures of the Pakistan Army, considering that Mujibur Rehman, the newly elected prime minister, had made it abundantly clear that he wanted to form a government in Islamabad, so as to supervise the political apparatus of the whole of the Pakistani state, rather than in Dacca, to rule East Bengal alone? In the first instance, Alavi had sought to explain this configuration.

But Pakistan was by no means the only state arising out of decolonization that was dominated by the military–bureaucratic apparatus rather than a bourgeois parliament. What were the mutual articulations of class forces, and what were the structural relations between classes and state apparatuses, which had led to this fairly generalized outcome? Alavi was sober enough not to think of decolonization as a sham, so that the more extreme ideas centered on the concept of '*neo*colonialism' were simply not available to him, even though the imperialist character of the world system was obvious enough. Furthermore, Alavi had little use for those Maoist kinds of theorization which took recourse to such formulae as 'semi-colonial, semi-feudal,' as if land, labour and production had not been fundamentally commodified during the colonial period and as if the onset of independence had made no substantial difference to either the state apparatus or the alliance of the colonizers and the so-called 'feudal' classes. As for the social structure of production relations, Alavi believed that commodification was a necessary consequence wherever colonial capital had taken hold in any considerable degree, so that the regimes that arose out of decolonization were essentially regimes of backward capital, and their incorporation into the global imperialist system could not but intensify the commodity form and the social relations arising necessarily out of that form. Meanwhile, he thought of decolonization, quite rightly, as an event of historic proportions, which had inaugurated fundamental shifts in the alignment of classes and structures of governance. What were these shifts? More specifically, why had decolonization led not to the rise of bourgeois republics throughout Asia and Africa, as problematics of the nation-state might suggest, but to a more generalized dominance of the military– bureaucratic apparatus, while the parliamentary form was stable only in very few instances, such as India?[5] On this issue, then, Alavi's theoretical intervention went far beyond the experience of Pakistan and sought to conceptualize the postcolonial state as such.

But then, quite aside from the experience in Pakistan and elsewhere, there was also the issue of theory. The term 'postcolonial' in Alavi's formulations arose, in the first instance, to address – and redress – the insufficiencies – indeed, inaccuracies – of terms such as 'neocolonial,' 'semi-colonial,' 'semi-feudal' etc. The lazy habit of 'posting' that became so common after poststructuralism had been commodified in the Anglo-American academy was simply not the issue. The 'post' in postcolonialism signified for Alavi the moment of a fundamental rupture that came with decolonization and therefore led to equally fundamental but also equally determinate rearticulations in the alignment of class forces and state apparatuses that now ensued on the national as well as global scales. To the specificities of structural rearticulation, as Alavi theorized them, I shall return presently. Let me emphasize, though, that the sort of inflation that has come about in literary theory with the publication of such books as *The Empire Writes Back* were also not available at the time. It has now become quite common to push the moment of postcolonialism back to the American Revolution, the decolonization of Latin America, the founding of Australia; indeed, according to some, postcolonialism begins with colonialism itself, with the earliest practices of resistance, perhaps as early as 1492.[6] The object of analysis for Alavi, and for those who participated in those debates, was more delimited: the independent states that arose out of the near-complete dissolution of the European colonial empires in Asia and Africa, during roughly the first fifteen years after the Second World War.

The problem of beginning a theoretical reflection was not exhausted, however, simply by taking up the issue of the state only and not that hold-all thing that we now call 'culture'; or by fixing a rather brief historical phase for investigation; or by distinguishing the postcolonial from the neocolonial, semi-colonial, etc. That was in fact the smaller part of the problem. The problem was the status of the Marxist theory of the state as participants in the debate respectively understood it. On one fundamental premiss most participants – certainly Alavi and myself – could readily agree: namely, that the explanatory power of classical Marxism does not reside in some transhistorical ability to provide an already existing conceptual apparatus to make manifest the meaning of historical events as they unfold long after the founding theoretical positions of classical Marxism were first assembled; the explanatory power resides, rather, in the claim that Marxist concepts possess sufficient systemic coherence and are sufficiently grounded in the historical process itself to be able to generate new concepts through self-criticism and through realignment with new events and knowledges that arise within the historical process. One could recall the quasi-Hegelian language of Sartre and repeat that the claim of Marxist knowledge is not that it constitutes a completed form of knowledge or yields a total understanding of the world, but that it is always in the unfinished and unfinishable process of totalizing itself and surpassing itself, so that its knowledge of the world is, by its very nature, at any given moment, incomplete. One could go farther than Sartre, in fact, and say that it is in the very structure of Marxist knowledge that every major event in history, every emergence of major new agents of history, every fundamental reorganization in the field of historical forces, must *necessarily* produce a crisis in the very structure of Marxist knowledge – a crisis that can only be resolved by introducing fundamental new departures within this structure. Decolonization was such an event, and it required theoretical realignment in the very framework of the existing theory of the state.

On all this one could readily agree. But implicit in that was another agreement: namely, that as one undertook the necessary surpassing, one could not simply bypass or take easy recourse to an infinite regress of heterogeneities; one had to *go through* the Marxist categories, in order to arrive on the other side, hoping that one had produced a knowledge that was not lesser but richer. One had to take stock, as a first step, of what one had at hand, as theoretical legacy and as historical experience. It was at this point of actual stock-taking – of theory and of history – that the most productive disagreements began. And, in relation to theory, disagreements began with the respective understandings of the theory of the state itself, in its classical form, before we arrived at the theory of the postcolonial state as such.

II

As I turn to the substance of Alavi's argument and my disagreements with some of his propositions, let me start by saying that his own thinking, rigorous as it was in many respects, was nevertheless marked by the debate on the theory of the state as this was then taking place between the late Ralph Miliband and Nicos Poulantzas. From each, he took a part of the argument about the capitalist state; but from each he took only that part that was the most useful for him as he set out to construct his own distinctive theory of the postcolonial state out of these disparate elements. According to Alavi, then, there were two main variants of the theory of the state in classical Marxism. Following Miliband, he proposed that the classical theory of the state was already given in the *Communist Manifesto*, what Miliband had called the *instrumentalist theory* – that is to say, in the language of the *Communist Manifesto*, the capitalist state was not much more than a managing committee for the affairs of the *whole* of the bourgeoisie. In other words, the state was, on this reading of classical Marxism, an instrument of the bourgeoisie, and what little autonomous leverage it had derived from the fact that it had to articulate the relatively distinct interests of the different fractions of this one class. But then, Alavi also took from Poulantzas the category of the *exceptional* state, especially the Bonapartist state but implicitly also dictatorship and fascism, which was *relatively autonomous* of the bourgeois class that was in normal circumstances the ruling class. Derived partly from Miliband and partly from Poulantzas, Alavi's understanding of the Marxist theory of the capitalist state, in short, was that it was in normal circumstances an instrument of the bourgeoisie, with little leverage of its own, while its *exceptional* form, the Bonapartist for example, gave it, provisionally, much relative autonomy.

This too was problematic. For, in taking up only parts of their arguments to integrate into his own formulations, Alavi had ignored the larger part of the arguments of each of his interlocutors. Miliband was then moving closer to left laborism, and the main burden of his argument was that the instrumentalist character of the Marxist theory of the capitalist state, developed as it was before the invention of the parliamentary form as the *normal* form of bourgeois rule, was quite inadequate for theorizing the modern capitalist state, which was *always* autonomous of the economically dominant class; to Miliband's credit, it must be said that he stopped far short of what we were to hear later from Laclau and others. But the more serious omission on Alavi's part was that he completely ignored the argument Poulantzas had put forth about the classical theory itself, even before his debate with Miliband began. Two elements of Poulantzas's position are worth recalling. First, he argued that Marx never formulated a systematic theory of the capitalist state, and that the elements of Marx's thought that give us the surest entry into such a theory are contained not in the polemical phrases of the *Communist Manifesto* but in the more mature theoretical writings, such as *Capital*, and especially in the historical writings. Poulantzas went on then to argue that far from thinking of it as the instrument of any one class, Marx had thought of the state in capitalist society as *a field of force* over which all classes of society struggled for dominance, so that the composition of the state at any given time reflected the balance of contending forces at that time; the making of the welfare state in postwar Europe, for example, could not be theorized according to this logic, as an action of the liberal bourgeoisie, whose *instrument* the state was supposed to have been, but had to be theorized as a *presence* of the working class within the state in the organizational form of the trade union and the theoretical and political form of social democracy. This postulation was connected, further, with the strict distinction Poulantzas maintained between the *abstract* level of theorization implied in the concept of 'mode of production' and the *concrete* level of theorization involved in the analyses of actually existing social formations. On the abstract level, which rested on the theoretically necessary assumption of a two-class schema of capitalism, the state *had* to be the state of the capitalist class only. But the concretely existing social formations, he argued, were (a) multi-class structures and (b) included not only the capitalist mode in the proper sense but also effective residuals of non-capitalist modes. An actually existing capitalist society was (a) one which included several classes other than the polar classes of bourgeoisie and proletariat, and (b) one in which capitalism was dominant over other modes but not universalized. This implied, then, that it was *normal* for an actually existing capitalist state (a) to be under the dominance of the bourgeoisie, but (b) nevertheless to reflect in its very structure and action the balance of class forces existing in society, and (c) to articulate the dominance of capital with the existence and effectivity of class forces drawn from those modes of production other than capitalism that were effectively present in the given society. The 'exceptional' state, according to Poulantzas, arose when this alignment between the state and the balance of class forces in civil society, hence the character of the state as a field of contention for such forces, broke down. Poulantzas did not directly theorize about the states of backward capital in the decolonized zones, but the implication clearly is that the presence of 'feudal' power in such states, alongside bourgeois power, was in itself quite reconcilable with the classical theory of Marxism and was indeed a feature of the capitalist state at earlier phases of its development, even in what are now the zones of advanced capital.

Meanwhile, Poulantzas had also argued that one of the fundamental functions of the modern state was the reproduction and redistribution of social agents for the various apparatuses of society and state, so that the ones who were assigned the task of staffing the state apparatuses played a significant role in articulating the class conduct of the state. It was with reference to this process of the location of particular human agents in apparatuses of the state that Poulantzas had emphasized the great importance of what he called the 'new petty bourgeoisie.' In turn, the enhanced role of the professional and state-associated petty-bourgeois strata was central to the arguments Poulantzas had put forward about the structural specificity of the modern type of the so-called 'exceptional' state, specifically fascism and dictatorship. In fascism, he argued, the exceptional intensification of the autonomy of the state, in relation to civil society, also meant an exceptionally powerful role for those class fractions that were materially present in the structure of the state as such.

Needless to add, Alavi ignored this part of Poulantzas's argument, and to his own peril, not only because the exercise of trying to combine elements of the otherwise antithetical positions of Miliband and Poulantzas left him with an overly simplified and largely inaccurate idea of the classical theory, but also because it led him to emphasize too exclusively, in a more or less functionalist manner, the *apparatus* of what he calls the 'military–bureaucratic oligarchy' in the postcolonial state and not the class projects of the professional petty bourgeoisie which have been so central in both the nationalist movements of anticolonialism and in the workings of the postcolonial state. More-over, it is only by conceptualizing the state as a condensation of the balance of class forces in an actually existing society that we can account for the vast differences among the various sovereign states that arose on the morrow of decolonization. Such differences were ex-ampled by the contrasting trajectories of India and Pakistan, respect-ively, as the two states emerged out of the partition of the British colonial empire. Thus, India became a bourgeois republic and a constitutional democracy, with very considerable commitment to independent economic development and a Fabian kind of commitment to (in Nehru's phrase) a 'socialistic pattern of society,' with the Communist Party of India (CPI) emerging as the main opposition party in the parliament after the elections of 1952, precisely because among all the formerly colonized countries India uniquely had the largest, most confident national bourgeoisie as well as the largest, best-organized movements of workers and peasants. The anticolonial movement had itself been premised on this combination, under bourgeois hegemony, which was then reflected in the character of the Indian state in the first phase of its postcolonial development. In

Pakistan, by contrast, parliamentary democracy was never secure, communism never legalized, commitment to independent development never made, precisely because the state that emerged out of Muslim separatism had neither a developed national bourgeoisie nor an organized working class. These were fundamental differences that one could have explained correctly only if one held a theory of the state that viewed *each* capitalist state as a condensation of the balance of class forces in the particular social formation of which it was the state.

Be that as it may. The normal capitalist state in Europe, for Alavi, is an instrument of the bourgeoisie; the exceptional state becomes, for circumstantial reasons, provisionally and relatively autonomous. This normalcy of the capitalist state in Europe arises, for him, from the circumstance that the revolutionary bourgeoisie in Europe stands in irreconcilable conflict with the feudal landowning classes, destroys its property base and dismantles the feudal state machinery, assembling a new bureaucracy under its own dominion as it proceeds to build its own territorially based nation-state; the military is its instrument for domestic control, for securing national frontiers against neighbors, and for territorial expansion and foreign conquest. The 'exceptional' state, such as the Bonapartist or the Bismarckian, even the fascist one, is a provisional deviation from this norm.

This so-called *normal* European state strikes me as an ideal-type, though I must hasten to add that Alavi is hardly the only one who has subscribed to this way of condensing the main contours of Western European history. It is much to be doubted that it was normal for bourgeois classes to arise as ruling classes before there were territorial states to rule, nations to administer, governments to make laws favorable for capitalist accumulation, intellectuals to naturalize the idea of nationhood. Bourgeois–aristocrat alliance, so marked in the British Restoration, was common enough in post-Napoleonic Europe as well, as was the incorporation of the landowning classes into the dominion of capital through capitalization of the ground rent and the *embourgeoisement* of those classes – far more common than the outright liquidation of those classes prior to the emergence of bourgeois rule.

That larger history we shall ignore, so that we may go on to specify just where the *difference* of the postcolonial state, for Alavi, lies as he proceeds to distinguish among three kinds of states: (1) the metropolitan state of the advanced countries, for example the British state inside Britain; (2) the colonial state that the colonizing bourgeoisie establishes in the colony, for example the British colonial state in India; and (3) the postcolonial state as it arises in the former colony after independence, for example the Pakistani or the Tanzanian state.

The metropolitan state inside Europe is marked, Alavi says, by the existence of a distinct ruling class, namely the capitalist class; by the location of this class inside the social formation and in control of the state apparatus; and by the subordination of all other classes, including the landowning class, to the bourgeoisie and its state; it is marked also, therefore, by an independent development in which not only is there proper articulation between departments of industry and between industry and agriculture, but there is also a marked tendency to complete the basic circuits of production and circulation, hence the main process of accumulation, within the national geographical space, which is then supplemented and greatly increased by colonial profit. The colony, by contrast, is marked, first of all, by a ruling class, namely the metropolitan bourgeoisie, that is located nevertheless outside the colony; second, by the existence of a state apparatus that is an instrument not of the indigenous propertied classes but of the externally based ruling class of the metropolitan bourgeoisie; third, and thanks to the highly repressive character of the colonial formation, by the great *overdevelopment* of the state apparatus and great *underdevelopment* of the indigenous propertied classes; fourth, by the relatively low development of the indigenous bourgeoisie and pro-longed power of large-scale landed property under colonial patronage; and, fifth, by a fundamental antagonism between the military–bureaucratic apparatus, as an instrument of the metropolitan ruling class, and the indigenous society, which the military–bureaucratic apparatus administers and represses on behalf of the colonizers. What happens, then, to this structure of colonial society after independence?

Alavi's specifications of the postcolonial state as a distinct type of capitalist state are structured along the axis of two basic postulates. The first is his proposition that the overdeveloped state apparatus, dominated by the repressive and administrative organs, hence by the military–bureaucratic oligarchy, survives intact into the postcolonial period, over and above the weakly developed indigenous bourgeoisie and the structurally backward class of landowners. There is thus a structural tendency for the state to dominate the whole of civil society, including its propertied classes. Supplementing this is his second proposition, to the effect that unlike either the colonizing state or the colony itself, postcolonial society is marked by the existence of not one but three ruling classes: namely, the metropolitan bourgeoisie, the indigenous bourgeoisie, and the landowners, none of which can rule by itself and which therefore coexist in a relationship of competitive collaboration, so that the postcolonial state, dominated by the

military–bureaucratic oligarchy, emerges as the exceptionally autonomous agent for mediating and accommodating the competing interests
of the respective ruling classes. This mediating role, and the space of
autonomy that it entails, only serves to accentuate the power of the
state apparatus in relation to the civil society that it dominates; indeed,
we might say, pushing Alavi's argument even further, that this
structural feature inhibits the proper constitution of civil society as
such, which finds it at least very difficult to emerge from under the
weight of what Marx once called 'the state vermin.' The continuing
presence of the metropolitan bourgeoisie *within* the newly independent
state is posited here not as a form of neocolonialism – that is to say,
continuation of colonialism in disguised form – but as a necessary
effect of the subordinated assimilation of the weaker capitalist
economies into the very structure of imperialism. The fundamental
departure from colonialism is signified, meanwhile, by the elevation of
the indigenous bourgeoisie and the landowners as ruling classes, which
position they had hitherto not occupied. The dominance of the
military–bureaucratic apparatus in the postcolony is surely premissed
on its prior overdevelopment during the colonial period, *vis-à-vis* the
indigenous propertied classes, but this dominance is now structurally
of a different order, in the sense that the apparatus is no longer simply
the instrument of the metropolitan bourgeoisie, which must now
accommodate itself to the domestic preeminence of this apparatus; and
it now dominates the indigenous propertied classes not because it
represents colonial authority over the indigenous society, but because
those classes are structurally weak while the state apparatus is much
more developed, and because those classes must negotiate with the
metropolitan bourgeoisie *through* the postcolonial state.

There is no gainsaying the fact that Alavi's is a powerful formulation,
and powerful especially in explaining what it had set out to explain,
namely, those structural features of the Pakistani state that accounted
for the dominance of the military–bureaucratic apparatus and which
not only eroded the possibility of building the supremacy of
parliamentary organs but had also contributed immeasurably to the
breakdown of the territorial state as such. Where, then, could one
dissent from so powerful an argument?[7]

III

First, the level of Alavi's generalization is much too sweeping. Some
elements of his argument are doubtless applicable far beyond Pakistan,

but the overall structure of the argument is not. He nevertheless presents the argument in such a way that it stakes a claim to being a general theory of the postcolonial state, while the case of Pakistan appears to be intended only as an illustration of a general process. This suggests that colonialism produced analogous structures of class forces and similar articulations of class and state apparatuses wherever it established its dominion, and that such structures and articulations were fundamentally different in countries that were not colonized. Both suggestions would seem at the least very excessive. Alavi's own purposes would have been better served if, in the very first instance, he had sought to construct a more flexible *typology* of postcolonial state forms instead of building so tight an argument structured singularly around the axis of the military–bureaucratic apparatus arising out of the colonial state and arbitrating the interests of the various ruling classes in the postcolonial phase. To give but one instance, the predominance of the military–bureaucratic apparatus in postcolonial Algeria arose not out of the French colonial state, which was effectively destroyed, but out of the army of liberation; direct control of this apparatus over the postcolonial economy was premissed, meanwhile, as much on the centralization of state power in the Nasserist fashion as it was on the fact that large-scale properties of the departed *colons* were taken over by the state itself.

The contrast between Pakistan and India is also instructive. The praisesongs for Indian democracy, which we hear from so many quarters, often neglect the enormous power of the bureaucracy there; and the roots of this bureaucratic power certainly go back to its genesis during the colonial period. But Alavi's characterization of politicians as middlemen who merely serve to propagate the policies set by the bureaucracy among the populace at large, and his further characterization of the parliamentary system as a mere façade that the military–bureaucratic oligarchy uses for perpetuating its own rule, is misleading in the Indian case on several counts. First, policies in India as the postcolonial state was first assembled after independence were not set primarily by the bureaucracy, and neither Nehru nor Patel could be considered a mere middleman. In the years when Nehru's power was secure – between 1952 and 1960, let us say – policies flowed much more from his office, from the parliament that he dominated, and from the bureaucrats he either handpicked or simply introduced into the policy-making institutions. All in all, the Congress Party itself has been a powerful enough *political* bureaucracy, and the Indian bourgeoisie has been strong enough to keep the civil bureaucracy more or less on leash; the military apparatus in India, no matter how large and no matter how great a share of the national surplus it consumes, has never been anywhere near the ruling institution that its counterpart in Pakistan has been.

But Alavi's insistence on the colonial origins of these apparatuses, and on their further elaboration in the postcolonial period, as mediators of the competing interests of the three distinct ruling classes, raises a much larger question about countries that were not colonized. The striking fact is that in India, which was colonized, and in Turkey, which was not, the middle decades of the nineteenth century witnessed the erection of remarkably similar institutions, apparatuses and class clusters: standing armies, civil bureaucracies, civil and criminal codes of the bourgeois type, laws of commerce and contract along European lines, the institution of private property in land, dependent industrialization, and so on. From the destruction of the janissaries in 1826, through the *tanzimat*, right up to and through the Kemalist regime, we witness in Turkey the elaboration of a massive state apparatus, overwhelming in relation to a rudimentary civil society. None of this has to do with postcoloniality. In Egypt, the construction of that type of state begins in the days of Muhammed Ali, in opposition to colonial incursions; passes through the cooperation between Khedive Ismael and the imperialist capital, then the Occupation of 1882 and the semicolonial status of the country, punctuated by the rise of a bourgeoisie based on the export of cotton; passes then through formal independence in 1923, and the continued division of power between the colonial authority, the Palace and the Wafd; finally culminating in the Nasserist military–bureaucratic apparatus, which arose as much from the traumas of the war of 1948 as from the need to arrest the growth of the Ikhwan on the right, the Communists on the left, and which was then vastly strengthened after the nationalization of the Suez Canal. Which of these moments does one privilege, and in what sense is the Nasserist military–bureaucratic state apparatus uniquely postcolonial?

Nor is the question of class and its articulation with the state apparatus quite so straightforward. With regard to Pakistan, Alavi offers a superb summation of the relationships between agrarian property and membership in the state apparatus. In his general theory, however, he distinguishes too sharply between the military–bureaucratic oligarchy on the one hand, and the three ruling classes of postcolonial society on the other. Whether in the Egypt of Muhammed Ali or the Turkey of the *tanzimat*, or even the one attempt at bourgeois revolution in Asia that actually succeeded, namely Japan under the stewardship initially of the Meiji, we find reforming and modernizing fractions arising from inside the traditional landowning classes who seek to build powerful state apparatuses so as to initiate a process of capitalist development as a project *against* colonial encroachment. In the initial phase of assembling the bourgeois state, membership in the upper layers of the military–bureaucratic apparatus almost always presumed prior membership in the upper layers of the traditional propertied classes; only at much later stages, when the apparatus as such was already in place, and when its expansion was greatly accelerated, mainly since the 1920s, did this relationship between class and apparatus get modified and the new professional petty bourgeoisie, arising from lower strata of property, begin to move sharply up the bureaucratic scale. This happened, in the larger countries such as India or Egypt, as much in the colonial setting as in the noncolonial one – but in Japan, where the breakthrough to industrial capitalism came rapidly, the pattern was, again, very different.

Two more points before I draw some conclusions. One is that the genetic view of the postcolonial state, which traces the apparatus back to its origins in the colonial state, has its limits. When Pakistan came into being, it had no navy, hardly an air force to speak of, and only a handful of army officers on or above the rank of lieutenant-colonel; by 1971, when the operation in Bangladesh came, it had over two hundred thousand men in uniform, and an air force that was not only flying the most sophisticated Western aircraft but was also confident that it could supply an army fighting a war of occupation two thousand miles away. In the event, the confidence proved to be illusory when the Indian military machine went into action, but the point I am making is that what mattered was not the *origin* of the military–bureaucratic apparatuses during the colonial period but their fundamental restructuring and vast elaboration in the postcolonial period itself. As time passes, decade by decade, those colonial backgrounds become more remote.

The last point I want to make in this chain of differences from Alavi's otherwise brilliant exposition is that the military–bureaucratic apparatuses of the postcolonial state display very different patterns of relationship with the metropolitan bourgeoisie, in different countries and at different stages of their evolution, thanks to the differential conditions that were internal to the respective countries but thanks also to the way power configurations in them were articulated with the prevailing global situation. It is striking, for example, that a theorisation of the 'postcolonial state' fails to take into consideration the sizable fact of the Soviet Union and the power it exerted on the global scene at that time, as an alternative pole of attraction *against* the metropolitan bourgeoisie. The turn of the Indian state toward non-alignment was not simply a hoax; it was a genuine attempt to gain a considerable degree of autonomy from the metropolitan bourgeoisie by establishing extensive economic and military relations with the Soviet bloc. Up to the time of Alavi's writing, the military apparatus of India was more closely aligned with the Warsaw Pact countries than with NATO. Internally, at the moment of independence, India commanded a large reserve of hard currency which underwrote its considerable independence from imperialist finance capital. In turn, such reserves underwrote the Nehruvian visions of independent development and nonalignment in the midst of the Cold War. There was, in other words, a certain correspondence between financial capacity and nationalist ideology. This, combined with the supremacy of the political bureau-cracy of the Congress Party over the military–bureaucratic apparatus of the services, meant that the metropolitan bourgeoisie had a very limited role in India, certainly until after the Gailbraith ambassador-ship and the Sino-Indian War of 1962, but also in some respects well beyond that point. Only since 1989 has the full integration of India into the military and economic structures of imperialism, in a fully subordinated position, begun, and this process of full subordination needs to be understood not only with reference to the evolution of class politics in India *since* decolonization but also in connection with the stagnation and subsequent demise of the system of the Comecon countries, which had previously underwritten Indian non-alignment and relative independence from imperialism. Meanwhile, this far-reaching adjustment with imperialism has been initiated not by the military–bureaucratic apparatus itself but by the political leadership and the upper layers of the bourgeoisie, with the full consent of the majority of the commercial and professional middle strata.

A plausible argument could be made that, thanks to its territorial extent, demographic size and level of capitalist development on the eve of decolonization, India represents in many respects an exceptional case. However, even if we discount such postrevolutionary states as Vietnam or Cuba, a comparative study with some substantial sense of periodization *since* decolonization, of such diverse countries as Indone-sia and Algeria, Ghana and Egypt, Iran and Libya, would demonstrate that the relationship with the 'metropolitan bourgeoisie' has in a great many cases been volatile and has depended, from one phase to another, more on the political character of a given regime than on some stable military–bureaucratic apparatus that keeps on mediating relations among the three mutually discrete ruling classes.

IV

Let me conclude this part of my argument. The point Alavi makes about the overdevelopment of the repressive and administrative apparatuses of the state, relative to the development of classes and of civil society as a whole, is a very important one. So is his emphasis on the historic shift that occurs in the moment of decolonization, from the dominance of an externally based ruling class during the colonial period, to the more complex distribution of power between the metropolitan bourgeoisie and the indigenous propertied classes after decolonization. Not the least important of his propositions is that in the case of politically independent but structurally imperialized formations, the state apparatus occupies a decisive and relatively autonomous position, not only because of its own overdevelopment relative to classes in civil society but also, more significantly, because it is through the agencies of this state that the interests of the metropolitan and the indigenous propertied classes are articulated and reconciled.

Having said all that, we must also recognize that the effort to organize our thoughts along the singular axis of colonialism/postcolonialism creates more problems than it resolves. We need, rather, to combine this particular distinction with many others in order to produce an integrated knowledge of a particular phase of global history. Societies like the Indian and the Turkish that have histories of large-scale imperial consolidations in their background, large agrarianate systems at their social base, and some rudimentary attempts at industrialization in the latter part of the nineteenth century, may have in some respects more in common as regards their histories of state formation, whether or not they were colonized, than societies that do not share these other attributes, colonialism notwithstanding. Both India and South Africa were colonized, but in very different ways, and even though there is a substantial Indian population in South Africa and Gandhi's own career began there, we cannot abstract some essential 'postcoloniality' from these very different experiences, now that India has been independent for roughly half a century and South Africa has just obtained its first black-majority parliament. The colonial form was by no means the only form of the dominance of European capital, nor did it function in the same way in different parts of the globe, so that as we now look back, it seems more appropriate to think of the many genealogies of this dominance than to speak of an undifferentiated 'postcoloniality.' This plea for historical specificity must be distinguished, however, from the kind of infinite regress of heterogeneity which is the fashion these days. My remarks on the comparative cases of India and Turkey would suggest, for example, that certain historical generalizations *can* be made, not on the basis of 'postcoloniality,' but on the basis of the insertion into the global capitalist system of societies that had many *other* similarities, despite the fact that one was colonized and the other not; the basis for generalization in this instance would be the history not of colonialism but of capital itself.

Two aspects of the debate that Alavi's theorization had provoked need to be summarized here at least in the most general terms. These had to do, first, with a number of very illuminating responses that centered on the empirical side of the African experience and sought to specify what was common and what was not; and, second, with a more theoretical slant which sought to displace the issue of postcolonialism with the more central issue of the typologies of state form that necessarily accompanied peripheral capitalist development itself – 'peripheral capitalism' being understood here not simply as a mode of 'underdevelopment' which would some day get developed, but as deriving its specificity from those structural characteristics which distinguish the working of capital in the periphery of the system from its workings in the metropolitan formations as such. The argument in the latter case was that contemporary state forms had much less to do with their origins in the colonial period and much more to do both with the way capital operates in particular types of social formations and how class forces contend over the political field that is condensed at any given time in the activities of the state. John Saul's arguments about Tanzania, or the more theoretically inclined arguments of Ziemann and Lanzendörfer, were presented as part of this problematic of historical differentiation within the overall typologies of the peripheral capitalist state. I might add that this shift of focus from colonial past to the past and present workings of capital itself, and from some virtually transcendent postcoloniality to existing structures of material power, is all the more essential because the independent states of Asia and Africa are structured now not in the form of a unitary Third World, nor as so many Others of an equally transcendent West, but along the axis of the differential and particularist interests of the ruling classes of each country, and also because contemporary subjectivities within those countries are structured much more in terms of their national particularities than of a shared postcoloniality. Each of the three wars between India and Pakistan; the Iran–Iraq War; the Iraqi occupation of Kuwait; the American invasion of Iraq; and the Saudi funding of the American invasion – all are instances of national bourgeoisies pursuing

their own particularist interests. It is only when the Angel of History
casts its glance back at Asian and African societies from its location in
Europe and North America, or when it flies across the skies of the
world on the wings of postmodern travel and telecommunication, that
those societies look like so many variants of a postcolonial sameness.

Be all that as it may. The merit of that debate was that it had involved
determinate objects of investigation, and the main conceptual term –
postcolonialism – also had, for the participants, a determinate and
more or less shared meaning. This determinacy of meaning of words
and objects of research made it possible, then, for disagreements to be
sharp, precise and fruitful.

V

As the terms 'postcolonial' and 'postcolonial*ism*' resurfaced during the
1980s, this time in literary and cultural theories and in deconstructive
forms of history writing, and as these terms were then conjoined with a
newly coined 'postcoloniali*ty*,' this resurfacing was combined with a
very postmodern kind of erasure: the lapsing from memory of the
history of the term's own origin. One no longer needed to know about
or engage with that earlier debate. This erasure involved a characteristically postmodernist indeterminacy of meaning as well, not in the
philosophical sense of indeterminacy but in the more mundane sense of
unclarity as to what words signify in simple lexical ways. In some
usages, the word 'postcolonial' still attempted a periodization, so as to
refer to that which came after colonialism – though this sense of
periodization was itself used differently by different critics. But the
word 'postcolonial' was to be used increasingly not so much for
periodization as for designating some kinds of literary and literary-
critical writings, and eventually some history writing, as *generically*
postcolonial, while other writings in those same domains of literature,
literary criticism and history writing presumably were not.

This aggrandized sense of the term, as connoting generic definitions
of periods, authors and writings, gathered force through a system of
mutual citations and cross-referencing among a handful of influential
writers and their associates. About Edward Said's sharp – and largely
erroneous – distinction between the so-called 'colonial' and 'postcolonial' intellectuals, I have written elsewhere at some length.[8] Earlier, I
referred to the influential book *The Empire Writes Back*, which

attempts an even more comprehensive global classification of the generically postcolonial. Gayatri Spivak's self-representation within this group is captured nicely in the very title of the collection of her interviews, which is simply called *The Postcolonial Critic* – with notable emphasis on the 'the.' Robert Young, who had until a decade ago devoted himself almost entirely to propagating French poststructuralism in the British Isles, with hardly a thought to spare for the erstwhile colonies, suddenly emerged as a leading theorist of what got called 'postcolonial criticism'. Even though he scarcely uses the term in his *White Mythologies*, the book signifies his first major awakening to the fact of imperialism, but in a world already populated by poststructuralist thought and punctuated by those three masters of postcoloniality – Said, Bhabha and Spivak – to whom he devoted the last three chapters of the book.[9] In turn, Gyan Prakash would then invoke Young's authority – and that of the Subaltern Studies group of historians among whom Gayatri Spivak more or less belongs, and who have been greatly applauded by Edward Said as the quintessential postcolonials in the essay I discussed in my book – in his own squabbles with David Washbrook.[10] In another sort of inflation, Homi Bhabha would cite Jameson's magnificent reading of Conrad's *Lord Jim* in *The Political Unconscious* to declare that Jameson himself was practicing 'postcolonial criticism'[11] – which is probably news to Jameson himself, considering that Bhabha says on the previous page that 'the postcolonial perspective resists the attempt at holistic forms of social explanation.'[12] 'Holistic explanation' (what Jameson more accurately calls 'totality') was, I thought, something Jameson prized particularly. Also, so far as I know, Jameson has never broken with concepts of history and progress, or with the further concept of modes of production, whereas, according to Gyan Prakash, the main virtue of 'postcolonial criticism' is precisely that it has abandoned the nationalist ideas of history and reason as well as the modes-of-production metanarratives of Marxism.

But within the field of literature, we also have, alongside 'postcolonial criticism,' the category of 'postcolonial writing.' This quite different, and in its own way equally common, usage refers simply to literary compositions – plays, poems, fiction – of non-white minorities located in Britain and North America, while efforts are now under way also to designate the contemporary literatures of Asia and Africa as 'postcolonial' and thus to make them available for being read according to the protocols that metropolitan criticism has developed for treating what it calls 'minority literatures.' It is in this sense that

British universities, for example, are currently in the process of institutionalizing that singular pedagogical object which is variously called 'new literatures,' 'emergent literatures' and 'postcolonial literatures.' In some ways, this specific sense of 'postcolonial literature' converges with the categories of 'multiculturalism' and 'minority literature,' even 'Third World literature,' as these categories arose somewhat earlier; but then, it also converges with the term 'Others' as it was used in the phrase 'Europe and its Others.' In at least one of the many nuances, 'postcolonial' is simply a polite way of saying not-white, not-Europe, or perhaps not-Europe-but-inside-Europe. In pedagogical practices, at any rate, the category 'postcolonial literature' functions as a latecoming twin of 'colonial discourse analysis,' while the term 'postcolonial critic' serves here, more or less in a Freudian sense, as the Name of the Father – that is to say, he who authorizes the formal separation, even a play of opposition, between the two entwined categories of 'colonial discourse' and 'postcolonial writing.' I should add that in the case of 'history,' as an academic institution, the word 'postcolonial' is reserved almost exclusively for the Subaltern Studies group, whatever that group at any given point may be.

Let me turn briefly, now, to the matter of the term's spatial and temporal applications. In a widespread usage, 'postcolonial' is the third term that simply follows 'precolonial' and 'colonial' in a tripartite division of history, much as colonialist historiography had once cut up the whole expanse of Indian history into Hindu, Muslim and British periods. 'Postcolonial' in this sense serves as an end-of-history term, just as the 'British period' was once supposed to last forever. But what I find truly alarming about this way of periodizing our history is that 'colonialism' becomes the structuring principle of such narratives, and all that came before it becomes a prehistory of colonialism itself, so that literally thousands of years of contradiction, sociality and creativity come to be gathered up under the singular heading of 'precolonial,' as if those diverse temporalities, those conflicts and principles of structuration, could now only be recalled in relation to the changes that the coming of the East India Company was to cause.

But equally surprising is the frequent *inflation* of the term, both spatially and temporally. In some usages, especially in much writing emanating from Australia, the terms 'colonial' and 'postcolonial' are applied not just to what is generally called the 'Third World,' but also to the United States, Canada, New Zealand, Australia itself, so that what remains to be done, I suppose, is to see how this singular thing, 'postcoloniality,' functions in the United States and in Vietnam, both colonies of Europe at one time or another. In another range of usages, I have seen the term 'postcolonial' applied to Western Europe itself, not only in the sense that the Basque country might have been colonized by Parisians but, more fundamentally, in recognition of the fact that the colonizing powers were European, so that the dissolution of the empires makes *them* postcolonial as well. Then, in a radical extension of meaning, London is said to be the postcolonial city *par excellence*, in the redoubled sense that it once was the capital of the world's largest colonial empire and that, now, large non-white minorities from the former colonies have come to reside within this metropolis.

This inclusion of countries like the United States among the postcolonies, and the fixing of the beginning of postcolonialism with the first moment of colonizing itself, serves of course to extend both the spatial and the temporal scope of postcoloniality quite considerably. But I have seen articles in a great many places, including the special issue of *Social Text* on postcoloniality, which push the use of the term 'colonialism' *back* to such configurations as the Incas, the Ottomans and the Chinese, well before the European colonial empires began; and then bring the term *forward* to cover all kinds of national oppressions, as for example the savagery of the Indonesian government in East Timor.[13] 'Colonialism' thus becomes a transhistorical thing, always present and always in process of dissolution in one part of the world or another, so that everyone gets the privilege, sooner or later, at one time or another, of being colonizer, colonized and postcolonial – sometimes all at once, in the case of Australia for example. This manner of deploying the term has the effect of leveling out all histories so that we are free to take up any of the thousands of available micro-histories, more or less arbitrarily, since they all amount to the same thing, more or less.

The fundamental effect of constructing this globalized trans-historicity of colonialism is to evacuate the very meaning of the word and disperse that meaning so widely that we can no longer speak of determinate histories of determinate structures such as that of the postcolonial state, the role of this state in reformulating the compact between the imperialist and the national capitals, the new but nationally differentiated labor regimes, legislations, cultural complexes, etcetera. Instead, we have a globalized *condition* of postcoloniality that can be *described* by the 'postcolonial critic,' but never fixed as a determinate structure of power against which determinate forms of struggle may be possible outside the domains of discourse and pedagogy.

Notes

1. *New Left Review*, no. 74, July–August 1972; reprinted in Kathleen Gough and Hari P. Sharma, eds., *Imperialism and South Asia* (New York: Monthly Review Press, 1973).

2. Sherry Girling, 'The State in Postcolonial Societies – Pakistan and Bangladesh. Comments on Hamza Alavi,' in *Working Papers on the Capitalist State*, San José, Milan, Berlin, Tokyo 2/1973, pp. 49–51; Majorie Pompermeyer, 'The State and Dependent Development'; and Immanuel Wallerstein, 'Comments on "The State and Dependent Development," ' in ibid., 1/73, pp. 25–7 and 27–8.

3. John Saul, 'The State in Postcolonial Societies,' in *Socialist Register 1974* (London: Merlin Press); reprinted in John Saul, *The State and Revolution in East Africa* (New York: Monthly Review Press, 1979).

4. Colin Leys, 'The "Overdeveloped" Post Colonial State: A Re-evaluation,' in *Review of African Political Economy*, no. 5/January–April 1976, pp. 39–48; W. Ziemann and M. Lanzendörfer, 'The State in Peripheral Societies,' in *Socialist Register 1977* (London: Merlin Press), pp. 143–177; Aijaz Ahmad, 'Class, Nation, and State: Intermediate Classes in Peripheral Societies,' in Dale Johnson, ed., *Middle Classes in Dependent Countries* (Beverly Hills: Sage, 1985).

5. Even for India, Alavi had argued that the parliamentary regime was more or less a 'façade' for bureaucratic decision making, and the politicians, he opined, were mere 'powerbrokers' whose main task was to facilitate negotiations between local or regional elites and the bureaucratic decision makers. There was certainly a grain of truth in this assertion, but, as I shall argue below, this view of the virtual irrelevance of the parliamentary process and the political parties strikes me as greatly exaggerated.

6. See Bill Ashcroft, Gareth Griffiths, and Helen Tiffin, *The Empire Writes Back: Theory and Practice in Post-colonial Literatures* (London and New York: Routledge, 1989), where the great broadening of the scope of application for this term begins early. Thus, already on p. 2 we read: 'We use the term "postcolonial," however, to cover all the culture affected by the imperial process from the moment of colonisation to the present day. So the literatures of African countries, Australia, Bangladesh, Canada . . . Malta, New Zealand . . . South Pacific Island countries . . . are all postcolonial literatures. The literature of the USA should also be placed in this category.'

7. What I offer here is a brief review of a particular debate in which a particular text of Alavi was of central importance. This is by no means a commentary on Alavi's work as such. In several later writings, he clarified and refined his ideas on this score very considerably. See, for example, his 'State and Class under Peripheral Capitalism,' as well as 'The Structure of Peripheral Capitalism' in Hamza Alavi and Teodor Shanin, eds., *Introduction to the Sociology of 'Developing Societies'* (London: Macmillan, 1982).

8. Aijaz Ahmad, *In Theory: Classes, Nations, Literatures* (London: Verso, 1992), pp. 204–11.

9. Robert Young, *White Mythologies: Writing History and the West* (London and New York: Routledge, 1990).

10. Gyan Prakash, 'Postcolonial Criticism and Indian Historiography,' *Social Text*, no. 31/32 (1992), pp. 8–20.

11. Homi Bhabha, *The Location of Culture* (London and New York: Routledge, 1994), pp. 174.

12. Ibid., p. 173.

13. *Social Text*, no. 31/32 (1992). See, in particular, Anne McClintock, 'The Angel of Progress: Pitfalls of the Term Postcolonialism,' who enumerates some of the 'pitfalls' in her opening pages and then goes on to inflate the meaning of the term 'colonialism' so markedly that all territorial aggressions ever undertaken in human history come to fall under this singular dispensation, thus erasing, among other things, the specificity of that capitalist colonialism which the nation-states of Europe uniquely produced.

2

'Getting to Know You': Travel, Gender, and the Politics of Representation in *Anna and the King of Siam* and *The King and I*

Caren Kaplan

'And what will you do, Janet, while I am bargaining for so many tons of flesh and such an assortment of black eyes?'

'I'll be preparing myself to go out as a missionary to preach liberty to them that are enslaved – your harem inmates amongst the rest. I'll get admitted there, and I'll stir up a mutiny; and you, three-tailed bashaw as you are, sir, shall in a trice find yourself fettered amongst our hands . . .'

Charlotte Brontë, *Jane Eyre*

If Europe and North America have gained strength and cultural cohesion through differentiating between a 'West' and a 'non-West,' how has Western feminist discourse operated in the field of cultural differences? Western women have been engaged in both imperialist and anti-imperialist enterprises.[1] Feminism, however, as an articulation of modernity, has an ambivalent relationship to empire. In the struggle to expand the realm of social and political power for women, Western feminism has sometimes relied upon the frontiers and zones of difference established through economic and cultural imperialism. For example, if colonial expansion brought unprecedented economic gain to the metropolitan centers of the West, a corresponding personal and political gain was won for Western women through the liberating activities and challenges of travel. It is worth exploring the costs and benefits of these gains. Celebratory treatment of Western women's travels erases or suppresses resistance to colonial discourse. The question before us, then, is how to read feminist texts that privilege the

33

liberatory and modernizing effects of travel. And what is the impact of this representational legacy of feminist travel discourse on relations between Western and non-Western women today?

When Westerners, particularly Western women who are struggling for social power, define themselves through or against constructed 'others,' the historical relationships between these constructed identities can be lost in romanticized or mystified discourses of modernization, sisterhood, and personal emancipation. Such mystifications obscure the distinctions between different modes of feudalism and modernity or between forms of purdah and slavery, for example, blurring our understanding of Western cultures as well as non-Western cultures. Even the terms 'Western' and 'non-Western' participate in this process of conflation and erasure, posing pure extremes against each other and reinforcing the notion that both 'West' and 'non-West' are unified, consistent categories frozen in configurations of unequal power relations.[2]

We can particularize our knowledge of colonial discourses by resisting the mystique of personal emancipation in Western women's travel discourse when that freedom is established over and against racist, exoticized images of non-Western women and men. Such a critical practice alerts us to the dangers of equating metaphors and conflating symbols rather than deconstructing the cultural production of such metaphors and symbols. A striking example of troubled gender relations within this complex network of colonial discourses occurs in the Twentieth Century Fox film versions of Anna Leonowens's late nineteenth-century travel memoirs, the 1946 *Anna and the King of Siam* and the 1956 musical, *The King and I*.[3] In Leonowens's memoirs and the literary and cinematic versions they engendered, the production of motifs such as sisterhood, harems, and romantic love mask the differences between North American slavery and Siamese concubinage while suppressing the histories of nationalist investments in notions of masculinity, femininity, and female solidarity. The feminist and abolitionist emblems that emerge from Leonowens's texts can tell us a great deal about power relations between men and women in England and the United States during the middle part of the nineteenth century. Such local concerns are displaced to the site of 'Siam' and to the narrative of development, emancipation, and education of Asian women and men. Each subsequent version manages the same displacement for slightly different ends, providing the feminist cultural critic with a map of shifting boundaries in the colonial discourses of race, gender, nationalisms and sexualities. What is lost in such displacements is the cultural specificity and subjectivity of the site or body that is appropriated for the ideological ends of the narrative. Thus, the story of Western women's liberation through travel and crosscultural contact enacts its own form of imperialist objectification through the mystification of historical inequities. The celebrations of individualism, modernization, romance, and sisterhood that mark all the versions of Anna Leonowens's sojourn in Thailand are a crucial part of the reproduction of colonial discourse in modernity, including our supposedly 'postcolonial' moment.

Colonial Harem Discourse and Western Ideologies of Sisterhood

Anna Leonowens's texts represent Western interests and powers at a crucial historical juncture. The mid nineteenth century marked the emergence of a modern women's suffrage movement in both England and the United States as well as the culmination of the abolitionist struggle to end the enslavement of Africans in the West. The intertwined histories of British and US abolitionism and women's suffrage contribute to the colonial discourses of Western women's travel; personal and social emancipation through self-determination could be symbolized as mobility or travel. If mobility and travel came to symbolize the middle-class myth of self-determination, the discourses of abolition and suffrage became deeply imbricated in the literature of Western women travelers. Notions of freedom and sisterhood helped form the ideological lens through which middle-class, Western women travelers viewed the world.

The profound changes that reconfigured the world through which nineteenth-century middle-class women moved included a shift from what Patrick Brantlinger has termed the 'altruism of the antislavery movement to the cynicism of empire building.'[4] Following Eric Williams's contention that British slavery came to an end only when the surplus capital needed to initiate industrialization was accumulated, Brantlinger links abolitionist movements to the early formation of empire. As the British began to see themselves no longer as the slave owners but instead as the 'potential saviors' of Africans, intervention on African territory became a 'moral, religious, and scientific' imperative.[5]

Although Anna Leonowens spent time in South and South-East Asia rather than Africa, the emergent mid-century imperialist ethos that Brantlinger describes can be traced throughout her travel writing. Brantlinger enumerates two key features of British antislavery discourse, both of which typify the narrative strategies of the first 'Mrs Anna' and all the literary and cinematic versions to follow: the revelation of atrocities and the posing of the narrator as the savior of the slaves or victims. Thus, Leonowens's texts combine paternalistic abolitionist sentiments with both nationalist and feminist appeals to a British, 'civilized,' way of life. The cinematic versions heighten the contrast between an enlightened Western civilization that emphasizes fair play and chivalrous 'respect' for women and a sinister, despotic culture that operates through deceit and the ill-treatment of women. The generic revelation of atrocities against women, therefore, transforms women into symbols of political conflict between nations, cultures, and economic interests.

Just as abolitionist sentiments could be appropriated to support the interventionist policies of empire, the suffrage rhetoric of freedom did not ensure equity for all women.[6] Race and class bias on the part of white, middle-class or wealthy suffragists left the majority of women out of the contest for political, economic, and social power even if their names, bodies, and spirits were invoked by the universalizing term 'women.' Leonowens's descriptions of the women in the Nang Harm (royal women's quarters) drew upon the available tropes of women as passive victims. In a critical alliance between abolitionist and feminist rhetoric and ideology, Leonowens fashioned a portrait of British womanhood in marked contrast to Asian women's lives, thereby transforming the conditions and possibilities of Western women's lives and illustrating the helpless dependency of non-Western women. Rather than focus upon patriarchal formations 'at home,' the colonial discourse of 'sisterhood' necessitated a binary opposition between the victims of Eastern despotism and Western womanhood. In particular, as Inderpal Grewal argues, British women not only viewed Asian women as the antithesis of their own desire for emancipation, they required documentation of their perceived superiority:

> By retaining these hierarchies and supporting the masculinist project of colonialism, the suffrage movement was able to evoke nationalist sentiment by making itself distinct from the colonized women even while indicating their exploitation and thus their similarity to them. Racial superiority and national pride, so integral in the habitus of empire, was often used as the basis for the demand for women's votes.[7]

One of the most powerful representational practices used in the process of differentiation between Asian and British women was the construction of the 'oriental' harem – a composite image of indolence and moral degradation that erased most differences between Middle

Eastern and Asian systems of purdah and sex segregation as well as class and ethnic distinctions within the particular cultures that endorsed polygamy. While there is a significant critical literature on the Victorian sexual sensibilities that contributed to the discourse of the colonial harem, less attention has been paid to the links between nationalist, feminist, and abolitionist agendas in the debates that contrasted the British 'home' and the 'oriental harem.'

Leonowens's role as a *producer* of colonial harem discourse hinges on her construction of a form of international sisterhood that legitimates Western intervention. As Grewal points out, women in purdah were viewed by British women as trapped in their homes, unable to enjoy the very mobility that brought Western women into contact with them.[8] Two different codes of sisterhood could be seen in operation in these encounters. The women in purdah recognized a similarity based on gender, admitting Western women but not men into their quarters. Leonowens's reaction to her admittance to the women's quarters at the king's palace typifies the second version of sisterhood in operation at such sites. She refuses to live in the 'harem' – insisting that she is different from the women who inhabit this part of the palace – and she indicts Thai patriarchy while promoting British masculinist policies as chivalrous and necessary for national and social health.

Leonowens's texts rehearse the standard harem discourse of 'getting inside' an enclosed or secret place and 'discovering the truth' through a moral or scientific expedition, justifying Western imperialism and its invasive tactics. The nineteenth-century Western depiction of Thailand itself reproduced the metaphorical structure of the colonial harem. In the 1860s, when Anna Leonowens was employed to teach in the king's palace, Siam, as Thailand was then known, was under tremendous pressure to increase trade with Western nations. Both France and England considered military occupation in order to ensure economic cooperation. Although the British came to enjoy privileged trade agreements with the country, Thailand was never formally colonized. Thus, from the point of view of the West, Thailand could be seen as 'inaccessible' and 'mysterious.' It cannot be accidental that the tale about Thailand that the West most loves to tell concerns a British woman who is able to 'get inside' and gain proximity to the center of Thai governmental power. If, as Grewal argues, the colonized countries were viewed as 'feminine' and 'weak' to bolster public support for military and economic intervention, the acceptance of Anna Leonowens into the Nang Harm feminizes the entire culture, suggesting that colonization (or Western modernization) can be achieved.

Anna's presence as one of the few Westerners in the kingdom as well
as in the palace itself is staged in each version not only as a drama about
culture shock and gender politics but also as a crisis in international
relations. Leonowens's struggle to live outside the palace compound in
a European-style 'home' of her own is staged in every version as a
morality play – a Western woman cannot live in a harem and, further,
no woman should live under such conditions. If the 'ideal' British
Victorian home functioned to create separate spheres for Western
women and men, the harem, which also operated through separation
and seclusion, was designated as barbaric. By the time Anna Leonowens published her books and embarked on a series of lecture tours in the
1870s, most Westerners were familiar with the primary tropes of the
'colonial harem': supine concubines, lush interiors, water pipes, and an
atmosphere of indolence and decadence. With the advent of inexpen-
sive photographic reproductions, what Malek Alloula has called a
'harvest of stereotypes' flooded Western marketplaces in the form of
postcards and book illustrations.[9] In Alloula's study of these postcards,
most of which were created in photography studios owned by
Europeans who paid prostitutes to model for them, the gestures of
orientalism taken from paintings by Ingres or Delacroix can be seen as
grotesque repetitions that mechanically discharge racist and misogynist
messages. The colonial postcard, with its focus on women in harems,
Alloula writes, 'is a naive "art" that rests, and operates, upon a false
equivalency (namely, that illusion equals reality). . . . It literally takes
its desires for realities.'[10] The harem clearly functions as a location
where Western preoccupations with gender, nation, and sexuality
expand and flourish.

Leila Ahmed extends Alloula's analysis, arguing that 'if an area is
culturally blank and populated by an irrelevant people' it is open to the
designs and desires of others.[11] In particular, she points out, the harem
or the practice of wearing a veil become synonymous for Westerners
with female oppression.[12] Thus, Western women ' "know" that
Muslim women are overwhelmingly oppressed,' Ahmed argues, 'without being able to define the specific content of that oppression, in the
same way that they "know" that Muslims . . . are ignorant, backward,
irrational, and uncivilized.'[13] These prejudices, she writes, become
'facts': 'manufactured in Western culture, by the same men who have
also littered the culture with "facts" about Western women and how
inferior and irrational *they* are.'[14] Ahmed urges Western feminists to
avoid hasty judgments about social practices like purdah and to resist
perpetrating the cultural images of enslaved harem females so popular
and influential in the West.

Ahmed's critique of Western representations of Middle Eastern harems is supported by Hanna Papanek's studies of South Asian purdah. Papanek, too, notes the uniformly negative evaluation accorded the practice of purdah by Western travel writers, missionaries, and reformers: 'What was overlooked in many of these partial views,' Papanek writes, 'was the extent to which female seclusion is integral to . . . other aspects of society.'[15] Because secluded women do not develop public systems of expression, the West cannot easily obtain access to their points of view. Yet, from the point of view of the indigenous culture, women in purdah are not necessarily excluded from powerful positions within the family and community. What is impaired, Papanek asserts, is their 'direct communication with the outside observer.'[16] With this kind of gap in public discourse, the only kind of discourse the West is willing and able to recognize as viable expression or constituting reality, fantasies come into play. Sarah Graham-Brown suggests that it is these fantasies about the harem that have done much to 'cloud understanding of the social, domestic and sexual lives' of indigenous women.[17]

Inderpal Grewal argues that both home and harem are significant terms in Western feminist discourse.[18] Travel, which entails leaving home, may serve a transgressive function for middle-class women, yet the Western woman traveler of Leonowens's era recuperated her respectability by focusing on re-establishing a 'home' abroad.[19] When the reader or viewer of a version of Leonowens's memoirs encounters Anna's battle with the king over his promise of a 'proper,' European-style house, an entire set of cultural assumptions about race, gender, class, and sexuality are called into play. Anna's dismay at finding herself living in the women's quarters of the palace is based on her association of the harem with loss of power, respect, and privacy. Once there, however, Anna 'discovers' that the women of the harem require her ministrations as much as the king's children do; that is, her mission is to teach the women of the Nang Harm the difference between a harem and a home.

The film versions of Leonowens's texts follow her nineteenth-century paternalist belief in enlightened intervention. In a recent essay on gender and filmic colonial discourse, Ella Shohat demonstrates the prevalence of the theme of the 'Western liberator' in films such as *The King and I*. This colonial rescue fantasy, she argues, 'links issues of sexuality to the justification of Western expansion.'[20] The liberator can only be a Western woman when Western men are absent, in which case, Shohat argues, the white woman's gaze becomes the 'civilizing center' of the film. Anna, a widow and the only Westerner inside the palace, demonstrates this civilizing function in a multitude of ways, but perhaps most powerfully vis-à-vis her relationships with both the king and the concubine Tuptim.

In the 1956 musical film, Anna's first opportunity to instruct the women in the harem arrives with her introduction to the women's quarters. Unlike Irene Dunne's stricken cry to her young son ('Oh Louis, I've brought you straight into a harem') in the 1946 film, Deborah Kerr's characterization of Anna elicits no anguished moments. Finding herself ensconced in the harem, this Anna firmly sets about introducing her primary concerns: freedom, autonomy, and a Christian conception of marriage and love. In an important early scene, Anna distinguishes herself from the women of the harem by discoursing on 'true' love, a category that she insists is only available through freedom of choice and association. Anna's picture of domestic romance – a sheltered young woman's one true love – is to be contrasted with the exotic romance of the harem – a sequestered woman's enslavement to an oriental despot. The introduction of Tuptim to the narrative at this early stage (earlier than in any other version) only emphasizes the contrast between Tuptim's limitations and Anna's freedoms. Already structurally linked to Anna's project – Tuptim is in love with Lun Tha and full of despair over her fate as concubine – she will legitimate Anna's Western viewpoints.

Tuptim's culturally liminal position also constructs her as similar to Anna in many ways. Because the narrative from the very beginning firmly establishes Tuptim's position as marginal – she comes from Burma in this version, a country that is not at all the same as Siam – her emotional distance from the system at work in the royal court is highly credible. Both Tuptim and Anna come from somewhere else. Both Tuptim and Anna have a single, true love. Unlike most of the other women in the harem, Tuptim already speaks English quite well. Tuptim, therefore, is a bridge between the women of the Nang Harm and Anna, the European. Yet, in the particular function of oppositions in this narrative, she cannot remain for long in her liminal, mediating role. Tuptim's situation will have to be resolved one way or the other. Since it is not possible for her to become completely Western (after all, she is the king's concubine, and thus, in the moral equation of the Hollywood film, 'degraded') or to reconcile herself to life in the harem, Tuptim will have to be sacrificed.

Tracing Tuptim's emergence as a central figure in the cinematic versions tells us a great deal about modern articulations of colonial and feminist discourses. A pivotal character in both film (and Broadway musical) versions, Tuptim does not appear anywhere in the first volume of Leonowens's memoirs, *The English Governess at the Siamese Court*. Significantly, Tuptim does not make an appearance until the second chapter of Leonowens's second book, *The Romance of the Harem*, a book that chronicles *many* instances of purported patriarchal brutality against the women of the harem. It is this second memoir that emphasizes the genre qualities of the abolitionist text to the greatest degree, focusing on Leonowens's 'heroic' efforts to rescue the wives and concubines of King Mongkut from their 'torment.' Margaret Landon's book *Anna and the King of Siam* pulls the story of Tuptim almost word for word out of Leonowens's text and inserts it towards the end of her novel, in the chapter titled 'The Slave Tuptim.' Leonowens's title for her chapter is more sensational: 'Tuptim: A Tragedy of the Harem.' With each version, the story of Tuptim moves from being one story among many to the paradigmatic case in the drama of women's and national liberations. As one 'tragedy of the harem' becomes *the* tragedy of the harem, we can track the specific investments in gender, race, and nationalism that emerge within the context of mid-twentieth century reconfigurations of empire.

Tuptim's Tragedy: The Mystification of Slavery in Harem Discourse

Tuptim's tragedy signals the attention of a contemporary Hollywood film audience because of her identification with an issue close to home, as it were: the abolition of slavery in the United States. In this sense, the construction of Tuptim as a martyred slave read through the lens of an abolitionist novel, *Uncle Tom's Cabin*, brings colonial discourse into conversation with North American nineteenth- and twentieth-century discourses of race and gender.

The conflation of the nineteenth-century Siamese harem with the institution of slavery in the United States is initiated by Leonowens in her memoirs and reproduced in the film versions, finding its apotheosis in the staging of the musical within the musical, 'The Small House of Uncle Thomas.' The fusion (and confusion) of British, Thai, and US social institutions continues in current scholarship and literary criticism. For example, Susan Morgan's introduction to the recent reissue of *The Romance of the Harem* argues that Leonowens increased her attack on the practice of concubinage in her second memoir not out of prudery, religious zealotry, or imperialist beliefs, but out of a deeply rooted opposition to the institution of slavery.[21] Morgan leaves no room for any interpretation other than that of Leonowens: 'Any defense of the social institution of the Siamese harem also involves, however unwittingly, a defense of the social institution of slavery: without slavery the harem could not exist.'[22]

Laura Donaldson's recent essay on the race and gender politics of *The King and I* critiques the ease with which such links between the enslavement of Africans in North America and the Siamese concubinage system can be made. Donaldson argues that the insertion of *Uncle Tom's Cabin*, as well as the metaphorical allusion to the biblical Exodus story in the musical, 'Westernizes' the film's concept of freedom, erasing any possible reading of Anna's intervention as imperialist.[23] In fact, as Morgan's reading of Leonowens demonstrates, the intertextual links between *Uncle Tom's Cabin* and *The Romance of the Harem* appear to obviate any cultural distinctions or historical differentiation. Leonowens, by posing as the heroine of her own romance, equates her own economic and emotional survival with the fate of the women she chooses to portray as in peril. By virtue of her own skill in surpassing so many difficulties, by her own stated belief in the independence and value of women's lives, and by her self-portrayal as firm but compassionate, Leonowens projects her own worldview within the context of the Nang Harm. Producing representations of Siamese women only as victims of patriarchal despotism, Leonowens displaces her own culture's struggles with patriarchal power and social inequities. The sisterhood that Leonowens constructs as part of her autobiographical strategy lends credence to whatever statements she makes about the Nang Harm; their story is as much her story and vice versa. Their 'freedom' is linked to her own.

In both films, Tuptim is structurally linked to Stowe's abolitionist novel. We see her holding the novel *Uncle Tom's Cabin* itself or writing and staging a musical version that allegorizes her own dreams for escape from the Nang Harm. The figure of Tuptim clearly equates North American slavery and Siamese concubinage, allowing the film audiences to make the same ideological link without examining or questioning the historical accuracy or logic of such a gesture. Even the king is portrayed as strongly interested in the civil war in North America, debating the virtues of slavery with Anna, and writing to President Lincoln to offer Siamese elephants to aid the Union side. Yet, neither of the film versions sheds any historical light on the system of compulsory labor in Siam during the nineteenth century or highlights the presence of slaves in the harem that belong to the concubines themselves. According to standard histories of Thailand, the only slaves whose purchase could not be obtained under any circumstances were primarily prisoners of war. The Siamese *corvée* system delineated compulsory labor for both 'freemen' and slaves. The social structure of nineteenth-century Siam, then, could be seen as a grid of obligatory relations between the people and their government. Slavery occurred on a continuum of obligatory labor and could be entered and exited through a variety of monetary and social compensations. Wendall Blanchard argues that since many entered slavery voluntarily (to pay off debts, through desire for protection in time of famine, etcetera), 'the line between slave and free was not rigid.'[24] The narrative of 'escape' and 'freedom' so intrinsic to the North American context where slavery was codified quite differently is more difficult to transplant to a feudal system of patronage. Yet both films, drawing upon Western discourses of freedom and individualism, transplant just such a narrative configuration. The grounds for this maneuver lie in Leonowens's own interpretation of the condition of the women in the royal harem and in Landon's gloss on the same issues.

Tuptim's case is, perhaps, the most extreme of all the imperiled women so graphically described by Leonowens in *The Romance of the Harem*. In a text filled with examples of Leonowens's successful interventions with the king on behalf of concubines and slaves, it is Tuptim's case which fails to end happily. Leonowens describes Tuptim's excruciating death preceded by monstrous torture to illustrate the capricious, unstable nature of King Mongkut. Despite the monarch's interest in 'Western' culture, his treatment of Tuptim appears to reveal the inherent evil in his position as absolute ruler and patriarch, as well as his essentially 'Eastern' qualities. Unlike his children, he is, finally, unteachable.

Tuptim's immolation clearly links her representation to the powerful trope of *sati* at work in the colonial imagination. Lata Mani has argued that the meaning and practice of *sati* shifted when British colonial intervention increased the stakes in Hindu fundamentalist traditions as acts of nationalist pride.[25] *Sati* became a subject of emotional debate in the context of the same intersecting discourses of nation, gender, race, and sexuality that constructed the colonial harem. Leonowens's brand of British feminism relied upon the sacrifice of what Gayatri Spivak has termed the 'self-immolating colonial subject' to mark the superiority of the 'good wife' or Western woman's way of life.[26] The obvious differences between India and Thailand, not the least of which are the differences between Hindu and Buddhist practices, are precisely the sort of distinctions which become fused in colonial discourse. Tuptim's fiery end epitomizes the colonial discourse of the harem: in the generalized ethos of Western imaginations, the greatest peril facing Asian women is death by fire. Nothing else so dramatically illustrates their difference from Western women; nothing but purgatory awaits pagans; and nothing less than Western modernization will prevent further 'tragedies.'

It is no surprise, therefore, that the film versions have gravitated to Tuptim's tale as a crucial subplot and even as a primary allegory for the story of crosscultural contact. Yet, serious objections to the factual possibility of Tuptim's execution have been raised for as long as Leonowens's text and subsequent versions have been in circulation. Margaret Landon herself mentions that Leonowens's books are viewed negatively in Thailand. In her 'Author's Note' at the end of *Anna and the King of Siam*, Landon tells of a friend in Thailand who revealed hidden copies to her, explaining that the government had tried to buy up all the copies to prevent their distribution. Feeling still ran high, she reported, during the 1920s and 30s.[27] In his book on King Mongkut, published in 1961, Abbott Low Moffat mentions that the publication of Landon's book in the 1940s reopened old wounds: 'Many Siamese were highly indignant. Old tales told by Anna, which they knew to be fictional, were being repeated to a new generation of admiring readers as apparently true stories.'[28] If this were not bad enough, Moffat continues, 'The subsequent versions . . . offered even greater distortions in portraying King Mongkut.'[29]

If King Mongkut must be textually produced as a kind of 'Simon Legree' in the conflation of discourses of Western slavery and Eastern harems, Tuptim is structured as a Christian martyr. Each version stages a slightly different rationale and ending, but in each text the king is identified as an inhuman despot while the concubine is shown to be willing to die for individual freedom and true love. In *The Romance of the Harem*, for example, Tuptim escapes the Nang Harm by disguising herself as a priest and hiding in her true love's monastery. Along with the priest she claims she loves, Tuptim is subjected to excruciating torture, all carefully detailed by Leonowens, before being dragged off and burned at the stake before a huge, cheering crowd. Leonowens describes the king as 'fiendish;' 'I saw that there was something indescribably revolting about him . . . and I was seized with an inexpressible horror of the man.'[30] Tuptim, on the other hand, is pictured as a docile, almost saintlike, martyr:

> Every torture that would agonize, but not kill, was employed to wring a
> confession of guilt from suffering Tuptim; but every torture, every pang,
> every agony, failed, utterly and completely failed, to bring forth anything
> but the childlike innocence of that incomparable pagan woman.[31]

In the 1946 film version, the Western investments in Tuptim's fate are expressed through Anna's struggle with the king over the conflict between tradition and modernity. When the king asserts, 'This shall be *my* affair,' his inability to give up absolute rule (as his predecessor in England did some centuries before) and his insistence on his own sovereignty inspire a blistering condemnation from Anna: 'You *are* a barbarian!' From this moment of 'truth,' the king's powers wane. Through its structuring gaze, the film confers upon Anna the power to destroy a symbol of both patriarchal authority and resistance to colonialism. Both the king and Tuptim, vestiges of an old order, are dead by the end of the film. The last scene shows Anna strolling with the new king, her former pupil, advising him on affairs of state; that is, helping with the process of Western modernization.

While the 1946 film exploits the image of captive, tortured female slave to the fullest extent, the 1956 musical film cannot betray its light-hearted agenda by burning established characters at the stake. Tuptim's punishment is forestalled by the king's illness: an illness that directly follows Anna's withering accusation of barbarism. In the film versions, Tuptim's transgressions and the king's behavior towards her propel Anna to a moral pinnacle, forcing the issue of commitment to Westernization. The king, who was not defeated in life, cinematically relinquishes his powers to the more 'modern' heirs; the combined forces of 'Mrs Anna' and Prince Chulalongkorn usher in an era of Western supervision. In the musical, the defeat of the king is not only symbolized by his own request to Anna to stay and guide the young prince but is underscored by a melodramatic scene of the women and children of the harem begging her to help them. The king may be incorrigible and Tuptim may be lost, but here are subjects to be saved – and the structuring of the request for salvation (an economic and cultural rescue rather than a strictly religious maneuver) from the subjects themselves represents a triumph of colonial discourse.

Travel, Gender, and Empire: Deauthorizing Colonial Discourses

Part of the power of all the versions of Anna Leonowens's memoirs resides in the 'truth-value' effect of the travel memoir as an autobiographical account.[32] Yet recent scholarship casts suspicion on the factual nature of Leonowens's narrative of her life in the Nang Harm and recalls earlier protests against the publication of the memoirs. The fact/fiction divide is heightened in this instance due to the great stakes in contests for credibility in the politics of colonial representation. The power to describe is closely linked to the right to rule. In Leonowens's case, when autobiography is deployed as 'truth,' the colonial discourse of travel moves from the depiction of 'customs and manners' to the articulation of 'ethnographic authority.'

Leonowens herself raises the issue of credibility and 'truth-value' in her preface to the first edition of *The Romance of the Harem*:

> 'Truth is often stranger than fiction,' but so strange will some of the occurrences related in the following pages appear to Western readers, that I deem it necessary to state that they are also true. Most of the stories, incidents, and characters are known to me personally to be real, while of such narratives as I received from others I can say that 'I tell the tale as it was told to me,' and written down by me at the time.[33]

Most of the critics and writers who have commented on Leonowens's memoirs in the years after their publication follow the line established in the passage above. For example, in her introduction to the reissue of *The Romance of the Harem* in 1952 (this time titled less sensationally, and even more authoritatively, *Siamese Harem Life*), Freya Stark (herself an intrepid explorer and travel writer) produced yet another layer of myth concerning the factual nature of Leonowens's book. 'The present volume,' Stark writes, 'completes the picture with tales that read like fiction, but are really the intimate, poignantly matter-of-fact accounts of the various lives around her . . .'[34] Susan Morgan repeats this gesture in her introduction to the 1991 edition; acknowledging the 'preposterous' nature of the tales, nevertheless, she claims: 'The irreducible factual basis of these stories is one woman looking at other women's lives, seeing how they are blighted, and being horrified.'[35] 'Their excess,' she concludes, 'is their gift.'[36]

For all the assertions of authenticity that surround every version of Leonowens's memoirs, the story of Tuptim, among other important narrative elements, is easily deconstructed. Tuptim's sentencing and execution incite the greatest protests and challenges because they are difficult to document. In his monograph on King Mongkut, A. B. Griswold argues that not only did such punishment as burning at the stake not exist in Siam at this time, such an extraordinary execution would certainly have merited mention in either oral or written accounts of that time period. The underground dungeons of the palace where Leonowens claimed the wayward concubines or their slaves were sometimes incarcerated are also dismissed by Griswold as a total fabrication.[37] The credibility of Leonowens's account is further weakened by other historians, such as Abbott Low Moffat, who record the important changes in law that King Mongkut instituted, including a humane ruling that allowed any member of his harem or any slave to gain their liberty by paying costs. Histories of Mongkut's rule also note that his harem was relatively small compared to those of his predecessors. Mongkut's son's decision to abolish slavery altogether and to eliminate bowing and other subservient gestures could easily be viewed as a continuation of the father's liberal policies. It is ironic, therefore, that this ruler has been immortalized in the West as an irrational despot who murdered a concubine by burning her at the stake rather than grant her freedom.

Whether Anna Leonowens deliberately fabricated this infamous atrocity or not is a less interesting question than challenging the apparently seamless acceptance in the West of literary and cinematic representations of enslaved Siamese women and childishly capricious Asian dictators. It is also important to consider what is at stake in the ease with which Western audiences accept the narrative requirements of the death of the King of Siam when Thailand, in fact, remained the only country in South Asia to avoid actual colonization by European countries. The intersection of colonial and patriarchal discourses legitimated Leonowens's monological 'documentary' account at the height of imperialist ventures. What forms of imperialist nostalgia influence contemporary feminist discourses of sisterhood in an era of postcolonialism?[38]

Writing in 1958, as part of a development project administered by the Southeast Asia Studies Program of Cornell University, a program designed to teach Thai people to read and write English, Prajuab Tirabutana described her reaction to photographs of Yul Brynner as the king of Siam:

> I had never seen the picture 'The King and I' but I saw some pictures in a magazine. And the attitude of the Thai king in those pictures made my ears burn hot. It was just the pictures, everyone knew that so why should Thai people pay much attention to it. And it was through these pictures that people all over the world would know Thailand. Of course, they would know and remember the name of our country well because they had to laugh at the queer and wild actions of their king. But the question was where did the man who told the actor to act that way get those manners from?[39]

In considering such a question, Westerners might keep in mind that the film and Broadway stage versions of Anna Leonowens's travel memoirs were viewed by North Americans who had been at war with Japan. The United States embarked on military interventions in Korea and what had been French Indochina during the height of the musical's popularity. By the time Prajuab Tirabutana's autobiography was in print and in distribution as a 'data paper' from Cornell University, North American troops were already present in Indochina. Both films end with deathbed scenes of the cinematic King Mongkut, scenes in which Anna is begged to stay in Siam and help bring about 'true progress.' It might not be insignificant that MacArthur was taking just such a stance in post-war Japan at the time that the first film was released. Through firm guidance, and above all, through continuous *presence*, a supposedly backward, 'barbarian' country could be brought under 'rational' Western management.

In posing questions about the specific historical significance of different versions of Leonowens's texts, I intend to raise larger issues about the way the West tells stories about modernization, imperialism, race, and gender. When a figure such as Tuptim is constructed as a romantic, tragic victim, the narratives of non-Western women in resistance against local and global forms of oppression are displaced. Ironically, both Leonowens's and Landon's texts provide more information about the gendered and class-based division of labor inside the palace than the two 'modern' films. Yet, none of the versions detail the limits and possibilities of women's lives inside or outside the palace walls beyond their symbolic function as objects of the West's moral absolutism. Western feminists could do more to assess what such failures in representational practices might mean in terms of our own narratives of international sisterhood and the politics of intervention.

There is a danger in accepting uncritically the binary opposition between 'West' and 'non-West' when critiquing feminist representatio-nal practices. The figure of 'Mrs Anna' elicits contradictory responses. Part memsahib, part feminist avenger and adventurer, the fictional-izations of Leonowens speak to the desire for a good mother or a powerful woman who can stand up to patriarchal authority. Laura Donaldson has argued that despite the legitimating codes of 'angelic motherhood' that surround the figure of Anna, Leonowens's authorita-tive writing on life in the Nang Harm becomes a 'weapon as powerful as a gun.'[40] Laura Green cautions against such a complete condemna-tion of Leonowens. If we only view Leonowens as the purveyor of racist, imperialist assumptions, Green argues, we miss the 'productive, rather than simply repetitive' power of the binary oppositions that come into play in Leonowens's texts – in fact, we miss the opportunity to deconstruct the hierarchies that represent themselves as binary oppositions.[41] Donaldson herself points out that the women of the Nang Harm are not the only subjects to be denied any complexity or agency. Anna's feminist stance in the 1950s musical is subverted, Donaldson argues, by the 'colonizing' of Anna 'as just another patriarchal object.'[42] In that film, despite Anna's status as a British subject vis-à-vis the women of the harem, she, too, is caught in the operation of the masculine gaze. Viewing the cinematic Anna's ideological positioning as contradictory and complex is just as important as contextualizing the subjectivity of the non-Western female characters. Reading Donaldson and Green together – in conversation, as it were – provides a hopeful moment in the Western feminist critique of colonial discourses.

Yet, it is Leonowens's memoirs that inspire powerful cinematic and literary versions and not the memoirs of the ethnographic subject, Prajuab Tirabutana, or the records of women whose experiences of modernization have not been unilinear or uniformly positive. Despite her own patriarchal conundrums, Leonowens's 'weapon' is indeed formidable, fashioned through two technologies: the technology of narrative – literally, the 'power of the pen' – and the technology of knowledge acquisition and dissemination that can be characterized as 'ethnography.'[43] Leonowens's moral authority and textual credibility rely upon these twin operations to convey both the 'customs and manners' material *and* the elements of romance and tragedy that combine to form the colonial discourse of travel, gender, and empire.

Such knotty questions of production and reproduction, location and dislocation, underscore the importance of feminist critical archeologies of colonial discourses. Reading versions of Leonowens's texts, we learn how to identify the connections between national narratives and domestic ones as well as between acts of tourism and imperialism. Linking gender and race to the construction of particular economies and lines of power provides feminist criticism with the opportunity to deconstruct mystifications of difference and similarity. The staging of colonial discourse in these films suppresses different versions of events and points of view in favor of a totalized message: hierarchical power relations are inevitable and necessary. In the musical version, the song 'Getting to Know You' signifies not only the benign wish to make an acquaintance but the siren song of surveillance and the precursor of cultural, if not military, intervention. In this sense, even in a supposedly post-colonial age, Anna Leonowens's tale reinscribes colonial discourse in every neighborhood video store.

Nostalgia for a 'past in someone else's country' produces conventional colonial discourse but not a transformative feminist critical practice.[44] The representation of travel is an intensely seductive form of colonial discourse for feminists when it articulates and celebrates mobility, independence, and the acquisition of knowledge. When one form of gender liberation is structured upon economic and cultural subjugation, viable feminist alliances are obstructed. We cannot begin to imagine alternatives to such forms of knowledge until the specific histories of colonial discourses are fully traced in all their connections and modes of operation. Feminist critical practice can retrieve an anti-imperialist tradition and build upon it, but not without understanding the densely tangled legacies of modernity. Acknowledging the politics of knowledge requires that we scrupulously examine the ways in which we get to know others, including literary and cinematic representations, so that the liberatory practices of alliance and crosscultural interaction can begin.

Notes

1. In 'Empire and the Movement for Women's Suffrage in Britain,' Inderpal Grewal analyzes the intersections of gender, race, and nationalism that create two, opposing suffragist responses to the project of British imperialism – pro- and anti-empire. This chapter can be found in Grewal's forthcoming 'Home' and Harem: Nationalism, Imperialism, and Women's Culture in Nineteenth Century England.

2. For a full discussion of the troubled binary oppositions 'West/non-West,' 'global/local,' and 'center/periphery,' see by Inderpal Grewal and Caren Kaplan, 'Transnational Feminist Practices and Questions of Postmodernity,' in Grewel and Kaplan, eds., Scattered Hegemonies: Postmodernity and Transnational Feminist Practices (Minneapolis: University of Minnesota Press, 1993).

3. Both films are based on Anna and the King of Siam (1944), Margaret Landon's best-selling fictional adaptation of Anna Leonowens's autobiographies. In The English Governess at the Siamese Court (1870) and its sequel, The Romance of the Harem (1872), Leonowens depicted her travels in Asia and her five years as governess to the children of King Mongkut. Landon's immensely popular novel inspired the Rogers and Hammerstein Broadway musical The King and I. In a longer version of this essay I discuss the cultural production of colonial discourse in each of these versions in terms of genre and industry histories.

4. Patrick Brantlinger, 'Victorians and Africans: The Genealogy of the Myth of the Dark Continent,' in Henry Louis Gates Jr., ed., 'Race,' Writing, and Difference (Chicago: University of Chicago Press, 1985), p. 185.

5. Ibid., p. 192.

6. See Paula Giddings, When and Where I Enter: The Impact of Black Women on Race and Sex in America (New York: Bantam, 1984); Angela Davis, Women, Race, and Class (New York: Random House, 1981); and bell hooks, Ain't I a Woman: Black Women and Feminism (Boston: South End Press, 1981).

7. Grewal, 'Empire and the Movement for Women's Suffrage,' p. 10.

8. Ibid., p. 25.

9. Malek Alloula, The Colonial Harem, translated by Myrna Godzich and Wlad Godzich (Minneapolis: University of Minnesota Press, 1986), p. 35.

10. Ibid., p. 44.

11. Leila Ahmed, 'Western Ethnocentrism and Perceptions of the Harem,' Feminist Studies no. 8 (Fall 1982), p. 522.

12. Ibid., p. 523.

13. Ibid.

14. Ibid.

15. Hanna Papanek and Gail Minault, eds., *Separate Worlds: Studies of Purdah in South Asia* (Delhi: Chanakya Publishers; Columbia, Missouri: South Asia Books, 1982), p. 5.

16. Ibid., p. 6.

17. Sarah Graham-Brown, *Images of Women: The Portrayal of Women in Photography of the Middle East, 1860–1950* (New York: Columbia University Press, 1988), p. 70.

18. For a full explication of this representational relationship in the nineteenth century, see Inderpal Grewal's *'Home' and Harem: Nationalism, Imperialism, and Women's Culture in Nineteenth Century England* (forthcoming).

19. See, in particular, 'Chapter 2: 'Home and Work,' in Margaret Strobel's *European Women and the Second British Empire* (Bloomington: Indiana University Press, 1991), pp. 17–33; and Helen Callaway, *Gender, Culture and Empire: European Women in Colonial Nigeria* (Urbana: University of Illinois Press, 1987).

20. Ella Shohat, 'Gender and the Culture of Empire: Toward a Feminist Ethnography of the Cinema,' *Quarterly Review of Film and Video*, no. 13 (Spring 1991), p. 63.

21. Susan Morgan, 'Introduction,' to Anna Leonowens's *The Romance of the Harem* (Charlottesville: University Press of Virginia, 1991), p. xxx.

22. Ibid.

23. Laura Donaldson, *'The King and I* in *Uncle Tom's Cabin*, or On the Border of the Women's Room,' *Cinema Journal*, no. 29 (Spring 1990), p. 62.

24. Wendell Blanchard, *Thailand* (New Haven: HRAF Press, 1966), p. 287.

25. See Lata Mani's 'Contentious Traditions: The Debate on *Sati* in Colonial India,' in Kumkum Sangari and Sudesh Vaid, eds., *Recasting Women: Essays in Indian Colonial History* (New Brunswick, NJ: Rutgers University Press, 1990), pp. 88–126.

26. See Gayatri Chakravorty Spivak, 'Three Women's Texts and a Critique of Imperialism,' in Henry Louis Gates, Jr., ed., *'Race,' Writing, and Difference*, (Chicago: University of Chicago Press, 1986), pp. 262–80 and 'Can the Subaltern Speak? Speculations on Widow-Sacrifice,' *Wedge* no. 7/8 (Winter/Spring 1985), pp. 120–30.

27. Margaret Landon, *Anna and the King of Siam* (Garden City, New York: Garden City Publishing Co., 1944), p. 338.

28. Abbott Low Moffat, *Mongkut, the King of Siam* (Ithaca, New York: Cornell University Press, 1961), p. viii.

29. Ibid.

30. Leonowens, *The Romance of the Harem*, p. 34.

31. Ibid., pp. 38–9.

32. For a full discussion of the ambiguity between fact and fiction in modern Western literature see Barbara Foley's *Telling the Truth: The Theory and Practice of Documentary Fiction* (Ithaca: Cornell University Press, 1986). For a discussion of the intersections between autobiography, gender, and colonial discourse see Sidonie Smith and Julia Watson, eds., *De/Colonizing the Subject: Politics and Gender in Women's Autobiographical Practice* (Minneapolis: University of Minnesota Press, 1992).

33. Leonowens, *The Romance of the Harem*.

34. Freya Stark, 'Introduction,' to Anna H. Leonowens's *Siamese Harem Life* (London: Arthur Baker Ltd., 1952), p. xiii.

35. Morgan, 'Introduction,' xxxvii.

36. Ibid.

37. A.B. Griswold, *King Mongkut of Siam* (New York: Asia Society, 1961).

38. See Renato Rosaldo, 'Imperialist Nostalgia,' in *Culture and Truth: The Remaking of Social Analysis* (Boston: Beacon Press, 1989), pp. 68–87.

39. Prajuab Tirabutana, *A Simple One: The Story of a Siamese Girlhood*, Data Paper no. 30, Southeast Asia Program, Cornell University (November, 1958), p. 38.

40. Donaldson, *'The King and I* in *Uncle Tom's Cabin*,' p. 61.

41. Laura Green, ' "Harassed and Indomitable": Gender, Empire, and the Myth of Anna Leonowens.' Paper presented at the Boundaries in Question Conference, University of California at Berkeley, October 6, 1991, p. 3.

42. Donaldson, 'The King and I in Uncle Tom's Cabin,' p. 56.

43. See James Clifford, The Predicament of Culture: Twentieth-Century Ethnography, Literature, and Art (Cambridge: Harvard University Press, 1988); and Mary Louise Pratt, Imperial Eyes: Travel Writing and Transculturation (London: Routledge Press, 1992).

44. See Arjun Appadurai, 'Disjuncture and Difference in the Global Economy,' Public Culture, no. 2 (Spring 1990), p. 4.

3

'Dark Enough fur Any Man': Bram Stoker's Sexual Ethnology and the Question of Irish Nationalism

David Glover

Cultural identities today bear the stamp of a dual process of deterritorialization. On the one hand, the breakup of old political empires and, on the other, the experience of mass migrations have together led to a loss of continuity in the popular consciousness of place, and the rise of new ethnolinguistic communities and nationalisms in their wake. Increasingly, people no longer imagine themselves and the communities to which they feel they belong in the ways they once did. Indeed, the scale of these changes can partly be gauged from the shifting etymology of the word 'ethnic' itself, for in pre-modern times it had a broad religious meaning that has now all but disappeared. Originally, an 'ethnic' community was one that stood beyond the Judeo-Christian pale, signifying its heathen or pagan Otherness. When a seventeenth-century writer such as Thomas Hobbes spoke of 'Ethnique Princes,' for example, he was not only drawing a rough-and-ready line between civilized peoples and unbelievers but also tacitly assuming the possibility of natural alliances between otherwise antagonistic dynasties and principalities. This usage persisted as late as the 1850s, but by then the term was already becoming freighted with new racial connotations stemming from the growing tendency in scientific discourse to think of humankind as irremediably fractured by moral, mental and biological differences. Superseding the stark division of the world into two broad ethico-religious camps, the impact of biological and anthropological theorizing effectively transformed 'ethnicity' into a concept that deterministically treated the human species as a set of irreconcilable racial types – hence the term 'ethnology' to designate the putative

'science' of race. The new meaning of 'ethnicity' was further complicated by its intersection with the growth of nationalism in the nineteenth
century (an '-ism' that only came into common English currency in the
1830s); consequently, when it was used synonymously for 'nation,' the
term 'ethnic' and its cognates helped to thematize nationality in
essentially racial terms.

In this essay I want to look more closely at the connections between
ethnicity and nation as they figure in the work of a writer not usually
associated with questions of national identity, the Irish novelist Bram
Stoker (1847–1912). Stoker lived through some of the formative years
of Irish nationalism and though he died nearly a decade before
independent statehood was achieved, he was a cautious, but convinced
advocate of Irish Home Rule from at least his early twenties. Despite
the difficulties experienced in the latter half of the nineteenth century,
Ireland produced 'a national movement powerful enough to lead one of
the first successful independence struggles within the British Empire, a
struggle which in turn became a model for other colonized nations.'[1]
But then, as now, that movement was a highly controversial one, and
Stoker's own troubled relationship to it underscores the divided
loyalties that categories of ethnic identity and national belonging have
often bequeathed to nationalism's potential supporters and subjects.
As a result, in Stoker's time European defenders of nationalist
movements were often deeply at odds with each other over Irish claims
to full self-rule. More specifically, though Ireland's radical intelligentsia and political organizations could boast a nationalist pedigree
second to none, the rationales emerging to justify such newly unified
nation-states as Germany and Italy seemed to pull in different and
sharply opposed directions.

For some, the German and Italian examples epitomized a progressive
and typically liberal spirit of nation building in which scatterings of
peoples and territories were being brought together ostensibly to the
benefit of the whole citizenry. If a nation was truly to flourish, such
liberals reasoned, it required an optimum size, though few agreed on
how this size could be determined. In practice, because of the
uncertainty inherent in this so-called 'threshold principle,' appeals were
also made to the cultural distinctiveness of race, language or customs,
positive sources of identity that could be taken as indicators that
national viability had been achieved. However, these auxiliary arguments were equally inconclusive. Mid-century discussion of Ireland
shows just how fuzzy both sorts of criteria could actually be. Whereas
the English liberal philosopher John Stuart Mill argued that its
population size alone was enough to validate Ireland's claims to

independence, Mazzini – the nationalist theoretician of the Young Italy movement – not only thought that the Irish were too few in number, but also felt that they were not sufficiently different from the English to be granted self-determination on cultural grounds. There is a double irony here, for after the Great Famine (1845–49), Ireland's population fell dramatically and cultural nationalism became an increasingly important strand in the independence movement, as attempts in the 1880s to 'de-anglicize' Ireland by reviving the Gaelic language clearly show. In this respect, Ireland provided a prototype for challenges to the expansionary and assimilationist premises inherent in the liberal theory of nations, as calls for national sovereignty based solely on ethnic, linguistic or cultural difference were heard with growing frequency towards the century's close.[2] Unfortunately, appeals to ethnic distinctiveness cut both ways, and one of the trickiest problems for cultural nationalists lay in knowing what sense to make of the new 'advanced' sciences of race whose pejorative judgments were typically used against them and other subject peoples, structuring the relationship between dominant and subordinate groups and underwriting racist and imperialist sentiments.

What is remarkable about Stoker's fiction is precisely its preoccupation with this instability of racial or ethnic signifiers, so that the ideal and the phobic are never as far apart as at first appears. Stoker is primarily known today as the author of *Dracula*, the classic vampire novel that has never been out of print since its original publication in 1897 – it surfaced in The *New York Times* bestseller lists as recently as December 1992, following the release of Francis Ford Coppola's film adaptation. The book's global success has tended to obscure both the range of Stoker's writing and its specifically Irish origins. Before discussing the role of ethnicity in his work, it will be necessary to sketch in some details of Stoker's social and literary background.

Dracula, superficially among Stoker's least Irish texts, is in fact the one that best locates him within a predominantly nineteenth-century tradition of writing that struggled obsessively with the cultural meaning of Ireland and Irishness: Anglo-Irish Gothic. In this local subgenre the social and psychic fears mobilized in the uncanny scenarios of English writers such as Ann Radcliffe and Matthew 'Monk' Lewis were subtly inflected into a monstrous vision of Ireland as imagined through the eyes of some of the poorer members of the Protestant Ascendancy, the country's socially and culturally dominant elite. Economically dependent upon Britain for their readers, and awkwardly placed in relation to Ireland's turbulent politics, these authors produced out of their cultural marginality a deeply hybrid fiction, marked by eerie displacements and curious evasions, in which commonplace Gothic tropes such as the evocation of a decaying, haunted mansion or a Catholic European setting could acquire disturbing new resonances in Irish Protestant hands. Dissimulation and indirection were thus definitive of 'a remarkable line among certain writers of the ascendancy, running from Charles Robert Maturin at the beginning of the century to Bram Stoker at its close: compounders of fantasies and tales of the grotesque, set everywhere save in Ireland.'[3] Figuratively, and even sometimes literally, this was 'a fiction of exile.'[4]

In Stoker's case this exile was more than symbolic. Much of his life was spent not only in England, but also on the road in his role as theater manager for the celebrated Victorian actor Henry Irving. Stoker's travels overseas helped to bring him fame as a writer on contemporary affairs. He turned his visits to the United States into lectures that subsequently appeared as one of his earliest publications, *A Glimpse of America* (1886). Praise for this strikingly eulogistic pamphlet by another traveler, the American H.M. Stanley, was especially valued by Stoker, and his admiration for Stanley and for the explorer Sir Richard Burton indicates the wider imperial context in which his writings need to be placed. In Stoker's romances the footloose adventurer, home from Australia, the Balkans, or South Africa, is a favorite device, and one of the most fascinating aspects of his fiction lies in its journeys. But, if the pleasures of travel shade into dreams of empire, what of Ireland, Stoker's colonial home during the first thirty years of his life? Though he led a life that seemed to position him securely at the center of fashionable English society, Stoker's Irishness was – like his countryman Oscar Wilde's – something he was able neither fully to embrace nor completely forget.

In a letter to Walt Whitman written when he was twenty-four and working as a civil servant in Dublin, Stoker – 'reared a conservative in a conservative country' – praised the poet's *Leaves of Grass* for taking him 'away from the world around me' and placing him 'in an ideal land, . . . your own land of progress.'[5] Part of Stoker's response to what he saw as the backwardness and even the philistinism of Irish life was of course to leave Ireland to seek his future elsewhere, as did three of his four brothers. Another was to adopt the convictions of an English liberal, attracted by such different figures as John Bright and William Ewart Gladstone (characteristically, Stoker later became a longstanding member of London's National Liberal Club and acquired a great many contacts in British parliamentary circles). So, when Irving hinted at the possibility of a job in the metropolis, Stoker wrote excitedly in his diary: 'London in view!'[6] Yet despite this cultivation of a certain emotional and physical distance from his homeland, he never ceased to identify himself as an Irishman, a supporter of its culture and its causes. Politically Stoker once described himself as a moderate, 'philosophical' supporter of Irish Home Rule, and during his student days in Dublin he was on good terms with members of the nationalist intelligentsia such as Sir William and Lady Wilde.[7] Though he eventually came to prefer Gladstone to the more militant Parnell, Stoker was sympathetic enough to Parnell's associate and critic, the Nationalist MP William O'Brien, to try to help get a dramatization of O'Brien's Fenian novel When We Were Boys (1890) onto the London stage. Stoker's efforts came to nothing, but O'Brien gratefully wrote to thank him for taking 'so genuine a liking' for the book and for his deep interest in the play, whose performance O'Brien believed 'would be of priceless value in the Home Rule fight.'[8]

Stoker's nationalist leanings were also reflected in his literary tastes. In addition to the obvious influence of Sheridan Le Fanu's Anglo-Irish Gothic tales on his writing (particularly Le Fanu's vampire story 'Carmilla'), Stoker evidently admired William Carleton's popular portraits of Irish peasant life. He kept, for example, an autographed presentation copy of W.B. Yeats's The Countess Kathleen in his valuable personal collection. In a similar vein, his wife Florence was a devotee of the work of Maria Edgeworth, sometimes said to be the first truly Irish novelist.[9] When Stoker published his first novel, The Snake's Pass, in 1890, just over a decade after arriving in London, it was understandable that he should have chosen to return to an imaginary Ireland for its setting. And he went to some trouble to build an audience amongst those readers who shared his political views on Home Rule, writing to the Irish journalist and politician Michael Davitt seeking a favorable mention for his novel in Davitt's newspaper the Labour World. On November 29, The Snake's Pass received a prominent review, possibly written by Davitt himself, praising it as 'a fresh, powerful, dramatic, intensely interesting story.'[10] But perhaps the most gratifying response came from Gladstone, 'whose magnificent power and ability and character I had all my life so much admired.' When Gladstone told him in private conversation how much he had enjoyed the book, Stoker was extremely touched that the Liberal leader should have found time to read 'an Irish novel' at the very moment when his efforts to resolve the 'centuries-old Irish troubles' were breaking down, 'one of the greatest troubles and trials of his whole political life.'[11]

In terms of its Irish pedigree, The Snake's Pass owes most to the writer William Carleton's work (revived and championed by Yeats in the same period as 'the greatest novelist of Ireland').[12] Stoker borrowed from novels like *Valentine McClutchy* (1845) and *The Black Prophet* (1847) to create a Carletonesque plot that pits a virtuous heroine and a noble young man against an evil moneylender, the gombeen man Black Murdock who loudly echoes such villainous land agents or middlemen as Carleton's Black Donnel or Val the Vulture. Seven years later, however, it is possible to see the full-blown melodramatic villainy of Black Murdock as a clear precursor of the more famous Count Dracula, even down to the 'livid scar' each bears on his face after a potential victim has attempted to fight back.[13] At a deeper level one can also see the Transylvanian topography of *Dracula* as a kind of inversion of the mountainous Irish terrain of *The Snake's Pass*. Coming as they do at opposite ends of the same decade, a decade of severe setbacks for the Home Rule movement, these two novels deserve to be read in tandem for the contrasting light each sheds on Ireland, its country and its people. Taken together they go to the heart of Stoker's ambivalence towards his native land.

The road into this comparison comes via the opening narrative device both books share: the journey into an interior that is also a journey of discovery. In *The Snake's Pass* Arthur Severn, the novel's orphaned hero, has 'been brought up in an exceedingly quiet way with an old clergyman and his wife in the west of England' (p. 11). On completion of a six-months' tour of Europe, he travels to the West of Ireland to stay with friends in County Clare. With time to spare the young man decides 'to improve my knowledge of Irish affairs by making a detour through some of the counties in the west' (p. 13). Spurred on by the spectacular beauty of the countryside, Severn gains self-knowledge by going out of his way, moving beyond the rather narrow horizons of his upbringing to receive a romantic education in love and adventure. Only when we place the pastoral idealization of Ireland that is integral to Stoker's narrative beside the complex tradition of Irish travel writing can we see what is missing. For side by side with 'the Victorian fashion for wild, uncultivated and picturesque landscapes' is a counter-tradition that finds expression in Thackeray's *Irish Sketchbook* (1843), Carleton's literary and sociological documentation of the Great Famine (*circa* 1847), or even Charles Kingsley's *Letters and Memories of his Life* (1877).[14] This counter-tradition sees Ireland as, in Kingsley's words, 'a land of ruins and of the dead.'[15] If that phrase makes us think of *Dracula*, perhaps one can see in Stoker's portrait of an imagined Transylvania some of the features of that other Ireland that *The Snake's Pass* omits. To be sure, *Dracula* also has its roots in other modes of Victorian travel writing, the more so since Transylvania came to Stoker secondhand through the painstaking library research that often undergirded his texts, packing them with odd correspondences and intriguing references. But Transylvania is manifestly a place of ruins (Dracula himself residing in 'a vast ruined castle') and of the dead (Dracula's hand, we are told, feels 'more like the hand of a dead than a living man').[16] There is, I want to suggest, a curious geographical doubling that passes between *Dracula* and *The Snake's Pass*; it hinges upon equivocations in the representability of Ireland and the Irish. In *Dracula* the opening scenes of natural beauty so much a feature of *The Snake's Pass* slide alarmingly into the awesomeness of the sublime, and this is of a piece with an instability in the inhabitants of Transylvania themselves, who oscillate between the 'picturesque' and the 'more barbarian,' between rude outdoor health and an uncanny sickliness ('goitre was painfully prevalent'). 'Some of them were just like the peasants at home,' writes the solicitor's clerk Jonathan Harker, recounting his first trip abroad in a letter to an anxiously waiting fiancée; but we might pause at this sentence to wonder where exactly home was.

The close attention Stoker gives to the physical description of people is especially interesting for the way in which it draws upon the ideas and vocabulary of ethnology, the Victorian 'science' of race and the closely related pseudo-sciences with which it overlapped. For example, one of the discourses that conspicuously left its mark on Stoker's entire output was that of physiognomy, the belief that there could be a scientific knowledge of a person's true nature based upon facial features and bodily outline. In the early letter to Whitman quoted above, Stoker enthusiastically notes their common interests, calling the American poet 'a keen physiognomist,' and also declaring himself to be a 'believer of the science' and 'in a humble way a practicer of it.'[17] And as late as 1908, in a newspaper interview with the young Winston Churchill, Stoker portrayed the then up-and-coming Liberal politician in strict physiognomic terms, drifting off, as he so often did, into cognate pseudo-sciences including phrenology and palmistry, giving a detailed account of Churchill's palms, fingers and thumbs to conclude (correctly as it turned out) that 'the man with such a hand should go far.'[18] Readers of *Dracula* will remember that the count's hands are an object of great interest too, but that there is a worrying indeterminacy about them: 'hitherto . . . they had seemed rather white and fine; but seeing them now close to me, I could not but notice they were rather coarse – broad with squat fingers' (p. 28). It is almost as if the signs of the times had gone awry, that science is inadequate to the task of reading the character of such hands correctly, defeated by the readiness of appearances to dissolve into their gendered opposite or to change dramatically their class or even their racial connotations. Significantly, Stoker clung to these 'sciences' of faces, hands and skulls even after they had begun to decline in intellectual respectability towards the end of the century. Their ideas consistently formed a central core to his view of the human sciences. As a result, the scientifically precise descriptions that are supposed to provide a measure of stability and certainty often turn out, like Dracula's hands, to be a site of anxiety and apprehension.

The difficulty of interpreting physical types, of sorting out their meanings and effects, lay at the heart of the conundrums of race and nation, and would have presented a displaced and divided figure like Stoker with a peculiarly sharp dilemma. For to be a 'believer' in physiognomy who was also Irish, let alone a 'believer' in Irish Home Rule – no matter how 'philosophical' – was to find oneself torn by a contradictory set of allegiances. Refurbished and given a new Enlightenment imprimatur, discourses like physiognomy and phrenology had once aspired to true scientific status as instruments of human progress that might be set alongside Newtonian physics. But by Stoker's time they were becoming increasingly racialized through articulation with the themes and theories of ethnology and racial biology. Physiognomy in particular was one of the main currents feeding into the representation of the Irish as a race apart, lower down upon the evolutionary tree than other European races, as the 'human chimpanzees' of Kingsley's horrified gaze or the 'white negroes' scorned by Carlyle. Not only did physiognomy lend scientific authority to such racist epithets, but equally perniciously, its descriptive conventions were directly carried over into drawings and sketches of the Irish as a folk.

In the abundant caricatures of Ireland in the English press during the troubled 1880s, the Irish were depicted as monstrously subhuman, as creatures of Neanderthal stupidity and cruelty, incapable of civilized life. Amongst the innumerable permutations generated by artists and cartoonists were Frankensteinian brutes and also vampires. While the Irish gave as good as they got by quickly reappropriating these images in newspaper caricatures of the monstrous English, they were never able to mobilize the full weight of an intransigently siminianizing discourse on so many and so varied levels as their adversaries.[19]

One can see Irish politicians strenuously attempting to counter English prejudices. There is in 'the Irish race of to-day . . . no taint of intellectual degeneracy,' William O'Brien told an audience in Cork in 1885. And in a later lecture he tried to tackle head-on what he called 'one of the grotesque assumptions of the opponents of Home Rule': 'that the Irish population is composed of two races who have never melted together, and can never by any possibility melt together,' namely, the English settlers and the Celts. For the truth was that the settlers had repeatedly 'defied English statutes to seek the hands of Irish wives,' with the result that 'in all ages [there] has been the breaking down of the barriers, the identification of the colonists with the natives.' On this view, 'Celtic genius' is strong enough to attract, disarm and absorb its English Other. As we will see, this was not in itself an unusual argument. Distinguished English commentators were prepared to argue along very similar lines, albeit with somewhat different conclusions. However, the terms of the racialized discourse in which O'Brien is caught, his tactic of replacing the lie of a rigidly necessary separatism by the truth of good breeding, forces him to invoke a more distant point on the racial hierarchy in order to make his case. The aim of 'English policy,' he says, has 'invariably' been 'to stand apart from the native population as disdainfully as an English regiment operating in the country of the Hottentots.'[20] But as the behavior of the settlers has shown again and again, the Irish are objects of desire, not objects of disdain: they are precisely *not* Hottentots. Unlike the African colonies, Ireland represents no unbridgeable divide, no low Other beyond the pale of civilization, but rather a neighbor of equal status. Fraternizing with the 'natives' can naturally only enrich and enliven the two populations as they co-mingle in what ought to be their parallel but independent national spheres. In short, race appears here in the form of an ethnology that has been thoroughly *sexualized*.

Stoker's two novels of the 1890s, written from his base in the English metropolis, cover the same discursive territory as O'Brien's speeches, but without the same confidence, the same élan. *The Snake's Pass* and *Dracula* commence from a shared epistemological standpoint, encapsulated in the figure of the Englishman abroad, but what is deeply problematic in both instances is any simple 'identification . . . with the natives.' Even in the less complex of the two narratives, *The Snake's Pass*, the path to true love has to be smoothed by some adroit racial and religious maneuvering in order to sanitize and rationalize the stirrings of desire. Norah Joyce, the untutored 'peasant girl' with whom Arthur falls in love, is made to inhabit an uncertain zone of sexual exoticism in which the invitational play of race has to be held in check by the dangerous sexuality of miscegenation. In Arthur's male imaginary, 'this ideal fantasy' (p. 51) bears the 'traces of Spanish blood and Spanish beauty' that can be found 'along the west coast of Ireland,' but a beauty brought to perfection by 'being tempered with northern calm' (p. 75). What Norah cannot be, however, as Arthur makes plain while discussing his sexual 'ideal' with Andy, his Irish driver, is 'all dark,' a 'nigger.' It is Andy who colloquially draws the essential discrimination, universalizing his and Arthur's own whiteness as the heterosexual norm: 'a girrul can be dark enough fur any man widout bein' a naygur.' (p. 101). But even this move is insufficient to secure Norah's nuptial respectability. In a land of priests, fairy tales, and legends of saints, she must also be distinguished as Protestant, and this denomination is then articulated with class to provide her with the necessary motivation and self-discipline to 'try so earnestly to improve,' to school herself out of her peasant background so as to rise 'higher and nearer to your level' (p. 157).

The Snake's Pass negotiates Ireland's history of successive invasions and the problem of its colonial status by condensing them into the quest for companionate marriage.[21] In Dracula, by contrast, the narrative of invasion is more directly engaged, and in consequence the risks to marital success are at once more lurid and more threatening. The English clerk Jonathan Harker's journey to Transylvania takes him into the heart of a darkness in which miscegenation is deeply inscribed in the country's history as a battleground between the warring tribes of old, and between East and West. Dracula's land gathers together 'every known superstition in the world,' making it 'the centre of some sort of imaginative whirlpool' (p. 10), a place of 'many nationalities' (p. 14), 'the whirlpool of European races,' where Count Dracula is the leader of 'a conquering race' in whose 'veins flows the blood of many brave races' (p. 41). When Dracula proudly narrates the bellicose history of his people, the imagery he employs is as much about the mixing as the spilling of blood, interspersed with peasant legends that imagine the savagery of invaders as descended from 'the blood of those old witches' who would mate 'with the devils in the desert' (p. 41). Jonathan Harker discovers a country that is still the victim of its own history, in which the inhabitants are terrified of and terrorized by the barbarian elements in their midst, a condition he soon comes to share. Wandering into the remotest reaches of the Castle Dracula, Harker sentimentally fantasizes a medieval idyll in which gentle maidens pine for their absent menfolk, only to find himself descending rapidly into nightmare. His chaste bachelorhood promises to be fatally compromised on the very threshold of his marriage as three seductive 'ladies' of the night suddenly appear, provoking in him a 'wicked, burning desire' that threatens to destroy all hope of respectable domesticity (p. 51). Though Jonathan narrowly escapes their clutches, he sees at first hand what these vampire women are capable of, for he is forced to stand by helplessly as they cannibalize a living child.

Once Jonathan realizes that he has become Dracula's prisoner, the conditions of his captivity are revealed as a microcosm of Transylvanian social and ethnic relations. Helping the count prepare for his journey to England and effectively guarding the castle are a band of gipsies or 'Szgany,' 'peculiar to this part of the world.' They proliferate throughout the region in their 'thousands,' 'fearless and without religion, save superstition' and speaking 'only their own varieties of the Romany tongue.' Capriciously allying themselves with any powerful nobleman and taking on his name, they are (records the horrified solicitor's clerk) 'almost outside all law' (pp. 55–6). In the crudely racialized ethnology of Stoker's day, this migratory way of life was seen as a cause of cultural backwardness 'destined to perish, the sooner it goes the happier for mankind.' Francis Galton, the statistician and later eugenicist, regarded what he called 'the nomadic disposition' as utterly 'alien to the genius of an enlightened civilization,' so that 'the primary qualities of the typical modern British workman are already the very opposite of those of the nomad.' Alien it may have been, but not so alien that this vision of progress could not contain the seeds of its own potential reversal. Side by side with the optimism of Galton and others was a sense of the precariousness of such advances, particularly in the light of the hardships of industrial life for the urban working classes, which were felt to be 'crushing them into degeneracy.' There was, warned Galton, a very real danger that those 'best fitted to play their part on the stage of life' would increasingly be 'crowded out by the incompetent, the ailing, and the desponding.'[22]

The spectre of bad blood and degeneration evoked by *Dracula*'s imaginary terrain and its sinister inhabitants always harkens back to an anxiety about the lineaments of national identity, about the health and vigor of a race. Like the vampire in late-nineteenth-century political cartoons, Stoker's narrative shuttles to and fro between settings, never settling into a definitive formulaic set of meanings, but rather exploiting political resonances of contemporary ethnology to create a sense of social and psychic terror. Put another way, one can see much of the fear that stalks the pages of *Dracula* as reflecting the underside of the liberalism to which Stoker adhered, a nightmare vision of unruly subjects who are unamenable to its formal democratic calculus. For insofar as liberalism's theory of citizenship is based upon a political rationality that conceives of rights and duties in both highly abstract and highly individualized terms, it seeks to deflect and devalue those collective demands and aspirations that arise out of the solidarities of particular communities. For example, the liberal jurist A.V. Dicey argued that the new male voters admitted through British electoral reform would be likely to see themselves primarily as 'citizens' or 'persons' rather than as proletarians loyal to their social class. To think of political representation in this bloodless way ('regardless of race, colour, or creed') is to be forever haunted by the return of those flesh-and-blood identities that liberalism seeks to neutralize or exclude. Consequently, a constant preoccupation of liberal thought has been the need for scientific study of the causes of what were seen as society's most deeply irrational currents, epitomized by the ebb and flow of city crowds, those mass phenomena most at odds with liberalism's preferred atomistic logic. By the turn of the century, the fear of degeneration so prominent in the work of Francis Galton had been so thoroughly absorbed by modern liberals and intellectuals that one of them, J.A. Hobson, could argue that, as the result of urban living, 'the popular mind had reverted . . . into a type of primitive savagery dangerous for modern civilization.'[23] As always, it is the language of race that names civilization's deepest fears and discontents.

In keeping with liberalism's gathering mood of insecurity, both *Dracula* and *The Snake's Pass* make a mockery of the law, throwing its agents into crisis. *The Snake's Pass* strongly implies that Ireland's troubles represent a failure of bourgeois legality, since the accusation against the usurer Black Murdock is that (like the English) he has 'made the law an engine of oppression' (p. 37). A man who filches other people's lands for his own selfish gain is popularly regarded as a common criminal ('that black-jawed ruffian, Murdock'), and it is therefore only poetic justice when he is finally swallowed up in an Irish bog, destroyed by his own greed and by the land he tries to steal. Similarly, in the legend of the buried treasure with which the novel begins, when the King of the Snakes is described as looking 'mighty evil' he is said to be 'as slow an' as hard as an attorney,' a sign of the law's disrepute ('I'm the whole govermint here') at the hands of a willful monarch (p. 21).

Dracula also is much concerned with legal matters. The novel is after all a quasi-legal narrative of the type popularized by Wilkie Collins in which the various characters, including several scientific experts and 'a full-blown' lawyer, offer testimony to the material facts they are supposed to have witnessed. Nevertheless, here too justice is far from certain, as the story's heroes are periodically obliged to flout the law in the interests of a higher moral code. At the beginning of the novel, the unsuspecting Jonathan Harker is even misled into believing that Count Dracula really 'would have made a wonderful solicitor' (p. 44). In a sense, this is exactly what happens: Dracula dresses up in Jonathan's suit and carries out his grisly nighttime pursuits while masquerading as a representative of English law.

From his very first appearance, Dracula's 'marked physiognomy' is a clue that he will ultimately be assimilated to the condition of a most uncommon criminal, a specimen belonging in the annals of the Italian criminal anthropologist Cesare Lombroso. Once *Dracula*'s protagonists have agreed that 'the Count is a criminal and of criminal type' – in other words that he is merely a creature 'of imperfectly formed mind' and can be outwitted (p. 406) – the way is cleared for the vampire's defeat. Stoker's explicit references to the emergent criminology of the 1890s is another pointer towards the national–racial context of his writing and to the terrors that lay at its threshold. Read against its original Italian background, criminal anthropology was intended to be a disciplinary tool of national consolidation, in which the study of crime provided for the diagnosis and the cure of a nation's moral sickness. If the dilemma for post-unification nationalists was expressed in the dictum 'we have made Italy, now we have to make Italians,' then what Lombroso's new science hoped to achieve was to demarcate sharply the eligible body of authentic citizens from its pathological Others – hereditary criminals, cases of atavism and degeneracy, and the criminally insane.[24] By mapping the distribution of criminal acts and criminal bodies onto the new national and regional space, 'criminal anthropology constituted at once a political geography, a conjectural history of civilisation, an evolutionary account of organisms and races.'[25]

Dracula speaks to the most troubled point in the whole criminological project: the difficulty of recognizing the criminal by sight. Famous for his elaborate taxonomic use of photography, Lombroso was forced to modify drastically his emphasis upon the so-called 'born criminal' whose 'natural' pathology was supposed to be clearly legible from the miscreant's face and body type. What is disturbing about the vampire is that he can be so hard to read, altering his 'marked physiognomy,' passing as an English gentleman. The terror inspired by Count Dracula is a terror of biological difference both masked and *manqué*. When Jonathan Harker sees the count in Piccadilly in broad daylight, in the heart of the British Empire, mingling amongst London's 'teeming millions,' his terror is that no one else knows that the count is a vampire (p. 215).

The vicissitudes of the law and its ethnological and criminological supports suggest a flawed modernity, a modernity still struggling with the powers of the past. When the protagonists of *Dracula* come together to swear a 'solemn compact,' they are effectively renewing the social contract, pledging allegiance not simply to each other as comrades in arms, but as members of a liberal bourgeois order. Despite the invocation of archaic symbols, the laying of hands on the 'golden crucifix,' their ceremony is a virtual rehearsal of liberal protocols. The pursuit of the vampire is 'serious work,' to be undertaken 'in as businesslike a way, as any other transaction of life,' and with all the characteristically modern freedoms: freedom of association, freedom 'to act and think,' and access to the 'resources of science.' 'In fact,' their leader Dr Van Helsing reminds them, 'so far as our powers extend, they are unfettered, and we are free to use them' (pp. 284–5). At the turning point of the novel, therefore, the modern subject is being reconstituted as a prelude to the final, heroic climax in which Count Dracula is driven back to his Transylvanian lair and destroyed.

But as we have seen, in Stoker's writing this same subject is hedged about with qualifications, limited by racial, sexual, or religious status. Femininity, for example, is normatively defined by its lack of 'the man's desire for action'; hence Stoker's repeated polemic against the suffragette and the New Woman. On this model male strength is confirmed by its mastery of feeling. As Arthur Severn puts it in *The Snake's Pass*: 'there are times when manhood must assert itself, even though the heart be torn with pity for woman's weakness' (pp. 125–31). Arthur's naturalization of his own desperate aggressiveness seems conventional enough, fixing the usual binaries — active/passive, strength/weakness, reason/emotion, masculine/feminine — firmly in place. Yet it is important to see that this asymmetrically gendered pairing in turn depends for its appeal upon a pathologized low Other to whom it comes perilously close while always overtly insisting upon its exclusion. Norah's 'Spanish blood' is 'tempered with northern calm' in order to block the delirious slide towards the Mediterranean and the African (p. 75).

Blurred at their edges, these oppositions start to take on new meaning once Ireland has been fully situated within the already racialized zone of 'northern calm.' The ordinary Irish 'nature' is 'essentially emotional,' and the sight of oppression will release 'a torrent of commiseration, sympathy and pity,' even to the point of tears (p. 37). The spontaneous show of emotion is partly explained here in terms of the rustic simplicity of rural life and is of course being explicitly marked as such by a modern metropolitan eye, an eye habituated to the exercise of scientific reason. Arthur is hopelessly in love, but his rationalizing reflexes even lead him to speculate that 'the wave theory that rules our knowledge of the distribution of light and sound, may well be taken to typify . . . the beating in unison of human hearts' (p. 122). Certainly, as in *Dracula*, *The Snake's Pass* intrudes a logical, procedural eye into a hinterland that is awash with superstition, setting a Protestant discipline against a Catholic worldview with its crucifixes, legends, and stories of saints. But in this imaginary Ireland – whose terrors are only fully unleashed in *Dracula* – there is an almost Rousseauesque reverence for the uncorrupted emotionalism of peasant life, idealized as a natural sign of simple goodness.

Although Stoker's treatment of the Irish national character never strays far from the received categories of his period, his beliefs are compromised by his own cultural affiliations. In *The Study of Celtic Literature* (1867), for example, Matthew Arnold had argued that 'the Celtic races' were best defined by their quality of 'sentiment'; 'quick to feel impressions, and feeling them very strongly,' they were 'keenly sensitive to joy and sorrow.' Celtic 'sensuousness' had 'made Ireland,' yet because 'the Celt' lacked 'the skilful and resolute appliance of means to ends which is needed both to make progress in material civilisation, and also to form powerful states,' its culture and politics were 'poor, slovenly, and half barbarous.' On these grounds Arnold claimed that the union of Great Britain and Ireland raised the possibility of a racial synthesis of Celtic emotion with Anglo-Saxon pragmatism, taking literature as a model of the higher reconciliation of opposites that might be achieved.[26] Writing over two decades later in the thick of the crisis over Home Rule, the kind of apologetics for the Act of Union represented by Arnold's new imperial subject presented Stoker with a dilemma. On the one hand, as an Irishman born into the Protestant middle class and a former civil servant for the Crown, Stoker was predisposed to make sense of the world through similar categories and oppositions. On the other hand, however, as a supporter of Irish Home Rule, Stoker was compelled to place a different valuation on Celtic sentimentality, complicating the identification of masculinity with strength of character defined against the flood of emotion.

The idea of the Irish as 'essentially emotional,' when taken together with references to tears as 'unmanly signs of emotion,' seems to suggest that the unguarded outflow of affect is a source of racial and cultural weakness (p. 90). At least, many Victorians in the 1880s and 1890s would have regarded it as such, for by that period ideals of manliness had largely been purged of any open expression of feeling in favor of a self-confident physical robustness that regarded any undue sensitivity with suspicion. 'What was taught and learned,' argues Raymond

Williams, was 'a new and rigid control, "self-control" – even weak men not crying and being very stiff and proud of it where much stronger men before them had wept when the feeling, the impulse was there.'[27] In Stoker's work, however, the point is that the men *do* cry, even if sometimes only 'surreptitiously' (p. 90). In vindication of the feminized Irish, the historically dominant version of Victorian masculinity is unpacked by reintroducing a complex emotional economy into the male body and psyche. That this is a dangerous and controversial move is shown by the defence of male hysteria in *Dracula*, where an uncontrolled excess of emotion is simultaneously treated as both frightening and reassuring. On several occasions male characters succumb to bouts of hysteria while under extreme pressure. The terror Jonathan Harker experiences as a result of his imprisonment in the Castle Dracula, for example, constantly threatens his sanity, 'destroy-ing my nerve' (p. 46). But the most elaborate account appears when Dr Van Helsing breaks down into 'a regular fit of hysterics' following the death of a young female patient at Count Dracula's hands. Shocking one of his medical colleagues by 'laugh[ing] and cry[ing] together, just as a woman does,' Van Helsing explains his disquieting behavior away as a spontaneous release from trauma and distress, a way of 'eas[ing] off the strain,' that is all the more natural because it comes unbidden. Nevertheless, this emotional self-surrender remains sufficiently sensit-ive for Van Helsing to later deny 'that it was hysterics' (pp. 209–12).

I have tried to show that Stoker's use of such 'sciences' as physiognomy and criminal anthropology – what one might call his ethnological imagination – are closely tied to the question of Irish nationalism in his fiction of the 1890s. The notions of masculinity and femininity, of degeneracy and good breeding implicit in these books all pass through the racialized discourse of moral and physiological difference so critical to late Victorian conceptions of the social body. Some years earlier, Stoker's hero and fellow physiognomist Walt Whitman had called for the renewal of America, based upon what he had termed a 'democratic ethnology of the future,' a 'science' with proto-eugenic overtones.[28] Like Whitman, Stoker invokes an ethno-logy that also reaches out to sexuality for its assumptions about national character and cultural identity: a sexual ethnology, in fact. Stoker's attempted merger between the expressive man of sensibility and the strong, steadfast man of action has to be understood as ultimately driven by anxieties about the Irish male as subject, just as the fantasy of Irish womanhood requires the careful management of national–racial hierarchies if its desired exoticism is not to be rendered impure and shameful. There is throughout Stoker's texts an obsession with unfixing the boundaries, with the attractions of liminality, in order that the lines of demarcation might be all the more strictly controled.

In the final analysis Stoker stretches the categories of gender and race to their conventional limits. And this means that he always runs the risk of unseating the familiar logic of difference, sending it spinning in new and frightening directions. For Stoker, there is a constant sense that the divide between the stable and the unstable is itself unstable, that the line cannot be held. Subjects and nations seem to oscillate between modernity and atavism, and no science of race or place quite promises to guarantee the former without the latter. Perhaps it is only fitting, then, that Stoker should be allowed the last emblematic word on this point.

In *The Snake's Pass* 'a shifting bog' is believed to hide buried treasure and at various moments comes to stand for the Irish homeland and its womanhood, the story of its past carrying sediments of the country's history of underdevelopment. In the novel the bog is a symbolic source of horror and laughter, knowledge and uncertainty. The engineer who surveys its movements offers a prognosis that is at once bleak and suggestive: 'Then with this . . . bog suddenly saturated and weakened – demoralized as it were – and devoid of resisting power, the whole floating mass of the upper bog might descend on it, mingle with it, become incorporated with its semi-fluid substance, and form a new and dangerous quagmire incapable of sustaining solid weight.' In this geological forecast, 'saturated' slips too quickly and too tellingly into 'demoralized,' bringing the sexual or the social body irresistibly to mind as if the decomposition of the land can only be properly grasped by somehow being mapped onto cultural fears. The muddled metonymic relation between the physical and the cultural conjures up a common geography of bodies and land masses, an equivalence still central to so much of nationalist discourse today. But once these raw materials of nations are 'weakened,' once they become 'devoid' of a truly masculine 'resisting power,' they lose their cultural solidity and identity, they 'become soft and less cohesive.' Nevertheless, Arthur's awed response at the prospect of witnessing such 'upheaval and complete displacement and chaos' in the Irish landscape reveals the implicitly sexual fascination as well as the terror invoked for Stoker by the spectacle of degeneration and decline: 'Really . . . you put it most graphically. What a terrible thing it would be to live on the line of such a change' (pp. 67–9).

Notes

1. David Lloyd, *Nationalism and Minor Literature: James Clarence Mangan and the Emergence of Irish Cultural Nationalism* (Berkeley: University of California Press, 1987), p. ix.

2. See E.J. Hobsbawm, *Nations and Nationalism Since 1780: Programme, Myth, Reality* (Cambridge: Cambridge University Press, 1990) for an overview of the history of nationalism. However, Hobsbawm argues for a linear, two-stage model of this history that seriously underestimates the early development of cultural nationalism and the importance of 'scientific' theories of race throughout the nineteenth century.

3. Thomas Flanagan, 'Literature in English, 1801–91,' in W.E. Vaughan, ed., *A New History of Ireland Vol.V: Ireland Under the Union, I: 1801-70* (Oxford: Clarendon Press, 1989), p. 495. For a careful statement of some of the problems of interpretation here, see Julian Moynahan, 'The Politics of Anglo-Irish Gothic: Maturin, Le Fanu and "The Return of the Repressed," ' in Heinz Kosok, ed., *Studies in Anglo-Irish Literature* (Bonn: Bouvier Verlag Herbert Grundmann, 1982), pp. 43–53.

4. See W.J. McCormack's analysis of J. Sheridan Le Fanu's later novels in 'J. Sheridan Le Fanu's "Richard Marston" (1848): The History of an Anglo-Irish Text,' in Francis Barker et al., eds., *1848: The Sociology of Literature* (Colchester: University of Essex, 1978), pp. 107–25.

5. *With Walt Whitman in Camden*, vol. 4, Horace Traubel, ed., (Carbondale: Southern Illinois University Press, 1959), pp. 181–5.

6. See Daniel Farson, *The Man Who Wrote Dracula: A Biography of Bram Stoker* (London: Michael Joseph, 1975), p. 36.

7. On Stoker's support for Irish Home Rule, see his *Personal Reminiscences of Henry Irving* (New York: Macmillan, 1906). Details of his friendship with the Wilde family can be found in Harry Ludlam, *A Biography of Dracula: The Life Story of Bram Stoker* (Slough: W. Foulsham & Co., 1962), pp. 32–3.

8. William O'Brien to Bram Stoker, July 30, 1890 (House of Commons, London). The Brotherton Library, Leeds.

9. Information regarding Stoker's library is taken from the Sotheby auction catalogue for July 7, 1913. On Florence Stoker's collection, see David J. Skal, *Hollywood Gothic: The Tangled Web of Dracula from Novel to Stage to Screen* (New York: W.W. Norton, 1990), p. 180.

10. *Labour World* November 29, 1890, p. 15. Like William O'Brien, Davitt was an early associate of Parnell who later took a critical, anti-Parnellite position. By this period he was urging readers of his paper that cooperation with Gladstone's Liberal Party was essential if Home Rule was to be won.

11. *Personal Reminiscences of Henry Irving*, Chapter XLV.

12. On Yeats, see Margaret Chesnutt, *Studies in the Short Stories of William Carleton* (Goteborg: Acta Universitatis Gothoburgensis, 1976), p. 7.

13. Bram Stoker, *The Snake's Pass* (Dingle, Co. Kerry: Brandon, 1990), p. 61. Subsequent references are given in parenthesis.

13. See Christopher Morash's Introduction to W.M. Thackeray, *The Irish Sketchbook* (Gloucester: Alan Sutton, 1990), pp. xiii–xix.

15. *Charles Kingsley: His Letters and Memories of His Life*, vol. 2, edited by his wife (London: Henry S. King & Co., 1877), p. 107.

16. Bram Stoker, *Dracula* (Harmondsworth: Penguin, 1979), pp. 24–6. Subsequent references are given in parenthesis.

17. Traubel, *With Walt Whitman in Camden*, vol. 4, pp. 183–4.

18. Bram Stoker, 'Mr. Winston Churchill Talks of His Hopes, His Work, and His Ideals to Bram Stoker,' *Daily Chronicle*, January 15, 1908, p. 8. For further discussion of Stoker's use of physiognomy, see my essay 'Bram Stoker and the Crisis of the Liberal Subject,' *New Literary History* no. 234 (Autumn 1992), pp. 983–1002.

19. See L. Perry Curtis, *Apes and Angels: The Irishman in Victorian Caricature* (Washington: Smithsonian Institution Press, 1971).

20. William O'Brien, *Irish Ideas* (London: Longmans, Green & Co., 1893), pp. 10–12, 115–16. Although O'Brien's later lecture, 'Toleration in the Fight for Ireland,' was delivered in Belfast in November 1892, the reference to Hottentots probably derives from a rabidly anti-Home Rule speech by the Conservative Marquis of Salisbury in May 1886, in which the Irish were compared to the Hottentots in their unfitness for self-government. On the place of the Hottentot woman in nineteenth-century sexual discourse, see Sander L. Gilman, 'Black Bodies, White Bodies: Toward an Iconography of Female Sexuality in Late Nineteenth-Century Art, Medicine, and Literature,' in Henry Louis Gates, Jr, ed., *'Race,' Writing, and Difference* (Chicago: University of Chicago Press, 1986).

21. The novel's romantic component is inextricably fused with the other main narrative line in *The Snake's Pass*: the quest for buried treasure left by French soldiers in the aftermath of a failed invasion. When Arthur asks Norah's father for his daughter's hand in marriage, Phelim Joyce declares that 'whin the treasure of Knockcalltecrore is found, thin ye may claim her if ye will an' I'll freely let her go!' (p. 145).

22. Francis Galton, *Hereditary Genius: An Inquiry into Its Laws and Consequences* (1869; reprinted London: Macmillan, 1914), pp. 334–43.

23. Cited in John A. Hall, *Liberalism: Politics, Ideology and the Market* (London: Paladin, 1988), p. 69. Hobson was particularly horrified by the upsurge of popular sentiment during the Boer War; he wrote *The Psychology of Jingoism* (1901) 'to explain how the mass mind could have been so manipulated into supporting rabid nationalism and war.'

24. The quotation is from Massimo d'Azeglio as cited in Hobsbawm, *Nations and Nationalism*, p. 44. On Lombrosian criminology in its Italian context, see Daniel Pick, *Faces of Degeneration: A European Disorder, c.1848–c.1918* (Cambridge: Cambridge University Press, 1989), Chapter 5.

25. Pick, *Faces of Degeneration*, p. 141. Lombroso's conventional hierarchy of races was central to his national criminological enterprise. In *The White Man and the Coloured Man* (1871), Lombroso claimed that 'only we White people have reached the most perfect symmetry of bodily form . . . Only we have created true nationalism . . . [and] freedom of thought' (quoted in Pick, p. 126).

26. Matthew Arnold, *The Study of Celtic Literature* (London: Smith, Elder and Co., 1912), pp. 84–8. From a different perspective, compare Michael Davitt's claim that Irishmen are 'warm-hearted, impulsive, and generous,' these being the 'distinguishing qualities of their race.' Editorial, *Labour World*, November 29, 1890, p. 8.

27. Raymond Williams, *The English Novel from Dickens to Lawrence* (1970; reprinted London: The Hogarth Press, 1984), p. 62.

28. Walt Whitman, *Democratic Vistas* (1871; reprinted New York: Liberal Arts Press, 1949), p. 37. In the subsequent paragraph Whitman gestures towards what would soon be called eugenics to underwrite his 'basic model or portrait of personality for general use for the manliness of the States': 'Will the time hasten when fatherhood and motherhood shall become a science – and the noblest science?'

4

Notes on 'Activist Photography'
Steven Cagan

In this essay I look briefly at some historical and critical issues important to understanding the meaning of 'political photography.' I take some steps towards a necessarily incomplete, tentative and personal definition of this somewhat treacherous expression. Finally, I look at my own practice as one possible model of photographic activism.

The invention of practical photographic technologies in the early part of the nineteenth century was the culmination of a centuries-long search for ways to use lenses as aids to drawing, and to allow objects in the 'real' world, or the light they emitted or reflected, to create a self-generated image.[1] The view of photographs as 'real' representations has had a critical role in the enormous impact photography has had in our ideological and material lives.

Photographs are generally seen as more 'realistic' than any painting or drawing. They *look* like more 'objective' or real representations, despite the almost-too-obvious limitations on their realism – they are two-dimensional; they portray the world in tones of gray or highly artificial color; they are the wrong size, still and silent; they are rectangles.

A well-known early daguerreotype shows an intersection in the Boulevard du Temple, in Paris. The contemporary audience – and we, to the extent we are able to shed our sophistication about visual imagery – was amazed by the realism of the portrayal. Yet it is in an important respect not only unrealistic, but a virtual lie. Anything that moved much during the long exposure required by the relatively insensitive photographic material left no 'trace' on the plate. Thus the 'empty' streets are a consequence of technological limitations – the streets were bustling. A favorite detail in this picture is the bottom half of a bootblack and almost all of his customers in the lower center, visible because they did not move much.[2]

There are some indications that as 'natural' and 'direct' as photos seem to us, the ability to 'read' a photograph is socially learned. Allan Sekula, in his ground-breaking article, 'On the Invention of Photographic Meaning,' refers to a study in which a mother in a 'bush' culture fails to recognize her child in photographs until the resemblance is explained.[3]

A broad critical consensus has emerged that photography is in some senses a language – conventional and artificial, requiring a socially agreed upon code for successful communication, etcetera. And yet there is something compellingly attractive – and true – in the common-sense view of a photograph's 'realism.' Any photographic image results from a direct brush with the physical world being represented. It is a product of that physical world's impinging on light-sensitive materials. While we may not think of this when we look at a snapshot, and many of us cannot even explain it, we sense there is a way a photograph is a *trace* of what 'was there' that can never be true of a drawing or painting – even if a particular painting or drawing is more informative or accurate than a particular photograph.[4]

Photographs appeal to common sense through our understanding that photographers have to go to the places they want to represent. 'Orientalist' painters could work in their Paris studios, rendering 'the oriental bazaar,' 'the harem,' or whatever struck their special sensibilities, but nineteenth-century photographers who picked up those themes had physically to go to Egypt or wherever. They brought back 'real' traces; the photographs are evidence that the photographer was actually there, and actually saw something. For photography, unlike non-lens media, the subject has to exist, or at least to have existed when the photograph was made. Because of this quality, snapshots of dead people or photographs of century-old buildings have a special way of letting us see into the past.

The power of photographs to convince us of their 'reality' is based on a paradox at the very heart of the medium: photographs both are and are not direct representations of the world; they communicate both 'directly' (almost) and through a mediated set of signs and codes; they give the *appearance* of 'realism' and they *are* 'realistic.'[5]

This special 'documentary' value of photographs was recognized from the very early days.[6] Indeed, one of the problems for early photographic artists was that their work was not considered 'real art' because it 'merely' provided an 'exact reproduction' of the world.

The widely accepted truth value of photographs was exploited in a number of ways starting in the mid nineteenth century. British photographs of the Crimean War were used as evidence of the neglect of soldiers' medical needs and well-being, helped in the efforts to raise relief for what Queen Victoria referred to as 'the mutilated,'[7] and contributed to the critique of the view of war as a civilized contest between gentlemen officers.

Photographs of Civil War battlefields by such well-known workers as Matthew Brady and Timothy O'Sullivan had similar effects although, paradoxically, the horrific presentation of what the photographers called 'the harvest of death' seemed to stiffen the resolve to win the war, even as it awakened consciousness of its brutal nature.

Later, US photographers were sent with expeditions to the West, especially in support of the movement to create national parks. The work of people like W.H. Jackson and Timothy O'Sullivan, among others, was very important in allowing members of Congress to believe some of the incredible stories about the natural wonders of the region.

The 'reliability' of photographs was so strong that before half-tone printing publishers relied on an authority lent by photographs even when they could not reproduce them, claiming that the images they used – wood-plate engravings or etchings – were 'based upon' photographs.

Even some of the photographs of the pioneer of social documentary photography, Jacob Riis, appeared in *How the Other Half Lives* in the form of woodcuts.[8] Actually, this book is a bridge between two eras, as it contains both fairly primitive-looking half-tones and line drawings.

The popular sense that photographs represent the world with a special realism has not diminished much over the years. Although there is a widespread understanding that photographs may be manipulated or misleading ('Photographs don't lie, but liars photograph'), and this certainly is an issue, the more subtle and ultimately more significant set of problems at the very heart of photographic communication are seldom addressed.[9] A few cases might indicate the enduring strength of our belief in the 'objective' quality of photographs, and what happens when it is violated.

The first case is that of the Farm Security Administration photographer Arthur Rothstein, who was accused of faking a photograph of a bleached-out cow skull on a cracked, arid field.[10] A newspaper hostile to the New Deal said Rothstein carried the skull around in his car, looking for an appropriate place to photograph it. He apparently denied the accusation, but admitted to having moved the skull. This created a scandal, and is a much-discussed incident to this day.[11]

One might argue that there *was* a drought, and even if Rothstein did move the skull, the result was just a more dramatic picture of the situation. But the scandal was produced not by the accusation that Rothstein had said something untrue, but rather that he had rearranged elements in a documentary photograph, thereby weakening the credibility of his image. Ignoring the fact that *any* photograph implies decisions (about what to include and exclude, camera angle, etcetera), the critics point to the alleged physical manipulation. They know that if the criticism is believed, the public will feel that Rothstein has betrayed them, and his credibility will be undermined.

The strength of this criticism is directly dependent on the strength of the belief that a documentary-looking photograph is a 'real' picture of what was 'really there.' The sense of betrayal that emerges is evidence of the grip that the notion of objectivity in photography still maintains. The less we believe that claim in the first place, the less scandalized we are by Rothstein's behavior. But the skepticism about photography's claim to objectivity widely – and correctly – held among scholars and media workers has not made major inroads in popular consciousness.

A second case relating to this is that of the well-known Civil War image by Alexander Gardner, 'Home of a Rebel Sharpshooter.' Gardner faked this photograph. It is a real corpse, but the man probably was not a sharpshooter but a common soldier. Gardner moved the body and gun about forty yards (after doing scholars the courtesy of photographing the body where he had found it), to create a 'better' image. This is an acknowledged photographic lie, and it continues to haunt photo documentarians and journalists.[12]

I am often asked, 'Did you really find it like that, or did you arrange it?' It is clear that my audience wants to believe that I have portrayed things very much as I have found them – and the more they agree with my point of view, the more important this is to them.

The depth of popular faith in photography's 'realism' is highlighted by a new challenge to its credibility from 'digitized' images – photographs that are optically scanned and reduced to binary information. Photojournalism is particularly embroiled in controversy over this new technology.

Publishers are enthusiastic about reducing the time and expense of producing, transmitting and publishing images. Some photographers and editors fret, as the ease of manipulation threatens the very evidentiary or 'documentary' quality upon which their journalistic utility is based.

This is not an abstract fear. *National Geographic* magazine has already changed two cover images: once, they straightened the badge on a Polish soldier's hat. Another time, when two Egyptian pyramids were slightly too far apart to provide a strong composition, they moved them closer together! These actions provoked a minor scandal, and *National Geographic* has promised not to do it again. Some editors have made public pledges that they won't alter images.

Not all editors are moved by these scruples. As part of the work of demonizing Saddam Hussein before the Gulf War, the *New Republic* ran a cover picture in which his moustache was trimmed to make him look like Hitler. In case readers missed the none-too-subtle manipulation (I do not know whether it was done by computer or by airbrush), the magazine laid a title over the picture with an unsubtle word play – the headline, 'FUROR IN THE GULF.' In this case, the editors actually gave the retoucher a credit, after the photographer. Because of our confidence in what a photographic image is, this portrayal is dishonest in a way that a caricature, no matter how offensive it may be, never is.

Before the days of computer manipulation, we knew about airbrush manipulations – the disappearance of Trotsky and Bakunin from Soviet photographs, the use of photomontage by Roy Cohn and Joe McCarthy, etcetera. And there are lies – then-Secretary of State Alexander Haig held up a photograph of burning bodies he claimed were the victims of Sandinista bombing of civilians; they were actually bodies burned by the Red Cross after a massacre by the Somocista National Guard of Nicaragua.

Discussion of such cases has generally ignored the more subtle and serious questions about photographic 'truth,' and failed to challenge the credibility of photographs, a credibility which, despite the insights of critical theory, has survived essentially unaltered since the beginnings of the medium.[13]

This look at how photographs are understood, or 'read,' was meant to suggest the importance of a complex and fundamental theoretical problem. The issue is not to demonstrate that photographs are 'really real' (that would be hard to do) or that they are not (which has been only too easy to 'prove'), but to look at the very powerful sense of reality and truthfulness that photographs create. Political criticism of documentary and other social photographic practices has largely been based on an assault on that appearance of reality, as well as on other covert ideological premises which function in the ways images are used and understood.

*

One of the most important theoretical challenges to the 'objective' or 'realistic' quality of photographic representation, based on semiotic theory, holds that photography is an inherently 'polysemic' medium, which depends on its context for its meaning. The notion of context here is a complex one; it includes not only the immediate physical surroundings of the image (students often mistakenly confuse 'context' and 'text'), but also such things as the culture and life history of the audience, both collectively and as individuals.[14] Some of the meaning-determining elements of context are brought willy-nilly to the encounter between image and viewer. Others are intentionally introduced by the photographer or the presenter of the image.

Photography never necessarily supports a particular 'reading' of its subjects.[15] The intentions of the photographer, the physical environment or setting of the images, the social and political ambience in which the images are presented and seen, the historical juncture, the knowledge or prejudices the audience has about the subject, and many other factors will effect the very meaning of the image. This notion of context as determinant of meaning is of particular importance in the kind of photographic practices that we are interested in.

There was a time when it seemed that an interest in political photography meant an interest in photography of 'political subjects' – social injustice, war, poverty, and movements and activities to change the world. This definition never really fitted; a great deal of what was consciously and explicitly 'political' had little to do with narrow definitions of social issues and political activism. As early as the worker photography movement of the 1920s and 1930s, a significant proportion of 'political photography' was really about nothing more than seriously and directly representing aspects of daily life, not only of the poor and the working class, but also of the powerful.

Still, the agenda for political photography was pretty clear. The goal was to portray political issues, to illustrate evils and goods, to educate the viewers and inspire them to action. There were radical photographers and liberal reform photographers, but most shared the sense expressed in Hine's well-known dictum (borrowed from Victor Hugo), 'What, then, is required? Light! Light in floods!' All this activity, whether its goal was to support radical or revolutionary movements or to lend strength to campaigns for reforms of capitalist society, shared a central perspective: the politics was in the content; this was the representation of politics.

In the 1970s a critical examination of documentary photography was launched, stimulated by still-important articles by people such as Martha Rosler and Allan Sekula in the United States, and a number of writers in England, as well as feminist media theory and the redevelopment of a self-conscious political photography movement. The work of these and later writers was a necessary corrective to a number of generally unexamined assumptions about the way documentary (and other socially engaged photography) has functioned. These included the notion that photography was a direct and unmediated representation of an objective 'reality;' that photographs carried inherent meanings, rather than depending on a set of socially determined codes and values; and that the good (generally reform-minded) motives of the photographers obviated any need to examine the multiple relationships among photographer, subjects and audience.

These critics required photographers to think about the way our work might unintentionally reflect and therefore reinforce, rather than challenge, social power relations. They insisted that we confront, rather than accept, photography's claim to represent reality directly. They made it clear that anyone with a serious political agenda in this area must examine the history of the medium, the directions of current practices, and both art world and journalistic assumptions about our work.

A call arose in Left critical work to move from considering 'the representation of politics' to examining 'the politics of representation.' I first saw this formulation in the pages of the British journal *Camerawork*. It succinctly describes the shift I have been discussing, a shift that was a necessary corrective to the kind of unconsidered and unexamined practice that has been all too common among political photographers.

This criticism stimulated us to turn our attention to more theoretical questions of the ways in which meaning is constructed in photographs, and the various levels and kinds of political analysis to which photographs and photography are susceptible. Socially engaged photographers and theorists began to consider how our work, by relying on traditional and ideologically charged understandings of images, may have conveyed meanings different from and even opposed to our intentions.

Of course, this concern was not born in the 1970s, but for many of us it was in those years that we began to address it. This was a serious and important development, as it required us to consider the effects of the way in which we worked, of our relationships with the history of our medium and the institutions which had grown within it, of the politics implicit in our aesthetic decisions, of a host of issues to which many of us had devoted relatively little attention before.

This development was, and is, good. Those political photographers who reject this challenge to our work do so at the peril of reproducing the problems that have by now been so very well laid out to us. The traditional rejection of theory by photographers is simply no longer tenable.

On the other hand, a problem has arisen over the last few years within some ongoing Left critical activity. Some writers (I specifically am *not* talking about Rosler or Sekula) have begun to focus so exclusively and so intensely on the way photography works – on the nature of photographic representation – that they have apparently lost sight of the larger political goals of many activist photographers.[16] Even worse, as part of a general wave of 'postmodernist' criticism, some have begun to deny the possibility of intervening in the real world through photography at all. Interestingly, and disturbingly, by their own route and for their own motives, some Left critics have begun effectively to arrive at the same conclusion as the retired curator of photography of the Museum of Modern Art, John Szarkowski – that photography has nothing important to say about major social/political issues.

My problem is not with the analytic work that has been done on the nature of representation, but in the development of a sense that *only* work that addresses the politics of representation – that is, which examines the construction of meaning in photography, the uses to which images are put, or the media in which photographic images appear – is accepted as politically valid or useful.

As an example of the way this problem develops, let us take the idea that all photographs (like all utterances) are in some sense fictions. This is a concept central to the newer criticism of photography: it is found in everyone from Susan Sontag and John Berger to less popularly known writers such as John Tagg. By now, for anyone with a radical view of photography, it has become an axiom.

This axiom must be accepted as true; it should affect the way we look at and use images; it is a position worth fighting for among those people who do not accept it. But it does not follow that we cannot use photographs to deal with the real world, as some writers would have it, and even less does it follow that there is no real world with which to deal.[17]

There is a too-common leap from recognizing that all languages and systems of discourse are essentially sets of conventions, codes, etcetera, to claiming that language cannot adequately deal with reality; this leap is excessive and unconvincing. Even those philosophers and critics who make the leap continue, after all, to attempt to convince us, and even more, to do so with language. And the further leap, made by some, to the position that there is no reality, or no knowable reality, is a conclusion that is not inherent in the important original analytical insight. It makes a joke of critical thought, and cruelly mocks the real people facing the real problems in their lives that socially committed photographers are trying to address.

While radical criticism has established that photography does not reflect reality in a *direct* way, it still reflects reality in a usefully mediated way – it still functions as a medium. So, for example, these same critics are likely to carry around photographs of their children or people they love or even (horror of horrors), places they have visited. The fact that the picture of Mom is not an unmediated reflection of reality does not deprive it of all use-value – or even of all truth-value. This paradox seems to me the interesting issue for activist photography.

Thus, an excess of zeal in applying 'deconstructive' and 'postmodern' interpretative methods has produced a failure to recognize the following three points:

1. Even if we deconstruct a 'text,' and learn from the deconstruction, the text still remains and may still demand a response.
2. Even if we determine that language is an artificial, conventional system of codes, it still does work, however imperfectly, as language – it does allow communication.
3. Even if photography is not a direct representation of reality, it still does make some reference to a reality which actually does exist. (I will not argue here for the existence of the world; for now I simply posit it.)

There used to be a little joke that illustrated the essential error in the commonsense reading of photographs – the (wise) critic or photographer would take a snapshot of his or her dog from their wallet and ask, 'What is this?' Somebody would answer, 'It's a dog,' and our theorist would pounce with the retort, 'No, it's a photograph of a dog!' This once seemed very telling to me. Now I think that despite the fact that this is only a photo, and that it is only through our adoption of socially determined codes that we can understand it to represent a dog, if it's a decent one we will none the less probably be able to recognize the mutt when we see it in the flesh.

On the one hand, radical criticism has made it inescapably clear that because of the importance of context in constructing meaning, politically motivated photographers must take responsibility for the contexts in which our images are seen, for the social ways their meaning is constructed for and by the viewer. We cannot rely on any inherent reading of 'what's in the picture'; to do so would be to revert to a hopelessly naive faith in the image.

On the other hand, however, it is clear that photographs do have meanings, that these various meanings, while determined not by the image alone but by its relationship with the contexts within which it is seen, are ultimately based on a connection between image and a reality which actually does exist. To deny these connections and instead insist that the medium itself provides the only interesting political topic is equally unsatisfactory.

The position I want to draw from this is one that a number of photographers take implicitly in their work, but it needs an articulated statement. I am not suggesting a course that steers between the two camps, but rather one that moves forward with one foot in each, that draws from the paradox a creative and challenging contradiction. One way out of the potentially paralyzing effects of 'deconstructing' discourses, and of the cynically superior passivity which is one of the visible outcomes of adopting a postmodernist critical stance, is what I want to call 'activist photography.'

I prefer the term 'activist photography' to 'documentary photography' for a couple of reasons: first, the range of activities that I see as seriously political extends far beyond what we normally understand as documentary photography. Second, many of the critical objections that have been leveled at documentary photography seem to me very much on target because of documentary's traditional acceptance of reformist solutions to social problems, its sometimes overwhelming optimism about the power of persuasion, and its almost universal acceptance of the very truth values in imagery that the radical critics are questioning.

If I am not totally carried away by the leap from a valid criticism of traditional documentary to an exclusive focus on internal, formal or aesthetic political breakthroughs, it is partially because I think that this leap ignores both the issue of the potential development of a Left – as opposed to liberal – documentary practice and the wide range of other activities that are indeed 'political' but fall in neither of the two recognized areas. Indeed, 'documentary' becomes a dismissive label, a category into which all work the critic dislikes can be dumped, tarring it with a brush that should be more judiciously applied. This use of the term 'documentary' as a broad, sweeping term of condemnation for all politically motivated 'straight' or 'naturalistic' photography is another reason I am eager to abandon the expression.

'Activist photography,' then, is a term for photography with a clear set of political agendas (perhaps including, but definitely not limited to, internal criticism of fields of art and media), which is most comprehensible as a range of practices within a framework provided by political activities, campaigns or organizations, which are to be judged primarily in terms of their contribution to these movements, and which finally listen to and try to assimilate and apply the cautions and lessons drawn by radical criticism.

The development of political photographic practice runs directly into the problem of an enforced distinction between 'art' and the communicative and socially exploratory functions of photography. It is a distinction that all of us who are trying to work in socially significant photography run into, often to our great pain, at irregular intervals. What I am particularly concerned about is that a given set of images, if shown in a gallery or published in the 'correct' places and formats, is seen as 'socially engaged' or 'political' *art*, while if the same images are used for their communicative value in publications or other media or venues which are directly political, they are seen in a very different, and often disparaging, way.

This distinction, deeply rooted as it is in the dominant understanding of what constitutes 'art' (an understanding promoted not only by the art establishment, but also by allegedly political critics and theoretical writers who disdainfully dismiss what they call 'instrumental' activities), raises for me the question of whether, after all, those of us who are interested in having a political impact through our work are really well served by photography's being accepted as 'art.'

During the Second Colloquium of Latin American Photography, in Mexico City in 1981, the US photographer, video-maker and theorist Martha Rosler was asked by a Mexican journalist how political photography is repressed in the United States – a serious question, considering the repression experienced by progressive photographers in some countries in Latin America. Martha's answer was, 'In the US, it's repressed by being hung in galleries and museums.' At first, this sounds like a flip response, but it gets to the heart of the problem that the very acceptance of political photography by art world institutions changes its meaning and effects.

The fact that my first and fundamental motive in photography has been to contribute to political movements for social change has prompted me to seek a political definition of my work that would satisfy the needs of an identity rooted in those political movements, and not in what has become a socially isolated and unengaged art world.

Sometimes it seems almost ridiculous to raise the question yet another time, What is political photography? (perhaps a species of the more generic question, What is political art?). But in fact the question refuses to die – or even go to sleep – and for good reason. The world keeps changing, politics changes with it, and we who are interested in the politics of our work – and even more those of us who are interested in pursuing political ends through our photography, criticism and theoretical work – simply never will have the luxury of resting.

Frequently we are asked to discard the category of 'political photography' (or 'political art') altogether, under the assertion that acceptance of the category implies accepting a 'ghettoization' of our work, or represents a distortion of the reality that all photography – like all art – carries a series of ideological and political meanings, and we should only be examining the political distinctions among various photographers and photographic activities.

Clearly, in one important sense all photography carries an ideological content, potentially serves political functions, and can be analyzed for both its political meaning and its political effect. Those who wish to avoid considering the political significance of their work – or of photography in general – often find a kind of ironic solace in this reality. 'We will accept your argument that everything is political,' they argue, 'but that really means that the word "political" has lost its meaning.' In a sense they are right, but in a much more important sense they are completely wrong.

I want to suggest the paradox that while everything is political, it is also true that there is a deep gulf which separates political photography from all other work. Again, those who are eager to avoid confronting politics suggest that 'political photography' is best understood as a genre or an approach, like landscape photography or pictorialism. This seems to me completely wrongheaded.

Why do I think I can have it both ways? How can I insist that everything is political, and at the same time that political photography is in a class of its own, and distinct from all other work? Actually, I'm not necessarily troubled by apparent paradoxes like this one, and would enjoy maintaining the contradiction as a dialectical relationship. But in this case, we get out of the paradox only too easily when we acknowledge that there is an equivoque in the word 'political.' When we assert that everything is political, we mean that everything is susceptible to political analysis – everything has a series of political contents and effects which are (in principle, at least) understandable. When we speak about 'political photography' as a separate activity, we are referring to work that has some political consequence as its explicit and acknowledged goal – this is the quality that separates it from other work whose politics is understandable, though it may be only implicit, and perhaps unintended. We can distinguish between work that is self-consciously and deliberately 'political' (that is intended to have a political effect, to intervene in a political or social issue, to support or be part of political activism) and work that is being analyzed as to its underlying and perhaps unacknowledged political content, dimension or effect.

But this definition of political photography is obviously incomplete. In the first place, at least most of the time, when we speak of 'political photography,' we are talking about photography that emerges from a Left, or at least liberal, political perspective. Much of what I am going to say would probably also apply to right-wing political photography, although in reality, especially since we live in such a deeply conservative society, the main Right agenda in this area is to deny the legitimacy of political analysis and/or of political goals in photography. The Right clings to arguments that 'true' or 'great' art is 'beyond' politics, that political analysis per se distorts the meaning of artistic or photographic activity; they suggest that political goals are either unrealizable or dangerous to both art and society (sometimes they make both of these arguments at once).

There is an assumption that underlies my approach: that we can in fact seriously consider the possibility of social activism in general and in photography. Of course, I don't take the position that the assumption of a political, oppositionist or activist stance, or the adoption of activist goals (for example, influencing the ideas or behavior of one's particular public) guarantees the effective realization of such goals – only that it is possible to define activist goals and develop criteria for trying to judge one's effectiveness. For some people, this may seem too obvious to talk about, but it is actually a position I have recently had to defend against the critical position that the 'postmodern condition' implies the impossibility of positing a politically active 'subject,' and that any notion of activism is therefore hopelessly naive, and ignores all the mediating factors that tend to reduce effectiveness.

I want to argue, then, for the validity and importance of a wide range of activities – including practices critical of the media, work that has 'political content,' and work that has the kind of interventionist motives I have already referred to. And what I am going to do now, perhaps somewhat immodestly, is to use my own work as one model for practice in that last area.

I came to this activity – what I'm calling 'activist photography' – not primarily as an artist concerned with social issues, but as a social activist who decided to work with photography within his movements. For nearly twenty years, most of my photography has been done within the framework of political campaigns and activities. This has produced a two-way process, naturally enough, in which my political goals and criteria shape the nature and goals of my photo work, and at the same time, the insights of radical photo criticism and art come to bear on the development of those same political goals and criteria.

For some time, my work had essentially two outlets: it was published in various media of the political movements I related to, and it was exhibited, mostly in street fairs and peace fairs, in my own community. The political goals of this activity were pretty clear, if perhaps somewhat unexamined. There were several of these, but they can roughly be expressed as two:

1. Providing visual materials for the periodicals, leaflets, posters, etcetera, of the movements in which I was working. The intended audiences included both the constituencies of those movements and people to whom we were reaching out.
2. Working with people who were trying to develop a cultural current within our general political movement. This involved very largely thinking of ourselves as *local* artists, which in turn presented a string of opportunities and problems. I still believe very strongly in this kind of activity – one that by the nature of the structure of the art world is not very much examined by critics.

The decline of early political photography projects in Ohio, the new prominence of Central America after the Sandinista victory in 1979, and the profound effect of a visit to Havana in the same year helped me to turn my attention to the Central America solidarity movement, where I have been active, both as an organizer and as a photographer, for over a decade.

This has had implications both for the way in which my images have been produced – my conditions of work – and for the ways in which they have been disseminated. In the first place, projects are launched not only because I am interested in them but sometimes because they fit the needs of the movement. Work I did for the project 'Let Nicaragua Live' (which involved photographing in several areas of Nicaragua in a campaign to raise money for local development programs), and (Figure 1) for the Salvadoran project PROCARES (which runs social services and training programs for refugees), was in response to

Figure 1. A young Salvadoran musician playing in the triumphant final concert of the new song festival, celebrated in El Salvador in April 1988.

their needs, and *their* specific requests. Some of this work fits closely into what I am personally interested in, some less so. Similarly, photographing the first new song festival in El Salvador, in 1988, was undertaken because it was needed and useful for the movement; this was not particularly important to me as a photographer – it didn't respond to my photographic interests very much. What it *did* respond to is my self-definition as an activist (Figure 2).

One of the very positive consequences for the conditions of production of this self-definition is that when I am in 'the field,' my relationship to the people I am photographing and working with is not so much that of a sympathetic, or even committed artist, as that of an activist. Questions, for example, about my 'right' to take pictures, and relations with my 'subjects' – issues very important to progressive photographers – are cast in a very special, and for me helpful, light. This is also a double-edged sword: my political commitments often require that I devote time to other activities, including translating or other tasks. I'm ambivalent about that because I want to 'be a photographer,' but I also want to be an *activist*/photographer.

My most successful project in the terms I have just mentioned is my current work. For nearly five years I have been working with a community of people from El Salvador, first when they were in a

Figure 2. Two examples of the use of my photographs in solidarity movement literature. Photographs from 1983 and 1985; literature produced in 1986.

refugee camp in Colomoncagua, Honduras, and now that they have returned to establish a new town in Morazán Department, El Salvador. I work as part of the organization that represents that community here in the United States, and I have done a great deal of photography within the community (Figure 3).

My images have been used primarily in numerous publications of the movement, both in the United States and abroad. Such uses clearly imply an acceptance by the audience, the users (sometimes that means me) and the photographer, that despite the insights of critical theory, photography continues to assert itself as a fairly transparent and direct representation of a world that really exists. It is also clear that such uses conflict with any sense of the images as 'autonomous' art pieces – both because of the ways in which they are 'read' and because of the ways in which decisions about their uses are made – frequently in collaboration with editors, writers, etcetera, and often without any serious input from me as photographer.

The most substantial of these publications is a book I have done with my wife about the Colomoncagua-Segundo Montes community. Published in the United States by Rutgers University Press, it is now about to be published in an up-dated version, in Spanish, in El Salvador.

Ciudad Segundo Montes

A New Community in El Salvador

Figure 3. The opening panel in the display about Colomoncagua/Ciudad Segundo Montes. Photographs from 1988–91; display produced in 1992.

I have also experimented, sometimes in collaboration with other activists, with other formats and kinds of distribution and display, in which directly political criteria play an extremely important role:

1. The most recent product of my work with the community of Colomoncagua/Segundo Montes is a photo–text exhibit on laminated panels. This show is for me an important experiment in outreach display methods. The laminated panels are relatively tough, and easily hung. They don't require a curator. They can be

Figure 4. Two young Salvadoran refugees in the camp at Mesa Grande, Honduras. From the series 'How Sad My People Seems' 1982–3.

displayed anywhere. They can be – and have been – hung in art galleries, but they are also appropriate for union halls, churches, schools, and my thus far unrealized aspiration, laundromats (Figure 4).

This is my second experiment with this medium – I had previously done such a display about factory closings in Ohio.

2. Another important activity for me – the only one that competes with publication, and in fact has probably overtaken it – is using slides in public talks, in schools, churches, and other places. One of the wonderful aspects of this work is that it is the one thing that probably most closely integrates my photographic and organizing impulses.

3. I do continue to produce some rather traditional displays of photographic prints, accompanied with text. One, called 'How Sad My People Seems,' about the situation of Salvadoran refugees in the camp at Mesa Grande, in Honduras, was created within the context of an international campaign to support the refugees' desire not to be relocated into the interior of Honduras. The display was erected at what was an annual spring street fair in Cleveland. The clear political motive – to get people to join a postcard-writing campaign – was what gave the display an activist edge.

Figure 5. Some of the postcards from the set produced for the Zelaya Norte
delegation of the Ministry of Culture of Nicaragua, 1985.

4. Another area of 'alternate display' for me has been the production of
   posters and postcards. These have a number of very attractive
   qualities: they can be produced to allow activists and people
   interested in the issues addressed to buy them cheaply, they can be
   produced and distributed as an organizing tool, they are a flexible
   and relatively quick resource to produce, and so on.

   The first set of postcards I did was for the tourism office in the
   Nicaraguan town of Estelí. There are very few postcards in that
   country, and they are a very useful thing for the people there – to
   give away and to sell – as well as something that people who visit,
   especially out of motives of solidarity, enjoy having.

   The delegate of the Ministry of Culture in the northern Atlantic
   coast area later asked me to produce a similar set. And recently, I
   was involved in the production of other cards for the campaign in
   support of the Salvadoran refugees in the camps at Colomoncagua
   and San Antonio, Honduras (Figure 5).

5. I have managed to get a few articles printed in the Sunday magazine
   of the Cleveland *Plain Dealer*. This work falls in between what is
   traditionally thought of as art and journalism. That is not too much
   of a problem for me. A more serious problem lies in the effects on

the content of an essay of the context of advertising and general shlock in the magazine. Once again in this work, I do not in any serious way challenge the notion that photography is a useful medium for representing the world. I think the benefits of publishing articles that report positively about some of the developments of the Sandinista revolution and negatively about the crimes of the *contra*, in a publication that is printed in half a million copies and widely distributed in my area, are so great that it is worth it to me to be pretty direct and trusting about words and images, and not deal with *them* as the issue at all. The same could be said about the wonderful intentional community of the refugees in Colomoncagua.

6. Sometimes, the work is used in ways I have no involvement in. The music festival in El Salvador mentioned above took place in government-controlled areas. Afterwards, it was important for revolutionary artists and culture workers in that country to be able to share the experience with the people in the zones under the control of the FMLN guerrillas. I found out several months later that the set of black-and-white contact sheets I had provided to the organizers had been circulating in the zones. Even later, when I visited, I discovered people who had seen them and described them (and through them, the events) with great enthusiasm.

All the activities I have been discussing share one important characteristic: they are rooted in – indeed, they are part of – an activist political practice. They spring essentially not from my highly considered understanding of what 'true' or 'correct' political practice should be, but from the exchange – sometimes difficult, as we shall see – between my ideas and desires and those of the movements, organizations and campaigns within which I work. Ultimately that is the only environment in which my notion of activist photography makes sense. I have come to wonder whether the frequent expositions of the inherent problems of the gallery for socially engaged photography ought not to lead us to conclude that it is no coincidence that the rejection of the possibility of activist intervention comes mostly from people well ensconced in the academy and the institutional art world.

Serious political activity always involves a set of goals and criteria for success. These vary very widely, depending on the nature of the activity, the ways in which it fits into larger strategies or campaigns, etcetera. I have already indicated that I think that there is no one correct line for Left or radical photography. And if I have my doubts about the effect of looking for the one correct line, even less do I accept that there is one correct *activity* to engage in.

This position gets me into trouble with some radical critics, who see it as a hopelessly bourgeois pluralism. To make the briefest possible argument for pluralism, let me simply ask, how are we ever going to move any serious numbers of people in this country or support their spontaneous motion, if we decide to restrict ourselves to struggling against hegemonic ideas within the extremely tiny and narrowly class-based world of art? Yet that very struggle is the only one which the 'correct-liners' are seriously interested in.

This leaves the problem of how we can establish reasonable goals and criteria for political work. I think we all understand that intentions are not sufficient; nor is identifiable political content enough. We need to know what happens to that content, what purpose we want it to serve, and whether in fact our intentions are realized by the particular forms, methods, arenas, we choose for our work.

To draw a few perhaps almost too obvious examples: if we do work that is essentially intended for an art world audience – which is going to be displayed in 'serious' art galleries or published in art journals – and we essentially ignore issues of concern to that audience, we are simply being irresponsible. On the other hand, if we are most essentially concerned about actually having a political effect in the world, supporting or helping to build a popular movement, and so on, we may ask ourselves about the political efficacy of being in the galleries in the first place. But bringing art world questions to a broader audience does not solve this problem – when we go into the broader world we have to address that world's questions.

It is a principle of radical educational theory as well as of radical organizing theory that you have to address people about issues that are of interest to them in terms they can understand – I think this may apply to radical art and cultural work as well.

A couple of examples may illustrate this problem.

The first relates to a conversation I had some time ago, when I participated in a small 'political art' show at Rutgers by mounting my second *Plain Dealer* article on board and hanging it. The most articulate response I got, one that was intended to be very supportive, was to ask me, 'Where did you get that?'

'I made it.'

'I know, but where did you take it from?'

'From the magazine in which it appeared. I wrote the article and made the photographs. It's my article.'

'I don't understand – isn't it an appropriation?'

Well, perhaps in the context of an art school gallery, I should have anticipated that response and done something to deal with it in the 'piece.' The political meaning of that article derived from the context in which it was seen and used – from the way it fitted into a concrete practice. In the art school, those kinds of political considerations were not very important, and the 'piece' had political relevancy only to the extent it addressed concerns about hegemonic art world practices and ideas.

The second example stems from a visit I made once with a political comrade, an intelligent, intellectual person who is nevertheless not involved in the art world, to look at the show 'This is Not a Photograph.' She looked at pieces of political appropriation of advertising by Richard Prince and Hans Haacke and asked, 'What are they trying to say? They're not doing anything but repeating the ad.' Some people here might say, 'But that's the strength of their statement,' but in fact, it is only a statement to those of us who are sufficiently immersed in this world to know where it comes from and what it is about.

This is a problem with a great deal of so-called 'public' art, both political and 'non-political,' which essentially simply puts art into another context, one in which the artist is not necessarily active or even at home, without taking into account the numerous assumptions that can safely be made when we know who our audience is.

Part of the approach to untying this knot of such differing strands is to get back to that apparently understood area of political intentions. Our intentions are broadly connected with our social position, and the social position of our work (which are not necessarily *exactly* the same). If I do an art work because I think it is a good way to raise an issue the art world has been ignoring, that is going to invoke a certain complex of goals and criteria. If I do a piece because an activist movement recruits me to do it, to satisfy some needs of theirs, a different (though perhaps overlapping) complex will be invoked. And if I do work as an expression of my own role within that movement, that is likely to invoke a still different complex. Our goal should be to try to understand, control, and work within the possibilities suggested by all those complexes of intentions, goals and criteria, and many more.

Thus, for example, the criticism (one that has been made) that my images are not 'viable' because they recall the aesthetic of Lewis Hine (whether this is true or not is another question) is based on the false assumption that most of my audience knows who Hine was, thinks about his place in the history of socially conscious photography, or cares about these issues. And yet, if I were producing work whose *primary* use was exhibition in the gallery, it would be arrogant and stupidly self-defeating not to take such a question into consideration.

This is not an easy course. We who are engaged in activist photography are pressured on one side by organizers and editors to produce easy, formulaic work that corresponds to their immediate needs (often, it feels, pressured to relapse into the kind of sentimentalized, condescending photography we are trying to avoid), while on the other side we are criticized by theorists for producing work that is too 'instrumental' and that assumes that serious participation in concrete political struggles is possible.

What we bring to these situations, however, is something very valuable and worth developing and defending. In our relationships with unions, community groups, issue-oriented movements, we are able to contribute a sensitivity to some of the complexities and problems in visual representation. Of course, our insights are often ignored by those we are working with – so this, too, becomes an area of real struggle, but one that also seems well worth the effort. In our relationships within the world of art and 'serious' photography, we are able to contribute a grounding in concrete social practice.

I expect – and hope – that photographic activity whose goal is to examine the ways photography, modernism, the gallery, etcetera, function in distorting visual representations will continue. I am equally confident – and hopeful – that work whose goal is to expose patriarchal, racist and imperialist concepts and values for an art world audience inherently limited in size and in political options, but which is none the less a significant arena of ideological debate and struggle, will continue to be produced. At the same time I hope that equal value will be given to work whose primary goal is to argue not within the art world, but within the arenas where progressive social justice groups and campaigns are trying to win support.

In the final analysis, a pluralistic approach within the resistance to the all-embracing cultural, ideological and political hegemony that we confront is the only stance which offers hope of success.

Even activist photographers must take to heart the insights of radical critics; I hope the same critics, and our friends in those institutions that are in a position to support our work, will valorize it and recognize its role. Photography committed to social change must speak with a multiplicity of voices, to a variety of audiences. We must recognize the need for different kinds of address, for working in different contexts, for having different priorities in varying projects. At the same time, we must look for the ways in which our different experiences can nourish each other's work.

It is precisely from the interplay between the insights of critical theory and the demands of organizing that the materials and practices of activist photography can be forged – or more properly, are being forged.

Notes

1. This is not the place to recount the history of photography, its early reception, and so on. For those who are interested, I can suggest the basic references. First, Beaumont Newhall, *The History of Photography*, fifth edition (New York, 1982). This is the standard text, although very unsatisfactory in serious ways. Naomi Rosenblum, *World History of Photography*, revised edition (New York, 1989), was a major step forward in this area, casting a much broader net, both geographically and in her areas of interest. Photographic history remains a difficult area – numerous books that pretend to be survey histories are little more than annotated anthologies, but there have been a few recent contributions to survey history worth mentioning (in no particular order): Gus Macdonald, *Camera: Victorian Eyewitness. A History of Photography: 1826–1913* (New York, 1979); Ian Jeffrey, *Photography: A Concise History* (London, 1981); Helmut Gernsheim, *A Concise History of Photography*, third revised edition (New York, 1986); Jean-Claude Lemagny and André Roullé, eds., *A History of Photography: Social and Cultural Perspectives* (Cambridge, 1987) (translation of *Histoire de la photographie*); Petr Trausk, *Historia de la fotografía en el siglo XX: de la fotografía artística al periodismo gráfico* (Santiago de Cuba, 1984) (translation of *Die Geschichte der Fotografie im 20. Jahrhundert ...*). It should perhaps not be surprising, though it remains disappointing, that the European surveys present much more work from central and east Europe than the US and British texts.

2. This is not a particularly new observation on this photograph – the first person to describe it in this way was Samuel F. B. Morse in a letter cited in William Welling, *Photography in America: The Formative Years, 1839–1900* (New York, 1978).

3. Sekula's 'On the Invention of Photographic Meaning' has been reprinted in various places; one handy source, useful in general, is Vicki Goldberg, ed., *Photography in Print: Writings from 1816 to the Present* (New York, 1981).

4. One artist who has tried to use this sense of photography's strong connection to its subject is the Chilean Eugenio Dittborn. He has also written on this physical link as the source of the medium's strength. Roland Barthes, in *Camera Lucida: Reflections on Photography* (New York, 1981) (translation of *La Chambre claire*) provides one of several useful discussions of the affective strength that photographs derive from our understanding of their 'reality.'

5. Barthes, of course, and semiotic theory in general, remain important sources for this view. A very useful, and somewhat critical, summary of critical thinking about photographic meaning and of the paradox is provided by Frank Webster, *The New Photography* (London and New York, 1985).

6. Well, perhaps not celebrated by everybody – photographic artists spent a great deal of time and energy during the nineteenth century trying to convince themselves and their audiences that what they were doing was not dependent on the very qualities of the medium that attracted everyone else, that they were 'creative' artists and 'craftsmen' (and craftswomen – this field attracted more women practitioners than one might guess). When W.H. Emerson finally had to recognize that photography was genuinely dependent on its own technology and on physical, optical and chemical laws, he published his pamphlet, 'The Death of Naturalistic Photography' in 1891 within black borders.

7. Frances Dimond and Roger Taylor, *Crown and Camera* (London, 1987). The roles of British and US war photographers of the era are discussed in, for example, Rosenblum and most photo histories.

8. Jacob Riis, *How The Other Half Lives: Studies Among the Tenements of New York*, 'With Illustrations Chiefly From Photographs of the Author' (New York, 1890, reprinted, 1904).

9. A good example of looking at the politics of photographic representation as essentially a consequence of conscious decisions on the part of photographers, designers and editors may be found in Gisèle Freund, *Photography and Society* (Boston, 1980) (translation of *Photographie et société*).

10. For a good introduction to this project (currently being revised in several recent publications), see F. Jack Hurley, *Portrait of a Decade: Roy Stryker and the Development of Documentary Photography in the Thirties* (Baton Rouge, 1972).

11. Amazingly, in his own survey book on documentary photography, *Documentary Photography* (Boston and London, 1986), Rothstein makes absolutely no reference to this incident – an indication that he has not yet understood its significance.

12. Macdonald, pp. 85–6.

13. For a more detailed discussion of this topic, see the very lucid article by Martha Rosler, 'Image Simulations, Computer Manipulations: Some Considerations,' in *Afterimage* , vol. XVII, no. 4, November 1989.

14. A good introduction to this topic is Allan Sekula's already-cited 'On the Invention of Photographic Meaning.'

15. This is the way some people have read Susan Sontag (*On Photography*, [New York, 1977]) and John Berger in some of his articles in the Left press.

16. Part of my argument here is inherently negative – that in the Left critical literature about photography produced over the last few years, with a few exceptions, most of the most published writers simply do not interest themselves in work that is best understood outside the range of interests I have been indicating. While I cannot provide a survey of the literature in this small space, I would suggest that readers look at materials in such publications as *Camera Obscura*, *Screen*, *Afterimage*, *October* and (lately) *Aperture*.

In a recent letter, a European photo curator with a strong interest in documentary work, wrote of his interest in 'try[ing] to move beyond the problematizing of representation [to] refocus issues of content.'

17. These are not straw opponents. I have been accused of believing that 'intervention is possible' by one well-known Left postmodernist critic, and the notions of people like Jean Baudrillard, who suggests that there is not a knowable 'real world,' are taken seriously in some critical exchanges.

5

Eurocentrism, Polycentrism, and Multicultural Pedagogy: Film and the Quincentennial

Robert Stam

Both inside and outside the academy, recent years have witnessed energetic debates about the interrelated issues of Eurocentrism, racism, and multiculturalism.[1] These debates have focused on diverse questions – the historical debate about Columbus, the academic debate about the literary canon, the pedagogical debate about Afrocentric schools – and have invoked many buzzwords: 'political correctness,' 'identity politics,' 'postcoloniality.'

In the North American context, multiculturalism has catalyzed an array of political responses, each with its favorite metaphors, many of them culinary: 'melting pot,' 'ethnic stew,' 'tossed salad,' 'bouilla-baisse,' 'stir-fry,' 'gumbo.' For neoconservatives, multiculturalism is code for 'left opposition' and 'people of color,' both ideal scapegoats now that the Cold War has ended. Neoconservatives favor an imagery of purity and 'standards,' of medieval fortresses defended against barbarian siege. Militant nationalists, meanwhile, favoring originary metaphors of cultural 'roots' and 'wellsprings,' regard multiculturalism ambivalently, both as co-optable by officialdom and as a plausible strategic instrument for change and national regeneration. Liberals, finally, invoke the well-behaved 'diversity' dear to college brochures, but reject the anti-Eurocentric drift of the more radical versions of multiculturalism. Positing the ideal of 'color-blindness,' liberals prefer metaphors evoking an innocuous pluralism, ceramic metaphors like 'gorgeous mosaic,' culinary metaphors like the 'smorgasbord experience.'

Although neoconservatives often caricature multiculturalism as calling for the violent jettisoning of the classics and of 'Western civilization as an area of study,'[2] the more radical versions of multiculturalism constitute an assault not on Europe but on Eurocentrism, definable as the procrustean forcing of cultural heterogeneity into a single paradigmatic perspective. Eurocentrism sees Europe as the privileged source of meaning, as the world's center of gravity, as ontological 'reality' to the rest of the world's shadow. Eurocentrism, like Renaissance perspective in painting, envisions the world from a single privileged point. It maps the world in a cartography that centralizes and augments Europe while literally 'belittling' Africa, and organizes everyday language in binaristic cultural hierarchies implicitly flattering to Europe (our nations/their tribes; our religions/their superstitions; our culture/their folklore).

Eurocentrism is the discursive residue or precipitate of colonialism, the process by which the European powers reached positions of economic, military, political and cultural hegemony in much of Asia, Africa, and the Americas. Colonialism took the form both of distant control of resources (French Indochina, the Belgian Congo, the US-controlled Philippines), and of direct European settlement (Algeria, South Africa, Australia, the Americas). Colonization *per se* preexisted latter-day European colonialism, having been practiced by Greece, Rome, the Aztecs, the Incas and many other groups. But while nations had often annexed adjacent territories, what was new in European colonialism was its planetary reach, its affiliation with global institutional power, and its imperative mode, its attempted submission of the world to a single, 'universal' regime of truth and power. Eurocentrism is ethnocentrism gone global.

As an ideological substratum common to colonialist, imperialist and racist discourse, Eurocentrism is a form of vestigial thinking that permeates and structures contemporary practices and representations even after the formal end of colonialism. Although colonialist discourse and Eurocentric discourse are intimately intertwined, the terms have distinct emphases. While the former explicitly justifies colonialist practices, the latter embeds, takes for granted, and 'normalizes' the hierarchical power relations generated by colonialism and imperialism, without necessarily even thematizing those issues directly. Although generated by the colonizing process, Eurocentrism's links to that process are obscured in a kind of buried epistemology.

Eurocentric discourse is complex, contradictory, historically unstable. But in a kind of composite portrait or 'ideal type,' Eurocentrism as a mode of thought might be seen as engaging in a number of mutually reinforcing intellectual tendencies or operations. (1) Eurocentric discourse projects a linear historical trajectory leading from the Middle East and Mesopotamia to classical Greece (constructed as 'pure,' 'Western,' and 'democratic') to imperial Rome and then to the metropolitan capitals of Europe and the United States. It renders history as a sequence of empires: Pax Romana, Pax Hispanica, Pax Britannica, Pax Americana. In all cases, Europe, alone and unaided, is seen as the 'motor' for progressive historical change: democracy, class society, feudalism, capitalism, the industrial revolution. (2) Eurocentrism attributes to the 'West' an inherent progress toward democratic institutions (Torquemada, Mussolini and Hitler must be seen as aberrations within this logic of historical amnesia and selective legitimation). (3) Eurocentrism elides non-European democratic traditions, while obscuring the manipulations embedded in Western formal democracy, and masking the West's part in subverting democracies abroad. (4) Eurocentrism minimizes the West's oppressive practices by regarding them as contingent, accidental, exceptional. Western colonialism, slave trading, and imperialism are not seen as fundamental causes of the West's disproportionate power. (5) Eurocentrism appropriates the cultural and material production of non-Europeans while denying both their achievements and its own appropriation, thus consolidating its sense of self and glorifying its own cultural anthropophagy. In sum, Eurocentrism sanitizes Western history while patronizing and even demonizing the non-West; it thinks of itself in terms of its noblest achievements – science, progress, humanism – but of the non-West in terms of the latter's deficiencies, real or imagined.

Needless to say, the critique of Eurocentrism is addressed not to Europeans as individuals but rather to dominant Europe's historically oppressive relation to its internal and external 'others.' It is beside the point to suggest that non-European people are somehow 'better' than Europeans, or that Third World and minoritarian cultures are inherently superior. There is no inborn tendency among Europeans to commit genocide, as some 'ice people' theorists would suggest – such theories merely invert colonialist demonizations – nor are indigenous or Third World peoples innately noble and generous. Nor should we believe in the inverted European narcissism that posits Europe as the source of all social evils in the world. Such an approach remains Eurocentric ('Europe exhibiting its own unacceptability in front of an anti-ethnocentric mirror,' in Derrida's words) while exempting Third World patriarchal elites from all responsibility.[3] Such 'victimology' reduces non-European life to a pathological response to Western penetration. It merely turns colonialist claims upside down. Rather than saying that 'we' (that is the First World) have brought 'them' civilization, it claims instead that everywhere 'we' have brought Diabolical Evil, and everywhere 'their' enfeebled societies have succumbed to 'our' insidious influence. The vision remains Promethean, but here Prometheus has brought not fire but the Holocaust, reproducing what Barbara Christian calls the 'West's outlandish claim to have invented everything, including Evil.'[4] My focus here, in any case, is less on intentions than on institutional discourses, less on 'goodness' and 'badness' than on historically configured relations of power. The question, as Talal Asas puts it, is not 'how far Europeans have been guilty and Third World inhabitants innocent but, rather, how far the criteria by which guilt and innocence are determined have been historically constituted.'[5]

The word 'Eurocentric' sometimes provokes apoplectic reactions because it is taken as a synonym for 'racist.' But although Eurocentrism and racism are historically intertwined, they are in no way equatable, for the simple reason that Eurocentrism is the 'normal' view of history that most First Worlders, Second Worlders and even many Third Worlders and Fourth Worlders learn at school and imbibe from the media. As a result of this normalizing operation, it is quite possible to be anti-racist at both a conscious and practical level, and still be Eurocentric. Rather than attack Europe *per se*, an anti-Eurocentric multiculturalism, in my view, relativizes Europe, seeing it as a geographical fiction that flattens the cultural diversity and hybridity even of Europe itself. Europe has always had its own peripheralized regions and stigmatized ethnicities, classes and genders (Jews, Irish, gipsies, Huguenots, peasants, women, minorities of color). And since Eurocentrism is a historically situated discourse and not a genetic inheritance, Europeans can be anti-Eurocentric, just as non-Europeans can be Eurocentric. Europe has always spawned its own critics of empire. Some of the European cultural figures most revered by today's neoconservatives, ironically, themselves condemned European colonialism. Samuel Johnson, the very archetype of the neoclassical conservative, wrote in 1759 that 'Europeans have scarcely visited any coast but to gratify avarice, and extend corruption; to arrogate dominion without right and practice cruelty without incentive.'[6] Even Adam Smith, the patron saint of capitalism, wrote in his *The Wealth of Nations* (1776) that for the natives of the East and West Indies, all the commercial benefits resulting from the discovery of America 'have been sunk and lost in the dreadful misfortunes which they have occasioned.'[7] Yet when contemporary multiculturalists make the same points, they are accused of 'Europe-bashing.'[8] Or the critiques are acknowledged, but then turned into a compliment to Europe, in a kind of 'fallback position' for Euro-narcissism: 'Yes, Europe did all those cruel things, but then, only Europe has the virtue of being self-critical.'

Eurocentric thinking, in my view, is fundamentally unrepresentative of a world that has long been multicultural. At times, even multiculturalists glimpse the issues through a narrowly national and exceptionalist grid, as when well-meaning curriculum committees call for courses about the 'contributions' of the world's diverse cultures to the 'development of American society,' unaware of the nationalistic teleology underlying such a formulation. 'Multiculturedness' is not a 'United Statesian' monopoly, nor is multiculturalism the 'handmaiden' of US identity politics.[9] Virtually all countries and regions are multicultural. Egypt melds Pharaonic, Arab and Muslim, Jewish, Christian/ Coptic and Mediterranean influences; India is riotously plural in language and religion; and Mexico's 'cosmic race' mingles at least three major constellations of cultures. Nor is North American multiculturalism of recent date. 'America' began as polyglot and multicultural, speaking myriad languages, European, African, and Native American. Colonialism emerged from a situation which was 'always already' syncretic (for example in pre-Inquisition Spain), and projected its own diasporas (European and African) and crisscrossing migrations into an already fluid cultural mix. Within this flux, 'majorities' and 'minorities' can easily exchange places, especially since internal 'minorities' are almost always the dispersed fragment of what were once 'majorities' elsewhere, whence the various 'pan'- movements. The expanding field of 'comparative intercultural studies' (North/South border studies, pan-American history and literature studies, Afro-diasporic studies, postcolonial studies) in this sense, recognizes these dispersals, moving beyond the nation-state to explore the palimpsestic cosmopolitanisms left in colonialism's wake.

What is missing in much of the discussion of multiculturalism is a notion of ethnic relationality and community answerability. Neoconservatives accuse multiculturalists of Balkanizing the nation, of emphasizing what divides people rather than what brings them together. That the inequitable distribution of power itself generates violence and divisiveness goes unacknowledged; that multiculturalism offers a more egalitarian vision of social relations is ignored. A radical multiculturalism calls for a profound restructuring and reconceptualization of the power relations between cultural communities. Refusing a ghettoizing discourse, it links minoritarian communities, challenging the hierarchy that makes some communities 'minor' and others 'major' and 'normative.' Thus, what neoconservatives in fact find threatening about the more radical forms of multiculturalism is the intellectual and political regrouping by which different 'minorities' become a majority seeking to move beyond being 'tolerated' to forming active intercommunal coalitions.[10]

I would distinguish, therefore, between a co-optive liberal pluralism, tainted at birth by its historical roots in the systematic inequities of conquest, slavery and exploitation,[11] and what I see as a more relational and radical *polycentric multiculturalism*. The notion of polycentrism, in my view, globalizes multiculturalism. It envisions a restructuring of intercommunal relations within and beyond the nation-state according to the internal and partially overlapping imperatives of diverse communities.[12] Within a polycentric vision, the world has many dynamic cultural locations, many possible vantage points. The emphasis in 'polycentrism' is not on spatial relations or points of origin but on fields of power, energy and struggle. The 'poly' does not refer to a finite list of centers of power but rather introduces a systematic principle of differentiation, relationality, and linkage. No single community or part of the world, whatever its economic or political power, is epistemologically privileged.

Polycentric multiculturalism differs from liberal pluralism in the following ways. First, unlike a liberal-pluralist discourse of ethical universals – freedom, tolerance, charity – polycentric multiculturalism sees all cultural history in relation to social power. Polycentric multiculturalism is not about 'touchy-feely' sensitivity toward other groups; it is about dispersing power, about empowering the disempowered, about transforming institutions and discourses. Polycentric multiculturalism calls for changes not just in images but in power relations. Second, polycentric multiculturalism does not preach a pseudo-equality of viewpoints; its sympathies clearly go to the underrepresented, the marginalized, and the oppressed. Third, whereas pluralism is premissed on an established hierarchical order of cultures and is grudgingly accretive – it benevolently 'allows' other voices to add themselves to the mainstream – polycentric multiculturalism is celebratory. It thinks and imagines 'from the margins,' seeing minoritarian communities not as 'interest groups' to be 'added on' to a preexisting nucleus but rather as active, generative participants at the very core of a shared, conflictual history. Fourth, polycentric multiculturalism grants an 'epistemological advantage' to those prodded by historical circumstance into what Du Bois called 'double consciousness,' to those familiar with both 'margins' and 'center' or even with many margins and many centers), and thus ideally placed to 'deconstruct' dominant or narrowly national discourses. Fifth, polycentric multiculturalism rejects a unified, fixed, and essentialist concept of identities (or communities) as consolidated sets of practices, meanings and experiences. Rather, it sees identities as multiple, unstable, historically situated, the products of ongoing differentiation and polymorphous identifications and pluralizations.[13] Sixth, polycentric multiculturalism goes beyond narrow definitions of identity politics, opening the way for informed affiliation on the basis of shared social desires and identifications. Seventh, polycentric multiculturalism is reciprocal, dialogical; it sees all acts of verbal or cultural exchange as taking place not between essential discrete bounded individuals or cultures but rather between mutually permeable, changing individuals and communities. (Henceforth, I will use the term 'multiculturalism' in the radical sense outlined here).

It is essential, above all, to make connections. We make connections, first, in temporal terms. Whilst the media treat multiculturalism as a recent bandwagon phenomenon unrelated to colonialism, it is important to ground the discussion in a longer history of multiply located oppressions. And where many literary studies of culture and empire privilege the nineteenth and twentieth centuries, we think it is important to trace colonialist discourse back to 1492 and even beyond. We need to make connections, second, in spatial/geographical terms, placing debates about representation in a broader context that embraces the Americas, Asia and Africa. Third, we need to make connections in disciplinary terms, forging links between usually compartmentalized fields (media studies, literary theory, reflexive and experimental ethnography, Third World feminism, postcolonial studies, Afro-diasporic studies, the diverse 'area studies'). And fourth, in intertextual terms, we need to envision the media as part of a broader discursive network ranging from the erudite (poems, novels, history, performance art, cultural theory) to the popular (commercial television, pop music, journalism, theme parks, tourist advertisements). Although progressive literary intellectuals sometimes disdain the lower reaches of popular culture, it is precisely at the popular level that Eurocentrism generates its mass base in everyday feeling. Fifth, in conceptual terms, we need to link issues of colonialism, imperialism and Third World nationalism, on the one hand, and of race, ethnicity and multiculturalism on the other, attempting to place often ghettoized histories and discourses in productive relation (avoiding, for example, the conventional practice of 'delinking' issues of racism from issues of anti-Semitism).

Our collective goal as educators, at this point, should be to 'deprovincialize' our students, and this in both temporal and spatial terms. To understand present-day representations, students need to understand the longer history of a colonialist discourse accreted and sedimented over centuries, traceable in part to typically Western binarisms and hierarchies but also traceable historically to the grand encounter of an expanding Europe with its African, Asian and American 'others.' A polycentric audiovisual pedagogy, in this sense, might play off Eurocentric self-idealizations against alternative perspectives, using film and video in order to deconstruct and subvert the Eurocentrism whose fundamental operations have just been outlined.

Columbus and Audiovisual Pedagogy

For just one example of such an audiovisual pedagogy, we might think about the recent quincentennial debates about the historical legacy of Columbus. These debates were crucial in terms of historical self-perception because the so-called Voyages of Discovery inaugurated modernity, catalyzing a new epoch of European colonial expansion which culminated in its domination of the globe. For many revisionist historians, 1492 installed the mechanism of systematic advantage which favored Europe against its African and Asian rivals. Prior to 1492, according to J.M. Blaut, a movement toward modernization was taking place in various parts of Europe, Asia and Africa. 'Proto-capitalist' cities were developing and linked in a network of mercantile–maritime centers stretching from western Europe to eastern and southern Africa and Asia. These centers were equal to Europe in demographic, technological, commercial, and intellectual terms. Non-European urban centers were also undertaking ambitious voyages, for example. Africans were sailing to Asia, Indians to Africa, Arabs to China. An Indian voyage went around the Cape of Good Hope and apparently 2,000 miles into the Atlantic *circa* 1420. After 1492, however, the massive injection of wealth from the New World, the use of forced indigenous American and African labor, and the advantage of new markets in the Americas, gave Europe the edge that turned it into a capitalist and colonialist giant.[14]

In this regard, the Columbus story is crucial to Eurocentrism, not only because Columbus was a seminal figure within the history of colonialism, but also because idealized versions of his story have served to initiate generation after generation into the colonial paradigm. For many children in North America and elsewhere, the tale of Columbus is totemic; it introduces them not only to the concepts of 'discovery' and the 'New World,' but also to the idea of history itself. The vast majority of school textbooks, including very recent ones, as Bill Bigelow points out, describe and picture Columbus as handsome, studious, pious, commanding, audacious. Young pupils are induced to empathize with what are imagined to be his childhood dreams and hopes, so that their identification with him is virtually assured even before they encounter the New World others, who are described variously as friendly or as fierce, but whose perspective is rigorously elided.[15] Only some voices and perspectives, it is implied, resonate in the world.

The 1992 Columbus debate was played out not only in the pages of newspapers and academic journals, but also in the realms of the visual media and popular culture. While the official quincentennial celebrations poured millions of dollars into the restaging of the colonial master-narrative, at the same time widespread activism subverted the official celebration. Columbus, as Gary Wills put it, got 'mugged' on the way to his own party. A group of Native Americans 'landed' in Holland, declared the land theirs, and set off after an El Dorado rumored to exist near the Rhine. In the United States, there were countless anti-quincentennial demonstrations and conferences, to the point that even major media took cognizance of the protests on their news reports on October 12.

The quincentennial period brought not only two adulatory Hollywood superproductions and a Public Broadcasting Service (PBS) special, but also a number of critical, revisionist features and protest documentaries whose titles reveal their anti-Columbus thrust: *Surviving Columbus* (1990); *Columbus on Trial* (1992); *The Columbus Invasion* (1992); and *Columbus Didn't Discover Us* (1991). Cinematic recreations of the past reshape the imagination of the present, legitimating or interrogating hegemonic memories and assumptions. The mainstream films devoted to Columbus prolong the pedagogic role of the pro-Columbus textbooks. Indeed, such films exercise more influence over the representation of Columbus (and thus over perceptions of colonial history) than any number of debates and protests. There is surprisingly little difference, in this respect, between the 1949 (British) David Macdonald film *Christopher Columbus* and the recent (1992) Salkind superproduction *Columbus: the Discovery*. Although almost a half-century separates the two films, their idealizations of Columbus are virtually identical. Both films portray Columbus as a man of vision, an avatar of modernity and the Christian faith struggling against obstacles of superstition, ignorance, and envy. Both films relay the old chestnut that 'they all laughed at Christopher Columbus, when he said the world was round,' when in fact most educated Europeans (and Arabs) knew very well the world was round.[16] Both emphasize

European antagonists, and especially the aristocrat Bobadilla, and thus displace attention from the more fundamental antagonism of Europe and the indigenous peoples. In both films, Columbus is charismatic, attractive, and a loving father, a man whose fundamental motivations are not mercantile but religious – to convert the 'heathen' – and scientific – to prove his thesis about the shape of the globe.[17]

The 1949 film, featuring Fredric March as Columbus, is almost comically teleological, in that it has Columbus speak anachronistically of the 'new world' at a time when the historical Columbus was unaware of its existence. Millions of benighted 'heathens,' the dialog informs us, are simply 'waiting to be converted.' Commentative music translates the film's Manicheanism into contrastive harmonies; the music associated with Columbus is choral/religious, that associated with the natives is ominous, provoking an acoustic sense of menace and encirclement. (The music's orientalizing overtones replay Columbus's own transfer of cultural stereotypes from East to West). When Columbus arrives in the Caribbean, the mass of natives spontaneously applaud the conquest of their own land and seem to acquiesce in their own enslavement. They immediately abandon their beliefs and their culture, it is implied, and embrace those of Europe as irresistibly and charismatically true. Their spontaneous genuflections translate Columbus's own phantasy – namely, that his reading of a text in Spanish to uncomprehending natives signifies a legitimate transfer of ownership – into veristic representation.

Although Columbus's greed led him to demand, upon pain of hanging, that every Taino man, woman and child over fourteen deliver, every three months, a hawk's bell crammed with gold, the film makes Columbus himself the outspoken critic of unfair trade practices. 'We are here to convert the natives,' he tells a greedy underling, 'not to exploit them.' Although the natives are supposedly played by indigenous people from the 'Carib reserve' on Dominica island, they never achieve the status of characters, nor is their acting credited. They literally have no voice, no language, no dialog, and no apparent point of view beyond cheerful collaboration with European designs.[18] Exhibited in the Spanish Court alongside the New World parrots, the Tainos show no discomfort with their role. Indeed, the parrots are granted more voice than the natives; they are allowed to squawk: 'Long Live the King! Long Live the Queen! Long Live the Admiral!'

The major elisions in *Christopher Columbus* include: the Inquisition; Columbus's involvement in the slave trade; the European massacres of natives, and native rebellions against the Europeans.

Although the film stages the well-known shipwreck of one of Columbus's ships, we are not told that the natives saved the shipwrecked sailors. ('What does America owe the Native Americans?', asks historian Francis Jennings; and answers: 'America owes them its very existence.')[19] The selectively empathetic voiceover laments the toll of death and disease *among the colonists,* but ignores the demographic holocaust that engulfed the Indians themselves. At the same time, the film sets up a clear class hierarchy, conveyed through the gamut of accents in English; from the elite British accent of the Old World courtiers, to Columbus's anglified but still American accent, to the cockney accents of the superstitious sailors. Non-European races are clearly devalorized, while women are eclipsed by the emphasis on the strong masculine leader, and even the sailors are pictured as a mutiny-prone rabble – all choices that convey attitudes toward contemporary social relations.

The very title of the 1992 Salkind film – *Columbus: the Discovery* – betrays its makers' contempt for all those who have objected to the term 'discovery.' According to its producer, the film is an 'adventure picture' combining 'aspects of *Lawrence of Arabia* and *Robin Hood*' and featuring 'no politics.'[20] The generic choice of adventure film, the intertextual reference to an orientalist classic, and the tendentious use of 'no politics' to mean 'no opposition politics,' are in keeping with the general tone of the film. That the Salkinds were the producing team behind the first *Superman* films (1978, 1981), *The Three Musketeers* (1974), and *Santa Claus – the Movie* (1985), and that the chosen director (John Glen) was a veteran of several James Bond films, might have forewarned us about the heroic paradigm into which Columbus was about to be placed. Since the film covers only Columbus's campaign to win Queen Isabella's support, his first voyage, and his return in glory to Spain, it can ignore the death by massacre or disease that befell thousands of Indians after Columbus's second voyage. From the beginning, Columbus is portrayed as the personification of individual initiative overcoming bureaucratic inertia. Despite the historical Columbus's arcane views about so many subjects (mermaids, cannibals, devils), he is portrayed as the voice of modern rationality. That the role is incarnated by a handsome actor (George Corraface) further enforces spectatorial identification. Symphonic European music constantly supports the swelling ambition of Columbus's enterprise, whilst virtually every scene adds a humanizing touch. At one point, Columbus gives a young Jewish cabin boy a free ticket out of anti-Semitic Spain. The natives, meanwhile, are reduced to mute, admiring witnesses who regard white men as gods. They barely speak to one another, and seem to have no vibrant culture. The film portrays the native women as flirtatious toward the Europeans, while the *mise-en-scène* exploitatively places their nudity center-screen. No full picture of indigenous life, or of their reaction to the conquest, is developed.

Ridley Scott's *1492: The Conquest of Paradise*, meanwhile, is erratically revisionist, yet fundamentally protective of Columbus's good name. Here the scintillating beauty of the cinematography enfolds the violence of conquest into the ideology of the aesthetic. The film makes token acknowledgements of the present-day controversies surrounding Columbus, but in highly ambiguous ways. Once again, Columbus (Gérard Depardieu) is the central figure, subjectivized through voiceover, sycophantic close-ups, and empathetic music; and once again, he is the voice of faith, science, and modernity. *1492* covers a greater number of Columbus's voyages (although the four voyages are reduced to three) and portrays him as being occasionally brutal as well as magnanimous. With sets built in Seville and Grenada, the film shows the final siege of the Moors in Grenada, and portrays Columbus, on the basis of no known historical evidence, as outraged by the Inquisition. Throughout we are sutured into his vantage point, while the music encodes a binarist perspective; choral music with ecclesiastical overtones cues sympathy for Columbus, while brooding dissonance subliminally instructs us to fear the natives despite an otherwise positive portrayal. And indeed, on some levels the film does pay respect to indigenous culture. The Indians speak their own language, and complain that Columbus has never learned it. A native shaman takes care of the European sick, and in general the natives act with gentleness and dignity, although there is no hint that Columbus helped eradicate complex civilizations. What looks like forced labor is shown, but Columbus's crucial role in it is obscured, while the film scapegoats an underling figure (a scheming Spanish nobleman who happens to look very much like an Indian) as the racist, and Columbus as his antagonist. With the upgrading of the native image goes a parallel upgrading of Columbus. An enlightened version of the traditional figure, he sympathizes with the Indians and treats them just as he treats Spanish noblemen. It is as if the film combined the personalities and ideologies of Columbus and Bartolome de las Casas, as if the 'discoverer' had been retroactively endowed with the conscience of the radical priest.[21]

The seven-hour PBS documentary *Columbus and the Age of Discovery* (1991), meanwhile, careens between occasional liberal-sympathetic images of indigenous people and a generally conservative glorification of Columbus's enterprise. The opening image of the ocean, followed by a caravelle, already positions the spectator within the perspective of the voyagers, those who made the 'encounter' possible. The orienting questions are: 'Who was the man Columbus?' and: 'Should we celebrate Columbus's achievement as a great discovery . . . or should we mourn a world forever lost?' The series thus confronts us with a dubious choice – celebrate Columbus or mourn a presumably vanished civilization – leaving no room for activism or solidarity in the present. Although the film does sporadically show some of the suffering generated by the Conquest, it explicitly exhorts us, in the final episode, to 'celebrate Columbus.' More important, the series is structured as a voyage/inquiry into the mind of Columbus. There is no attempt to explore the cognition and understanding of the indigenous people. The series's subplot, meanwhile, revolves around the mobilization of the energies of the modern participants (shipbuilders, navigators, cartographers, historians) who reenact Columbus' first voyage in replica vessels under the auspices of the Spanish Navy. Why would people today be so psychically and financially 'invested,' one wonders, in literally following in Columbus's tracks, if his voyage did not speak to them in quasi-mythic terms? Attitudes, one suspects, are being replicated along with the ships. (Entrepreneurs have often replicated the *Nina*, the *Pinta* and the *Santa Maria*; did they ever replicate a slave ship?)

The contemporary critique of Columbus is sometimes said to be anachronistic and unduly prosecutorial, a question of seeing Columbus through modern eyes, as if it were a question of a misplaced historical paradigm.[22] But this 'critique of the critique' misses the point, first, because many of the European documents are self-indicting in their nonchalant reporting of European cruelties; second, because the critique of Columbus does not involve adopting a modern perspective but rather a *different* perspective, namely that of the native peoples and that of Columbus's critics in his own time. (Although history is written by the winners, the winners often quarrel.) It involves endorsing the opinions of Spanish legal scholars like Melchor Cano, who argued in 1546 that Spaniards had no right to take indigenous property for 'even if the inhabitants of [a] region hold things in common, foreigners cannot take possession of them without the consent of those who live there.'[23] It involves endorsing the views of religious dissenters such as Padre Antonio Vieira in Brazil, who in a letter (April 4, 1654) to Portugal's King John the Fourth called the domination of the indigenous peoples the 'original and capital sin of the Portuguese State.'[24] It involves adopting the perspective of Dominican friar Antonio de Montesinos, who in 1511 in Santo Domingo, before an audience of royal officials of Santo Domingo which included Columbus's son Diego, excoriated the 'sterile consciences' of the Spaniards and the 'tyrannical atrocities' imposed on 'innocent people.'[25] It involves endorsing the perspective of Father Francisco de Vitoria, who in his *Relectio de Indis* rejected the concept of 'discovery,' and argued that conquest gave the Spanish no more right to American territory than the Indians would have if they claimed and conquered Spain.[26] At the same time, it would be wrong to idealize the various Christian dissenters from conquest. (Roland Jaffe's film *The Mission*, for example, over-draws the contrast between racist mercenary colonialists and compassionate Jesuits like Father Gabriel who build schools and shelters and defend the natives from slavery.) The critics did not renounce the Christian colonization of the native soul or the colonial enterprise in general; their denunciation was limited to genocidal practices and the fact of enslavement.

The present-day debates echo those of the past. Even the debate about the word 'discovery' is not new; in 1556, the Spanish regime officially decreed the substitution of the word *descubrimiento* (discovery) for the forbidden word *conquista* (conquest). The ritual sacrifices of the Aztecs, by the same token, were then and are still now ritually invoked (for example in *Newsweek*'s 'Columbus Special Issue') to 'justify' European conquest and mask those 'sacrificed' on the altar of European ambition. The Aztec sacrifice rationale has certain difficulties, however, in that it (a) falsely suggests that Europeans conquered *in order to* cleanse these regions of such practices; (b) fails to explain why Europeans also slaughtered other peoples not accused of such practices (the 'friendly' Arawaks were destroyed along with the 'fierce' Caribs); (c) fails to explain why, if conquest constitutes a normal retribution for cruel practices, Europe would not itself be the object of such retribution for having practiced the Inquisition, slavery, torture at the rack, drawing and quartering, witch-burning and countless other misdemeanors. Equally, the fact that indigenous groups occasionally feuded or fought is said to justify European conquest, while the interminable squabbles of European nations are never seen as justifying the conquest of Europe by Native Americans.

In any case, the anticolonialist argument does not stand or fall on the moral qualities of native peoples – their humanity is sufficient. In Columbus's time, the Spanish priest Bartolome de las Casas witnessed the massacres of the Indians by the conquistadores, which he registered in a book, addressed to King Charles V in 1520, and entitled *The Devastation of the Indies: A Brief Account*. De las Casas described nothing less than a massive genocide which reduced the native population in the first thirty years after Cortez's landing from 25 million to 6 million souls. De las Casas is the subject of at least one feature-length film: Sergio Olhovich's *Bartolome de las Casas* (1992). Structured as a series of flashbacks conveying the protagonist's evolving attitudes toward the New World and its native inhabitants, the film emphasizes the priest's contradictions rather than his heroism. Olhovich stages the debates between Sepulveda and de las Casas as a theatrical encounter between the king and his two counselors, one of whom, de las Casas, criticizes conquest and enslavement in the name of what he sees as the charitable core of the Christian faith, the other of whom, Sepulveda, speaks in the name of the material interests of the Crown. When de las Casas argues that Spain should leave the New World to its original inhabitants, Sepulveda retorts that such a magnanimous gesture would only lead to a reversion to barbarism and idolatry. Rather than idealize de las Casas, Olhovich uses the Brechtian procedure of placing critiques of his character in the mouths of his adversaries. You claim you defend the Indians, says one critic, but you are yourself an *encomendiero* (a holder of rights over slaves). Nor does the film obscure the fact that de las Casas at one point called for Africans to be imported as slaves, a suggestion he later came to regret. When de las Casas is granted control of part of the coast of Guatemala in order to put into practice his democratic ideals, the project turns out to be quixotic, an exercise in futility given the larger historical forces at play. The film ends with the reading of a kind of final testament, in which de las Casas calls for the Spanish to restore the stolen wealth to the Indians, for priests to learn indigenous languages, and for Spain to restore dignity to the 'natural lords of these lands.' A reflexive epilogue has the camera pull back and reveal camera and cast as a cross of light covers the dead priest.

Revisionist Film and the Quincentennial

Only recently have films begun to offer a critical perspective on the conquest. A proleptic anti-quincentennial film, Glauber Rocha's *Land in Anguish* (1967), an allegory about contemporaneous Brazilian politics, satirically reenacts the arrival of Brazil's Columbus – Pedro Cabral – on the shores of Brazil in the year 1500. The right-wing figure of the film (named Porfirio Diaz after the Mexican dictator who slaughtered thousands of 'Indians') arrives from the sea, suggesting a myth of national origins. Carrying a black banner and a crucifix and dressed in an anachronistic modern-day suit, he is seen alongside a priest in an old Catholic habit, a sixteenth-century conquistador, and a symbolic feathered Indian. A huge cross is fixed in the sand as Diaz approaches it to kneel and perform a ritual evoking, for the Brazilian spectator, the famous 'first mass' celebrated in the newly 'discovered' land, but in an anachronistic manner that stresses continuities between the *conquista* and modern oppression. Yoruba religious chants pervade the soundtrack, evoking the 'transe' of the Portuguese title and suggesting, perhaps, an Afro-indigenous link.[27]

Land in Anguish anticipated a number of more recent revisionist historical films, set in the initial period of conquest, which relativize and even invert colonialist perspectives on the Conquest. The Mexican film *Cabeza de Vaca* (1989) tells the story of Alvar Nuñez Cabeza de Vaca, the shipwrecked Spaniard who went by foot from Florida to Texas. The film's source text, Alvar Nuñez's *Relación de los Naufragios*, already relates the Conquest as a story of failure. Inverting the usual roles, Nuñez portrays the Spaniards as vulnerable, as losing control, weeping, supplicating. And while a phantasmatic cannibalism usually serves to justify European exploitation, here it is the Spanish, as occasionally did occur, who cannibalize one another, and the natives who watch in horror.[28] Although the film version fails to humanize the Indians, it does expose the underside of European religious proselytizing, and shows the conquistadores, not the natives, as the real cannibals. The Venezuelan film *Jericó*, meanwhile, largely adopts the indigenous perspective, while respecting the languages, histories, and cultural styles of the indigenous groups portrayed. Jericho's story evokes what was actually a not infrequent occurrence during the first centuries of conquest – the case of the European who 'goes native.' In Mexico, Gonzalo Guerrero, a Spaniard kidnapped by Indians in the Yucatan, ultimately became a Cacique with tattooed face and pierced ears.[29] And in North America, as Hector de Crevecoeur noted, thousands of Europeans became 'white Indians' (to the point that some colonies passed laws against 'indianizing'), while 'we have no examples of even one of these Aborigines having from choice become Europeans.'[30]

Jericó concerns a Franciscan priest, Santiago, the lone survivor of a sixteenth-century expedition led by the cruel conquistador Gascuna, in search of the mythic Mar del Sur. Although Santiago hopes to spiritually conquer the Indians, he is in fact spiritually conquered by them. While their captive, he comes to question European attitudes toward religion, the body, the earth, and social life, and finally renounces his evangelical mission. Whereas most Hollywood films have the 'Indians' speak a laughable pidgin English, here the natives laugh at the priest's garbled attempt to speak *their* language. In the end, Santiago is retaken by the Spaniards, who regard his 'going native' as a form of madness and heresy. What makes this revisionist captivity narrative so subversive is that it transforms what official Europe regarded with fear and loathing – indigenous culture – into a seductive pole of attraction for Europeans. (The real purpose of the Inquisition, suggests Jorge Klor de Alva, was not to force the indigenes to become Europeans, but to keep Europeans from becoming *indigenes*).[31]

A number of revisionist films assert links between past and present-day oppressions and resistances. The Cuban–Peruvian epic *Tupac Amaru* (1984) evokes indigenous resistance to Spanish-European domination in Peru, specifically the eighteenth-century Inca rebellion led by José Gabriel Condorcanqui Tupac Amaru, whose story is told in flashbacks from his trial by the Spanish.[32] A direct descendant of an Inca emperor whose name he borrowed, Tupac Amaru led a broad-based messianic rebellion against Spanish rule. (The first Tupac Amaru was beheaded by the Spanish in 1572). In 1781, the second Tupac Amaru entered the main plaza of Cuzco and announced that he was condemning the royal Corregidor Antonio Juan de Arriaga to the gallows. A few days later he issued a decree liberating the slaves and abolishing all taxes (*encomienda*) and forced labor (the *mita*). After a number of victories, he was betrayed and given over to the royalists, who had him drawn and quartered in the four directions of the Inca empire, symbolically dismembering the indigenous reign which he was trying to install. The film begins and ends in Cuzco's central square, for within Inca cosmology, Cuzco was the center or navel of a universe that stretched anthropomorphically across a vast territory. The Spanish conquest, by decapitating the Inca, introduced a period of confusion and darkness, transforming the anthropomorphic figure of the Inca empire, the *Inkarri* in Quechua, into a grimacing, contorted figure of pain, and delegitimizing Cuzco as a center of power.[33] The film shows the Spanish punishment of Tupac Amaru and his family, watched by a distressed, benumbed indigenous crowd. (The historical torture and quartering of Tupac Amaru and his family was prolonged from 10 a.m. to 5 p.m. on May 18, 1781). We hear a pronouncement in Spanish: 'The proceedings of this trial shall be destroyed. Not a trace shall remain of these unfortunate events nor a vestige of this accursed race.' The camera swirls vertiginously, as if translating the despair of the crowd, after which the film segues into a black-and-white flashforward to a similar crowd, this time a modern-day political rally in 1975, held in the same square in which Tupac Amaru was assassinated. The film thus contradicts the Spanish prophecy that 'not a trace shall remain' and instead installs the terms of Inca prophecy, as a poem speaks of the head and body of the dismembered *Inkarri* coming back together in an apotheosis of liberation.

The Venezuelan film *Cubagua* (1987), an adaptation and update of the 1931 novel by Enrique Bernardo Nuñez, uses tripled characters to move back and forth between the sixteenth century, the 1930s, and the present, in order to show the continuities of exploitation. *Cubagua*'s male protagonist lives three different lives in three different periods: in 1520, as Lampugnano, an Italian helping the Spaniards extract pearls; in 1930, as an engineer helping North American oil companies; and in 1980, as an engineer working for a transnational company extracting minerals in the Amazon. His female counterpart, Nila, is a victim of the Spanish in the 1500s, a resistant chief's daughter in the 1930s, and an anti-imperialist journalist in the 1980s. Together, the characters help compose a portrait in transhistorical time of a country that has been colonized and neocolonized, but that has also displayed diverse forms of cultural and political resistance.[34] The Brazilian film *Ajuricaba* (1977), similarly, tells the story of Ajuricaba, eighteenth-century chief of the Manau tribe, who fought against his people's enslavement, and finally leapt to his death rather than be captured. The film stresses historical continuities by shuttling between Indian resistance in the eighteenth century to resistance against multinational companies in the present. Lastly Dos Santos's *How Tasty was my Frenchman* (1971) performs an 'anthropophagic' critique of European colonialism, using cannibalism as a metaphor to suggest that contemporary Brazilians should emulate their Tupinamba forebears by devouring European technique in order better to use it against Europe. Partly based on diaries written by Europeans such as Hans Staden and Jean de Lery, the film concerns a Frenchman who is captured by the Tupinamba and sentenced to death in response to previous massacres inflicted by Europeans upon them. Before his ritualized execution and cannibaliza-tion, he is given a wife, Sebiopepe (a widow of one of the Tupinamba massacred by the Europeans), and he is allowed to participate in the tribe's daily activities. In the last shot, the camera zooms in to her face as she emotionlessly devours her Frenchman, despite the fact that she has developed a close relationship with him. This final image is followed by a citation from a report on genocide by Europeans. Subverting the conventional identification with the European prot-agonist of the captivity narrative, the film systematically cuts off all the conventional escape routes, maintaining an ironically neutral attitude toward the protagonist's deglutition.

A number of films use avant-garde inflected tactics to critique European conquest. Lourdes Portillo's *Columbus on Trial* (1992) has the chicano group Culture Clash perform a contemporary indictment of a Don Corleone-like Columbus. Kidlat Tahimik's work-in-progress *Magellan's Slave*, whose alternate title is *Memories of Overdevelopment*, is premissed on the speculation that the first man actually to circumnavigate the globe was a Filipino slave that Magellan picked up in Spain, and who completed Magellan's project after Magellan died. But the most outrageously avant-gardist of the anti-quincentennial films is Craig Baldwin's *O No Coronado!* (1992), which is framed as a historical flashback within Coronado's mind as he falls off his horse – an apt metaphor for the carnivalesque dethroning performed by the film. Baldwin focuses on one of the more inept and deluded of the conquistadores, the one whose desperate search for the chimerical Seven Cities of Cibola led him into a fruitless, murderous, journey across what is now the southwest of the United States. To relate this calamitous epic, Baldwin deploys not only costumed dramatizations but also the detritus of the filmic archive: swashbucklers, pedagogical films, industrial documentaries. Found footage from diverse costume epics takes us back to the Old World origins of New World conquest in the Crusades and the *reconquista*. Educational footage of an atomic test site – located in the same region perambulated by Coronado – is accompanied by a female voiceover pronouncing the prophecies of Native American seers ('Earthquakes shook the world . . . fear was everywhere'). Coronado is portrayed as a Eurotrash exemplar of colonialism, whose avatars are evoked through the 'prior textualizations' of tacky costume dramas and sci-fi films: Vincent Price (incarnating the Inquisition), the Lone Ranger, Charles Bronson. The film ends with images of nuclear explosions, evocative of the apotheosis of instrumental reason, and of a lone Indian using a reflecting mirror as a weapon, an evocation of the minimal resistant means available to the weak.

Native Americans have also begun to make historical films from an indigenous point of view. George Burdeau's *Surviving Columbus* (1990) narrates the initial encounter between the conquistadores and the Zuni, giving pride of place to Zuni narratives and perspectives within a communal atmosphere of domesticated storytelling. The conquistadores, as seen from a Zuni perspective, become abstracted, depersonalized, Goyaesque figures of menace. Bob Hick's *Return of the Country* (1984) provocatively overturns Eurocentric assumptions, reversing an oppressive situation long familiar to Native Americans – but this time it is Anglo language and culture that are outlawed, and the courts, the congress, and the presidency are all in indigenous hands. Neil Goodwin and Lena Carr's *Geronimo and the Apache Resistance* (1988) tells the story of the Apache leader through commentary from present members of his tribe. A number of didactic documentaries finally, tell the story of the Conquest from the perspective of the conquered: Tainos, Mayas, Aztecs, Mohawks. *The Columbus Invasion: Colonialism and the Indian Resistance* combines sixteenth-century images with contemporary interviews of Native Americans to convey the indigenous perspective on the Conquest, citing a Maya prophecy that indigenous peoples, after five hundred years of suffering, will unite, as the 'eagle of the north meets the condor of the south.' *Columbus Didn't Discover Us* cinematically 'realizes' that prophecy by recording a pan-indigenous encounter held in the highlands of Ecuador in July 1990. The British documentary *Savagery and the American Indian* sees the puritans from an indigenous perspective, inverting the trope of savage 'wildness,' by positing the Europeans, rather than the Native Americans, as wild, at the same time satirizing the litany of ethnocentric prejudice by having it pronounced by the backlit, bearded mouths of the 'hairy men.'

The most remarkable recent development in relation to the larger relations between Europeans and the native peoples of the Americas has been the emergence of 'indigenous media,' that is the use of audiovisual technology (camcorders, video cassette recorders – VCRs) for the cultural and political purposes of indigenous peoples. The phrase 'indigenous media' itself, as Faye Ginsberg points out, is oxymoronic, evoking both the self-understanding of aboriginal groups and the vast institutional structures of television and cinema.[35] Within indigenous media, the producers are themselves the receivers, along with neighboring communities. Occasionally, videos are sent to distant cultural institutions or festivals. The two most active producers of indigenous media production in the Americas are native (especially Arctic) North Americans (Inuit, Yup'ik) and the Indians of the Amazon Basin (Nambiquara, Kayapo). Indigenous media, while not a panacea for the social ills afflicting native peoples, is an empowering vehicle for communities struggling against geographical displacement, ecological and economic deterioration, and cultural annihilation.[36]

In Brazil, the *Centro de Trabalho Indigenista* (Center for Work with Indigenous Peoples) has been working in collaboration with indigenous groups since 1979, teaching videomaking and editing, and offering technologies and facilities in order to protect indigenous land and consolidate resistance. In Vincent Carelli's *The Spirit of TV* (1991), the Waiapi people, newly introduced to television, reflect on ways that video can be used to make contact with other peoples and defend themselves against the encroachments of federal agents, goldminers, and loggers. Taking an eminently pragmatic approach, the Waiapi ask the filmmakers to hide their weakness to the outside world; 'exaggerate our strength,' they say, 'so they won't occupy our land.' In *Arco de Zo'e* (Meeting Ancestors, 1993), Chief Wai-Wai recounts his visit to the Zo'e, a recently contacted group whom the Waiapi had known only through video images. The two groups compare hunting and weaving techniques, food, rituals, myths and history. The film communicates the diversity of indigenous cultures – Chief Wai-Wai has difficulty adjusting to the total nudity of his hosts, for example. *Like Brothers* (1993), lastly, recounts the cultural exchange between the Parakateje of Para and their relatives the Kraho of Tocantins. The two groups exchange information and strategies for maintaining their language and identity and for resisting Euro-Brazilian domination. In all the films, the 'outside' spectator is no longer the privileged interlocutor; video is primarily a facilitator for exchange between indigenous groups. On a secondary level, 'outsiders' are welcome to view these exchanges and even support the cause in financial or other ways, but there is no romantic narrative of redemption whereby the raising of spectatorial consciousness will somehow 'save the world.' In these videos, the First World spectator must become accustomed to 'Indians' who laugh, who are ironical, and who are quite prepared to speak of the absolute necessity of killing non-Indian invaders.

Among the most media-savvy of the indigenous groups are the Kayapo, a Go-speaking people of central Brazil who live in fourteen communities scattered over an area roughly the size of Great Britain. When a documentary crew from Granada Television went to Brazil to film the Kayapo in 1987, the Kayapo demanded videocameras, VCR, monitor and videotapes as the quid pro quo for their cooperation. They have subsequently used video to record their own traditional ceremonies, demonstrations, and encounters with whites (so as to have the equivalent of a legal transcript). They have documented their traditional knowledge of the forest environment, and plan to record the transmission of myths and oral history. For the Kayapo, as Terry Turner puts it, video media have become 'not merely a means of representing culture . . . but themselves the ends of social action and objectification in consciousness.'[37] The Kayapo not only sent a delegation to the Brazilian Constitutional Convention to lobby delegates debating indigenous rights, but also videotaped themselves in the process, winning international attention for their cause. Widely disseminated images of the Kayapo wielding video cameras, appearing in *Time* and the *New York Times Magazine*, derive their power to shock from the premiss that 'natives' must be quaint and allochronic ('real' Indians don't carry camcorders).

In the Granada Television documentary *Kayapo: Out of the Forest* (1989), we see the Kayapo and other native peoples stage a mass ritual performance to protest the planned construction of a hydroelectric dam. One of the Kayapo leaders, Chief Pombo, points out that the name of the proposed dam, '*Kararao*,' is taken from a Kayapo war cry. Another, Chief Raoni, appears with the rock star Sting in a successful attempt to capture international media attention. At one point a woman presses a machete against the company spokesman's face as she scolds him in Kayapo. Another woman, in a remarkable reversal of colonialist *écriture*, tells the spokesman to write down her name, reminding him that she is one of those who will die. The spectator enamored of 'modernity' comes to question the reflex association of hydroelectric dams with an axiomatically good 'progress.'

The case of the Kayapo reminds us that polycentric multiculturalism cannot simply be 'nice,' like a suburban barbecue or teaparty. Any substantive multiculturalism has to recognize the existential realities of pain, anger and even rage, since the multiple cultures invoked by the term multiculturalism have not historically existed within relations of equality and mutual respect. A polycentric perspective would recognize not only difference but even irreconcilable difference. The Native American view of the land as a sacred and communal trust, as Vine Deloria points out, is simply not reconcilable with the European view of land as alienable property. The descendants of the slave ships and the descendants of the immigrant ships cannot look at the Washington Monument, or Ellis Island, through exactly the same viewfinder. But these gaps in perception are not unbridgeable; they do not preclude community answerability, alliances, dialogical coalitions, intercommunal identifications and affinities.

Central to polycentric multiculturalism is the notion of mutual and reciprocal relativization, the idea that the diverse cultures in play should each come to perceive the limitations of their own cultural perspective. Each group offers what Bakhtin calls its own 'excess seeing;' hopefully they come not only to 'see' other groups, but also, through a salutary estrangement, to see how it is itself seen, not in order to completely embrace the other perspective but at least to recognize it, acknowledge it, take it into account. By counterpointing cultural perspectives, we practice what Michael Fischer calls 'defamiliarization by crosscultural juxtaposition.' But historical configurations of power and knowledge generate a clear asymmetry within this relativization.

The powerful are not accustomed to being relativized; most of the world's representations are tailored to the measure of their narcissism. Thus a sudden relativization by a less flattering perspective is experienced as a shock, an outrage, giving rise to the hysterical neoconservative discourse of victimization and reverse discrimination. Subaltern groups, in contrast, are not only historically accustomed to being relativized, they also display a highly relativizing, even irreverent attitude toward the dominant culture. Multiculturalism should not be seen as a favor, something intended to make other people feel good about themselves; it also makes an epistemological contribution. More than a response to a demographic challenge, multiculturalism is a long-overdue course correction, a gesture toward historical lucidity, a matter not of charity but of simple justice; it is not a gift, but an indispensable part of the global decolonization of cultural life.

Notes

1. This essay is based on selected passages from a forthcoming book, *Unthinking Eurocentrism: Multicultural Studies in the Media Age* (London and New York: Routledge), co-authored with Ella Shohat.

2. For Roger Kimball, multiculturalism implies '. . . an attack on the idea of common culture, the idea that, despite our many differences, we hold in common an intellectual, artistic, and moral legacy, descending largely from the Greeks and the Bible . . . it is this legacy, insofar as we live up to it, that preserves us from chaos and barbarism. And it is precisely this legacy that the multiculturalist wishes to dispense with.' See Roger Kimball, *Tenured Radicals: How Politics has Corrupted Higher Education* (New York: Harper, 1990), Postscript.

3. See Jacques Derrida, *De la grammatologie* (Paris: Minuit, 1967), p. 168.

4. Barbara Christian, from a paper presented at the 'Gender and Colonialism Conference' at University of California, Berkeley (October 1989).

5. Talal Asad, 'A Comment on Aijaz Ahmad's *In Theory*,' *Public Culture*, vol. 6, no. 1 (Fall 1993).

6. Samuel Johnson, *The World Displayed*, quoted in the Yale edition of *The Works of Samuel Johnson*, vol. 10, *The Political Writings*, edited by Donald J. Greene (New Haven: Yale University Press, 1977), p. 421.

7. Adam Smith, *The Wealth of Nations* (New York: Random House, 1937), p. 590.

8. Thomas Jefferson, similarly, called in his own time for the study of Native American culture and languages in schools, yet the multiculturalist call for a 'curriculum of inclusion' is caricatured as 'therapy for minorities.' On Jefferson's interest in Native Americans, see Donald A. Grinde Jr and Bruce E. Johansen, *Exemplar of Liberty: Native America and the Evolution of Democracy* (Los Angeles: American Indian Studies Center, 1991).

9. For a critique of ethnocentric multiculturalism, see George Yudice, 'We Are *Not* the World,' *Social Text*, no. 31/32 (1992).

10. The phrase 'intercommunalism,' to the best of my knowledge, was first used by the Black Panthers.

11. See Y.N. Bly's *The Anti-social Contract* (Atlanta: Clarity Press, 1989).

12. Samir Amin speaks of economic polycentrism in similar terms in his book *Delinking: Towards a Polycentric World* (London: Zed Books, 1985).

13. For a similar view, see Joan Scott, 'Multiculturalism and the Politics of Identity,' *October*, no. 61 (Summer 1992), and Stuart Hall, 'Minimal Selves,' in *Identity: the Real Me* (London: ICA, 1987).

14. J.M. Blaut, *The Colonizers' Model of the World: Geographical Diffusionism and Eurocentric History* (New York and London: Guildford Press, 1993), pp. 153–213.

15. Bill Bigelow, 'Discovering Columbus, Re-reading the Past,' in *Rethinking Columbus*, a special quincentenary issue of *Rethinking Schools* (1991).

16. See Hans Konig, *Columbus His Enterprise: Exploding the Myth* (New York: Monthly Review Press, 1976), pp. 29–30.

17. Some of the material on quincentennial and anti-quincentennial films appeared in *Cineaste*, vol. XXX, no. 4 (1993). See Robert Stam: 'Rewriting 1492: Cinema and the Columbus Debate.'

18. The production notes for *Christopher Columbus* speak of an intermediary between the Europeans and the 'Caribs,' a former Cambridge graduate, Douglas Taylor, who 'settled among them, married a beautiful young Carib girl . . .' Taylor, we are told, became the 'uncrowned King of the Carib reserve.' Thus the venerable trope of the innate natural leadership qualities of white Europeans, reproduced in such films as *Tarzan* and *King of the Cannibal Island*, is recycled in the humble form of production notes.

19. See Francis Jennings, *The Invasion of America: Indians, Colonialism and the Cant of Conquest* (New York: Norton, 1975).

20. See Bernard Weinraub, 'It's Columbus Against Columbus, With a Fortune in Profits at Stake,' *New York Times* (May 21, 1992), C17.

21. For a similar critique of the Ridley Scott film, see Andrew Cornell's review in *Turtle Quarterly* (Winter 1993).

22. See for example Kenneth Auchinloss's introductory essay ('When Worlds Collide') to the Columbus Special Issue of *Newsweek* (Fall/Winter 1991).

23. Quoted in Anthony Pagden, *Spanish Imperialism and the Political Imagination* (New Haven: Yale University Press, 1990), p. 24.

24. Quoted in Leanardo Boff, *America Latina: da Conquista a Nova Evangelizacao* (Sao Paulo: Attica, 1992), p. 64.

25. Quoted in Bartolome de las Casas, *History of the Indies*, translated and edited by Andree Collard (New York: Harper and Row, 1971), p. 184.

26. See Carlos Fuentes, *The Buried Mirror* (Boston: Houghton-Mifflin, 1992), p. 134. Stephen Greenblatt quotes passages from *De Indiis* in which de Vitoria makes similar arguments.

27. Rocha's use of African music, as if it existed in Brazil prior to the arrival of Europeans, is extremely suggestive, reminding us that 'continental drift' theory suggests that Brazil and Africa were once part of a single land mass, and also anticipating Ivan Van Sertima's theory that Africans arrived in the New World 'before Columbus.' At the same time, Rocha deploys the music as part of an ironic reversal, since the Yoruba chants are repeatedly associated with the dictatorial figure of Porfirio Diaz. Although Europe posits African religion as irrational and hysterical, the film seems to suggest that in fact it is the European elite that is irrational and hysterical. Recent revelations about the 'black magic' rituals in which recently impeached president Fernando Collor, whose power in the Alegoas region goes back to the *capitanias* of the conquista, would stick pins into dolls representing his political opponents, confirm and literalize Rocha's prescience.

28. For a critical analysis of the accounts of Alvar Nuñez' and other Spaniards of the Conquest, see Beatriz Pastor, *Discurso narrativo de la conquista de America* (Havana: Casa de las Americas, 1983). For information on Spanish cannibalism, see David E. Stannard, *American Holocaust: Columbus and the Conquest of the New World* (New York: Oxford University Press, 1992), p. 216.

29. Quoted in Stephen Greenblatt, *Marvelous Possessions: The Wonder of the New World* (Chicago: University of Chicago Press, 1991), p. 141.

30. From Hector St John de Crevecoeur, *Letters from an American Farmer*, quoted in James Axtell, *The European and the Indian: Essays in the Ethnohistory of Colonial North America* (New York: Oxford, 1981), p. 172.

31. Lecture, New York University, October 9, 1992.

32. In Quechua *tupac* means the 'real thing,' while *amaru* means 'serpent.' 'Tupac Amaru' is also the name of a rap group denounced by former US Vice-President Dan Quayle.

33. I am indebted to Miriam Yataco and Euridice Arataia for their interpretations of the film in the light of Andean cosmology. For more on the Inkarri, see Gordon Brotherston, *The Book of the Fourth World: Reading the Native Americas through their Literature* (Cambridge: Cambridge University Press, 1992).

34. I would like to thank Emperatriz Arreaza-Camero for providing me with a videotape of *Cubagua*. Her essay '*Cubagua*, or the Search for Venezuelan National Identity' provides a historically informed, in-depth study of the film. See *Iowa Journal of Cultural Studies* (1993).

35. See Faye Ginsberg, 'Aboriginal Media and the Australian Imaginary,' *Public Culture*, vol. 5, no. 3 (Spring 1993).

36. Indigenous media has remained largely invisible to the First World public except for occasional festivals (for example the Native American Film and Video Festival held regularly in San Francisco and New York City, or the Latin American Film Festival of Indigenous Peoples held in Mexico City and Rio de Janeiro).

37. See Terence Turner's fascinating account of his longstanding collaboration with the Kayapo in 'Visual Media, Cultural Politics and Anthropological Practice,' the *Independent*, vol. 14, no. 1 (January/February 1991).

6

Postmodernism and Revolution: A Central American Case Study

Román de la Campa

I

In the spring of 1993, a United Nations-sponsored Truth Commission on El Salvador published a lengthy and carefully researched report. It documents the killing of seventy-five thousand men, women and children during ten years of revolutionary and civil war. The story, thus far, remains largely ignored by print journalism, television and even academic journals in the United States. Murray Kempton, an American journalist whose elaborate prose and heightened political sensitivities frequently adorn the pages of the *New York Review of Books*, writes that 'the Commission's report is so far available only in Spanish and is hard going for the monolingual majority of Americans whose social standing qualifies them for opinions worth taking seriously.'[1] He adds that 'to defer the English translation may, of course, be an exercise of diplomatic tact, since it spares the feelings of those official Americans, past and present, who were at best guilty bystanders and at worst willing partners to these crimes.'[2]

The conflict in El Salvador is but one of many that have sprung up in Central America and Mexico during a recent era that seems almost forgotten, even though its effects are still very much with us. It is an era of novel military and semiotic deployments: stealth bombers flattened the El Chorrillo neighborhood in Panama, and the term 'contras' inflicted semantic attrition on Nicaragua's revolutionaries. It is therefore striking to find mainstream journalists focusing on texts with the word 'Truth' on the title page, or sympathizing with claims of justice made by revolutionary movements. One could say that postmodern indifference still encounters some opposition in residues of liberalism. But what about the assumptions behind Kempton's conviction, that is, his call for a return to an almost natural nexus between educated readers, the national language as monolingual register, and a magnanimous foreign policy?

Aside from the question of whether Latin America was ever really a beneficiary of such largesse, one has to wonder about the proposition that an English version of the UN Truth Commission's report might mobilize clear and sensitive reporting by the global information networks centered in the United States. Few in the United States will have failed to notice the almost decade-long stream of English-only Iran/Contra broadcasts on Ted Koppel's 'Nightline'. Yet it is clear the American people could not be more unfamiliar with the Central American revolution that has so preoccupied the country's foreign policy during the past fifteen years. Except for a handful of writers and solidarity organizations, the text of Central America's revolution and its historical roots appear to have met with indifference or contempt, both among the masses and among the more educated sectors of the American population.[3]

A yearning for liberal values like Kempton's may be more symptomatic of an ongoing debate over national identity in Anglo-America than a sign of concern for the future of Central America. Intense culture wars now define US national politics. Debates over ethnic identity, levels of immigration, and welfare eligibility dominate the political discourse of both parties. Recently, the new chairman of the National Endowment of the Humanities issued a conciliatory call to redefine American pluralism through a series of sponsored conferences.[4] Indeed, Kempton's doubts about the future of journalism underscore a growing sense of uncertainty in the era following the Cold War about the impact of media tele-technology, particularly on language and on how we understand history. Worldwide 'techno-mediatic power' now constitutes a 'dogmatic orchestration,' observes Derrida in his latest essay, 'a power that at the same time, in a differentiated and contradictory fashion, *conditions and endangers* any democracy.'[5]

As with many other contemporary revolutionary movements, Central America's has been translated into a political culture of neoliberalism that reads Third World claims for redress as nothing but chronic conflicts of underdevelopment, inexplicable civil wars, or irrational residues from outdated master narratives. But it would be inaccurate simply to hold mass culture responsible for such indifference. Impatience with underdevelopment, poverty and subaltern claims from the

Third World (or minority populations in the First World) is also found in academic culture, including that of postmodernism. In the context of a neoliberal economics and neoconservative politics, academic research has been absorbed by the 'manic triumphalism' of a dominant discourse that basically preempts contestation.[6] Whether or not deconstruction can avoid becoming an unwitting contributor to this hegemony remains an open question. The answer may ultimately depend on whether its insights are in any way applicable to cultural and social projects that are politically engaged. It is evident, however, that the languages of humanistic understanding have become much more withdrawn and equivocal about their relationship to the world in the past few decades; and the social sciences appear to have abandoned their claims to comprehensive explanatory power of the social realm in order to embrace the wisdom of market forces. Current theories of reading and writing bear witness to these historical tensions, a critical juncture that has solicited new ways of producing and understanding knowledge, particularly as defined by Euro-American research centers. Yet it is Jorge Luis Borges – perhaps more than any other twentieth-century writer – who has come to exemplify a post-liberal academic humanism, a paradigm committed to showing the artifice implicit in all historical constructs, particularly those that aspire to universal value or pretend to foundational truths. His undeniable influence on postmodern Western philosophy has been acknowledged by Paul de Man, Jacques Derrida and Michel Foucault, while his specific Latin American cultural bearings are often discounted in the process – as if Borges were just another European author.[7]

Many current First World philosophers and theorists have found an indispensable source of inspiration in stories written by Borges during the 1930s and 1940s. But the relationship between his world, his texts and those decades is often ignored by them. None the less, one could argue that what best defines his uniqueness is his Latin American provenance, a historical sense of political and intellectual liminality now observed on a global scale. It is often said that one of the principal features of postmodern times is a global culture in which the First World can find itself represented in authors that come from the Third World, or what used to be categorized as such. But what about Borges's specific alterity, that is, his links to the modes of historical experience characteristic of a hybrid modernity, the product in large measure of Argentina's rapid process of industrialization after the Great Depression? Does it not undergo erasure when incorporated into a global literary canon administered through English-only translations and criticism, and informed by an inchoate multiculturalism or a new postmodern aesthetics?

A story about Borges during one of his visits to a US campus has him asking a student if he had read the *Arabian Nights*. Without a second thought, the student responded that he hadn't any need to study Arabic, to which Borges replied, in deadpan fashion, that he hadn't either, but that he'd managed to read it in night school.[8] At first glance, this brief anecdote may seem like just a bit of Borgesian irony aimed at utilitarian and isolationist modes of education that place insufficient value on learning foreign languages. Borges, like Murray Kempton, could be said to yearn for a world governed by educated, if not refined readers. But Borges, who is often simplistically portrayed as an Argentinian aesthete with aristocratic European tastes, was a Latin American writer for whom the experience of Anglo-American liberalism was much more distant than the hybrid forms of academic and political cultures that characterize his part of the world. His work, in form and content, defies all existing discursive genres, unless it may be understood perhaps as embodying a characteristically Latin American experience with contradictory, and often foreign, teleologies. It is this culture, so laden with ludic uncertainty, that was masterfully 'trans-created' by Borges into cerebral essays and detective narratives riddled with epistemological twists. In that light, his *Arabian Nights* story could also remind us that successful acts of reading and understanding are not simply guaranteed by any given 'natural' or 'national' language, but are produced by one's ability to sift through the layers of linguistic and ideological interplay always implicit in speech acts.

Reading Borges cannot fail to reveal that reading, whether literature or history, can become a treacherous and contentious undertaking from which one may gather both knowledge and pleasure. One of his most famous stories, 'Tlön, Uqbar, Orbis Tertius,' posits that nations and even continents can originate out of bibliographical accidents, and defines reality as not a 'concourse of objects in time and space but a series of independent acts' to be strung together at will by readers and writers.[9] But how is this insight employed when we look at what his literature portends for non-literary modes of reading and writing, or when it is applied to war-torn areas like Central America, whose current experience would seem to require a distinction between the immediacy of historical agency and the sedimentation of literary appreciation? Does Borges necessarily stand, then, for reading as a figure of designification, bound to unmask all social constructs as impertinent pretenses?[10] Are his powerful insights into the verbal construction of discourses transferable to a world in which aesthetics and politics are much more tightly intertwined than was the case in his? In short, how do contemporary theories of language and history that take their inspiration from writers like Borges allow for an understanding of differences embodied in multiple and complex texts such as revolutions?

II

Current theoretical wisdom holds that history's complicity with language disallows any attempt to look upon the realm of experience as if it were free of emplotments. Texts beget more texts; hence, the importance of contesting the canon, for any as yet unrecognized experiences – or narratives – remain adrift, unread and 'un-inscribed' in history, in a state of marginality or illegitimacy. Current revolutions face this sort of discursive cul-de-sac. They perform, unclaimed, in the space vacated by great narratives and ideas. They are thus – by definition – untenable or undecidable at a time when self-reflexive designification occupies the Western tradition. At this juncture, it would seem crucial, if not strategic, to examine how contemporary revolutions continue to write themselves; that is, it would seem crucial to investigate their textual nature, for they manifest themselves in discursive form to the majority of the world's inhabitants.

Reading revolutions in this fashion could perhaps allow one to explore relationships between literature and politics in ways that are generally shunned by both modes of organizing knowledge. With this aim, and assisted by the thought that revolutions are neither inevitable nor anachronistic, I took to rereading the biography of Ernesto Che Guevara, another renowned Argentinian writer, though of texts different in kind from those of Borges. A series of unsuspected connections immediately caught my attention, particularly the fortuitous encounters experienced by this bohemian rebel, beginning in 1954 with the Jacobo Arbenz regime in Guatemala, where Che witnessed an elected social democratic government suddenly overturned by a CIA-sponsored local general. Che had gone there as a political tourist in a stopover on a somewhat aimless journey of discovery as he hitchhiked northward across that 'other' America south of the Rio Grande. Partially politicized by this experience, he was forced to leave Guatemala, moving on to Mexico instead of returning to his native land.

What struck me most about this tale was not the obvious radicalization experienced by Che in Guatemala, but his subsequent encounter in

Mexico with the Castro brothers, who had been released from a Cuban prison by another CIA-sponsored local general. After that, it was not surprising to learn that Che ultimately joined the Cubans' mission in Mexico, a prelude to the 1956 insurrectionist invasion that would later become the Cuban Revolution. It did seem interesting, however, that all the knowledge and training in guerrilla warfare gathered by Che, the Castros and their comrades came to them from a man called Alberto Bayo Giroud, a veteran of the Spanish Civil War who had fought in Africa and various parts of Spain in the 1930s and 1940s. An engaging story, I thought, with a widening field of references that suddenly crossed oceans and bounced naturally from the fifties and sixties back into the thirties: Che's life, Guatemala, the Cuban Revolution, the Spanish Civil War. Up to this point, tracing and documenting these links seemed like an almost self-referential plot, followed easily enough through Che's biographers, as well as through many academically established histories such as Hugh Thomas's volumes on the Spanish Civil War and the Cuban Revolution.[11]

Some time later, however, while reading Donald C. Hodges's *Intellectual Foundations of the Nicaraguan Revolution*, I found the story taking a somewhat different path.[12] Hodges tells us that Colonel Alberto Bayo Giroud had also trained expeditionary forces against two other well-known generals during the forties: Nicaragua's Anastasio Somosa and Rafael Leónidas Trujillo of the Dominican Republic. I also learned that one of Bayo's books, *150 Questions for a Guerrilla*,[13] was employed as a training manual for Che and the Castros in Mexico, and that it later inspired Che to write his own famous text titled *Guerrilla Warfare*,[14] which the CIA has used to instruct guerrillas for invasions in Central America and the Caribbean ever since. But of greatest importance is the revelation that Bayo's influential text was actually a transcription of Augusto César Sandino's political–military experience in Nicaragua, which Bayo gathered after leaving Spain in 1939 from veteran Sandinista legionnaires still alive after their leader's assassination. On matters of literary history, Borges's story of Tlön and Uqbar concludes that critics often invent an author and then 'determine most scrupulously the psychology of this interesting homme de lettres . . .'[15] Thus, I asked myself if such a pursuit of bibliographical references could ultimately turn Sandino into the author of all Latin American guerrilla wars since the thirties, with the Cuban (1959) and then the Nicaraguan (1979) victories as his major works, and many other less successful attempts interspersed between? Had he, indeed, provided a textual force that has been read, chased and fought over during half a century all over Central America and the Caribbean Basin? But what about the source of that oral tradition kept alive by his remaining soldiers spread throughout Central America, which Colonel Bayo ultimately gathered into a book that later begot all those other texts and revolutions? Was there an important missing link to Sandino himself prior to Bayo's scriptural rendition of the oral tradition? Or should revolution be regarded as an experiential register of both oral and written discourse, a deeper structure that disseminates simultaneously through either code?

In time, I wondered if this intricate web of unsuspected permutations would deepen the implicit lesson in Borges's *Arabian Nights* reference? Could revolution claim the Latin American archive of fiction and history as a limitlessly translatable narrative? Was that the legacy of Latin America's abortive brushes with modernity? I even wondered if the story of Tlön and Uqbar, which was written in Argentina around the same time as Bayo's guerrilla manual, could in some allegorical way be read as Borges's own way of translating Sandino's historical concerns with nation building. Borges's story, after all, does formulate a response to the overt social realism predominant in Latin American literature at the time, though a deconstructive one.[16] His inventions of countries like Tlön have been commonly interpreted as an early (1940) manifestation of a postmodern disbelief in modernity's master narratives. In Latin America, however, such incredulity may not just inform a new literary frontier that negates dead-end political utopias, but may also instance yet another attempt to construct or imagine autonomous communities. Deconstruction, Derrida reminds us, is a radicalization, and as such it is 'always indebted to the very thing it radicalizes.'[17]

The labyrinth of textual and experiential articulations involving Che, Bayo, and Sandino, among other writers and revolutionaries, suggests a new way to approach that famous last paragraph of Paul de Man's essay 'Literary History and Literary Modernity,' where de Man seems to claim that history is nothing but texts, 'even if they masquerade in the guise of wars and revolutions.'[18] For Latin America, as well as for other peripherally modern societies, this formulation becomes particularly significant when altered somewhat to read that history reveals a propensity toward revolutions, even if its best articulations often masquerade in the guise of novels and short stories. To reorient de Man's thought in this direction also avoids a strictly literary definition of what 'texts' are – a comprehensible, though not necessary, shift of emphasis for a postmodern recasting of literariness and a broader understanding of intertextuality.

Thus changed, this formulation may serve as a timely reminder of the ideological investment inherent in all definitions of textuality, including that which understands reading and writing as an exclusive testimony to literary dissemination or epistemological performativity. As death, hunger, persecution, structural inequalities and sheer exploitation continue to enter the world of discourse and narratology, postmodern deconstructions of revolutionary events and contexts come under closer scrutiny.[19] Needless to say, in the process of emplotment into larger narrative units, experiences involving revolutions are also prone to manipulation and the will to produce meaning for the sake of histories, literature, biographies and constitutions. But even after the passage of time necessary for such encoding, with attention shifted to the verbal nature of generic features and authorial inscriptions, the reading of revolutions can still pose considerable challenges, particularly for readers positioned in Euro-American research centers. Such readers are bound to encounter texts still calling for various forms of identity, or for political programs heavily invested in the discourse of modernization – precisely the features that postmodern exegesis eschews from afar. How then to critique the potential pitfalls of essentialism without trivializing such historical claims or acknowledging them as mere fictional ruses?

III

Borges, Che Guevara, Colonel Bayo, Sandino and Farabundo Martí (leader of the Salvadoran revolution during the 1930s), despotic generals, death squads, US interventions and nationalist fervor – all are characters and episodes that accent a rich narrative constellation from the 1930s and 1940s. In typical Latin American style, this was a time when both politics and literature paved the way for a non-synchronous brush with the avant-garde, a period often overshadowed by the current emphasis on the area's 'novelistic boom' since the 1960s. As the persistent fame of Borges and Sandino attests, those earlier decades await interested readers with unsuspected connections. Naturally, one could also search further back for intertextual relations, say, to the earlier Mexican revolution and its likely influence on the thought of Sandino, which Donald Hodges has explored in a more recent book on this Central American revolutionary.[20] Followers and precursors alike are susceptible to inscription and discovery, Borges would remind us in the story of Tlön and Uqbar. And, I hasten to add, following de Man, this sort of fungible, open-ended intertextuality obtains for revolutionary as well as literary history.

Readings of Rubén Darío provide an interesting example. A turn-of-the-century Nicaraguan poet whose exquisite lyricism is often claimed as the bedrock of Spanish American modernism, Darío has been regarded as an apolitical, if not reactionary, aesthetic icon – an assessment reminiscent of the way Borges is often characterized. Heated debates about Darío's place in Latin American cultural history have raged for over seventy years, until the Sandinista revolution – armed with a forceful rereading of his work – claimed him as a primary source of inspiration. Suddenly, Darío became another precursor of the Sandinista movement and its love for poetry as a form of cultural revolution. Sergio Ramírez, a Sandinista military leader as well as an accomplished novelist, observes:

> The revolution rescues Darío, not from oblivion but from false idolization, because Darío has always been authentically present in the popular imagination as the source of a pride more intuited than understood, as the figure of the 'great poet,' the genius of unknown acts who could triumph over any rival, over death itself: the poet of poets, the fabulous creator of impossible rhymes and images. Because poetry as such, and poetic inspiration, are values which the Nicaraguan people esteem without limit.[21]

This sort of rereading reintroduces the interplay of political and economic demands into the realm of literary history that deconstruction generally dissolves or invalidates. Such rereading, however, may also point to possible blind spots in deconstructive modes of thinking about the relationship between language and history, particularly as these are assimilated in literary circles. If modernity's master narratives no longer obtain on a social or epistemological plane, perhaps the realm of relative autonomy granted to literature and the arts since the Enlightenment should also come under scrutiny. What then is the place for a readership that sees itself integrally linked to a process of revolution simultaneously driven by cultural and socioeconomic interests?

Central America's contemporary revolution configures an archive of stories with a northern point of origin that frames the century, as the Mexican revolution gathers its residual force in a new Chiapas chapter. This archive reveals an extraordinary intertextual range whose pertinence often goes unnoticed in postmodern renderings of literature, philosophy or history. One need not privilege any of these revolutionary stories politically, present them as transcendent utopias, or fail to acknowledge the failures of regimes that have come into power under their aegis, in saying that they constitute a textual epicenter from which much writing issues.

Indeed, when viewed from a cultural rather than a purely political perspective, the multilayered text of the Central American revolution becomes especially pertinent to postmodern configurations. It has responded to more than sixty years of tremendous military and political upheavals, often augmented, if not induced, by direct external interventions. But its corresponding cultural history has left a legacy rich in aesthetics as much as politics, in oral tradition, in ethnic and religious transculturation, as well as in elite and popular cultural hybridization. Whether under neocolonial or postcolonial frameworks of understanding, such a cultural history marks a special instance of that non-synchronous mixture that characterizes societies in which peripherally modern and postmodern cultures coexist, often in the most difficult circumstances.

With the advent of multiculturalist representation, a handful of Central American writers have obtained notoriety in Euro-American literary circles. Newly translated editions and anthologies often include Roque Dalton, Rigoberta Menchú and Ernesto Cardenal, although, characteristically, they often present these authors as isolated individuals. Serious reflection on the common cultural history that unites them has been scarce, giving way, instead, to various modes of literary analysis all too readily predisposed to praise or condemn any context that links literary and revolutionary values. One notable exception, in the United States, would be John Beverley and Marc Zimmerman's *Literature and Politics in the Central American Revolution*, which offers a comprehensive look at the rich tradition of poetry, 'testimonio' narratives and other cultural forms from the region, but not for the sake of a loosely periodized panoramic survey. The authors argue that this literary core is a primary agent of revolutionary articulation, not just an expression or a representation of economic and political developments, as is generally understood by traditional bourgeois or Marxist aesthetics. Most important, Beverley and Zimmerman bring to light how reading revolution as cultural articulation presents a particular challenge for any attempt to understand postmodernism in Latin America, for it shows how precapitalism, neoliberalism, deconstruction, feminism, and ethnic identity struggles – among other integral elements of social reality – all simultaneously inform Central America's hybrid texts.

The area's best-known authors are not the only ones who can be approached from this moving vantage point. It can also encompass other readings, such as those produced by a wide array of literary critics, artists, journalists, and social scientists who have journeyed there through texts and other forms of representation. Reading a revolution, perhaps more than any other text, may also be a way of reading oneself, of reading how one approaches that disquieting and heterogeneous form of otherness. For a closer look at such readings, I have chosen three influential travel narratives written by Latin and Anglo Americans over the last twenty-five years. They focus on Guatemala, Nicaragua and El Salvador, arguably the three primary sites of Central America's revolution since the 1920s. They are: Eduardo Galeano's *Guatemala, Occupied Country* (1967), Julio Cortázar's 'Apocalypse at Solentiname' (1976), and Joan Didion's *Salvador* (1983).[22] Each of these writers traveled to Central America and turned his or her experience into a text that traverses similar boundaries between the literary and the political. More specifically, each attempts to give artistic form to an encounter with revolution.

IV

Though not a professional historian, Uruguayan Eduardo Galeano has become one of the most prolific and comprehensive writers of Latin American history. His use of literary devices to dramatize key moments in the area's history has considerable appeal in Latin America itself. His texts, however, have eluded mainstream distribution channels in the US academic market for Latin American literature and social science. In those circles, Galeano's work has been judged as neither history nor literature, perhaps because professional intellectuals remain too bound by unchanging ideological presuppositions and schematic economic outlines. Galeano's panoramic histories of Latin America often depict the role of Europe and the United States as wholly motivated by imperialist interests. None the less, his *Open Veins of Latin America* (1965) has probably reached a wider Latin American audience than any other historical account of the area.[23] It articulates economic history since colonial times into a crafty narrative form that non-academic readers appreciate as much for its literary qualities as for its historical knowledge.

During 1967, after he had spent two months in Guatemala, Galeano's firsthand accounts of guerrilla camps were serialized in various Spanish American countries, Italy and the United States, before being published in book form. *Guatemala, Occupied Country* tests the difficult balance of history, novel writing and journalism characteristic of travel literature with questions about the relationship between intellectuals and revolution. Though written in the sixties at a time when many of today's most acclaimed Latin American 'boom' novelists were active sympathizers of Cuba's revolution, Galeano's text departs significantly from the more strictly existential explorations of political commitment then employed by Mario Vargas Llosa, Ernesto Sábato and Edmundo Desnoes. What we see, instead, is an early version of a type of 'testimonio' literature that has since become a genre in Latin America. Galeano's text privileges accounts of social histories and oral traditions, emphasizing collective experiences of subjects and classes generally denied a voice.

Galeano's writing poses many of the interesting formal dilemmas that characterize this type of literature of the subaltern, as well as some forms of anthropological writing. As with Rigoberta Menchú (whose experience has been transcribed by Venezuelan Elisabeth Burgos in *I, Rigoberta Menchú: An Indian Woman in Guatemala*), or the *Autobiography of a Run Away Slave*, in which the Cuban novelist Miguel Barnet presents the experience of former slave Esteban Montejo, Galeano finds that he must give way to the Other. This is doubly difficult in his case, since he does not intend to camouflage the implicit privilege of his voice as that of a distant editor. He first presents the guerrillas as the primary subject of his study, and then attempts to earn the right to speak for them through his first-person narrative. His strategy would seem to challenge any simplified understanding of testimonial writing as non-literature or as a genre through which the social can be transparently transmitted without textual complications.

The bulk of the material is a historical critique of socioeconomic conditions in Guatemala since the thirties, a thorough discussion of imperialist and oligarchic collusion to exploit the land and the people, and a detailed speculation on how the Mayan 'Indians' might integrate themselves with the campesinos as a new subject of history to guide the guerrilla insurrection and ultimately the revolution. All of this extensive analytical work flows initially from the author's third-person omniscience. The sections are interspersed with various dialogs, interviews and other discrete first-person interventions that introduce the author and various guerrillas as individual speakers. Galeano's voice, however, remains in the background as that of a passive interlocutor. To accent this self-effacement, he casts himself as a weak and alien Other who must recognize his limitations and suffer in dangerous jungles before his voice can attempt to speak with proper credentials.

Galeano dramatizes his shortcomings on the very first page: 'I am ashamed because I am cold,' he writes as he travels through the mountains on his way to the guerrilla camp,

> Walking, even if my leg muscles are as hard as fists, is better than any futile attempt to sleep on top of the foliage with nothing to cover myself and my sweat freezing over my body. By contrast, there is not an ounce of sweat in the bodies of my companions, and for them neither cold nor sleep matters.[24]

It is important to observe the exclusive emphasis Galeano places on his cosmopolitan condition. It is the one form of otherness that seems to concern him, as if bridging the world of intellectuals and revolutionaries were his sole object. Ethnic, national, and even linguistic elements of difference are ignored, even though they are crucial factors separating the Uruguayan writer from a Guatemalan guerrilla force. At this stage of Galeano's writing, one can detect an overarching identity that glosses over crucial differences, imbued by a Latin American insurrectionist discourse and a sixties male aesthetic. Later articulations, such as Che's 1967 experience with Bolivian Indians and the Sandinista struggles with ethnic and gender issues during the seventies and eighties, illustrate the need for a sobering corrective to this unilateral perspective.

But Galeano's mode of self-legitimation as an intellectual in the guerrilla world is of particular interest because it deviates from the example set by Fidel Castro and Che Guevara – both intellectuals in their own right – who abandoned their professions, thereby symbolizing the sacrifice of privileged positions necessary to overcome class boundaries with campesinos and other insurrectionists. By joining the guerrillas as fighters, not as lawyers or medical doctors, Fidel and Che appear to forgo their roles as professional intellectuals, a category whose value the Cuban Revolution has continued to stigmatize, even after assuming power. One could always question whether leading a guerrilla band or institutionalizing a revolution does not incur a certain level of privilege, even an intellectual one, through which prerevolutionary or new class privileges are maintained. But in any case, it is particularly instructive to see Galeano assert the role of professional writer in a revolutionary context during the sixties, even when he recasts himself as an organic intellectual whose legitimacy will be determined by his utility to the guerrilla cause.

In a later scene, Galeano outlines the profile of a politically committed writer in greater detail. The narrator's access to the city as a foreign journalist turns into an opportunity for urban spying. As his voice grows more familiar with the world of guerrillas, it suddenly reveals how he can aid their cause with crucial information from the city.

> The vice-president of Guatemala, don Clemente Marroquín Rojas, talked to me about napalm, in an informal interview. It wasn't hard to gain his confidence, it came to me effortlessly thanks to my extraordinary likeness with a friend of his, someone named Newbery, who'd been in exile with him in Honduras . . . That's how I found out that a squadron of North American planes, with North American pilots, had dumped North American napalm over a Guatemalan mountain and returned to Panama without landing here.[25]

Ironically, Galeano's most available weapon derives from the power attendant upon his journalistic craft, in combination with his physical likeness to the enemy. This important note of self-reflection turns this scene into an interesting contradiction, for it reveals the limitations implicit in the author's project of self-denial. His usefulness derives particularly from his status as outsider, as cosmopolitan writer whose class and ethnic features allow him to pass unnoticed among the oligarchy. One could conclude that he has failed to bridge the worlds of writer and revolutionary after all. On the other hand, one could also read this fact as Galeano's mode of traversing, rather than sacrificing, the way revolutions understand the roles of writers and intellectuals, after having incurred risks and put his commitment to various tests.

V

In contrast to Galeano's attempt to bring art to the revolution, Julio Cortázar's 'Apocalypse at Solentiname' could be seen as an experiment in bringing revolution to the world of art. But the story is also a travel narrative that retells an exploratory visit by this Argentina-born writer to Solentiname, Nicaragua, in 1976, three years before the Sandinista victory. Cortázar, a world-renowned novelist and short-story writer, is best known for *Hopscotch* (1964), one of the most influential contemporary Latin American novels, notable for its experimental treatment of theory and jazz, and for its self-referential awareness of the reader's role in deciphering the text.

For Cortázar, who lived most of his adult life in Paris, the Nicaraguan revolution became a genuine passion, mostly because of its reliance on cultural and spiritual revival for political awakening. Neither surrealism, which significantly influenced his earlier work, nor the Cuban revolution, to which he felt some attraction at first, intrigued him the way Nicaragua would in his later years. By the middle 1970s, his curiosity brought him to Solentiname, an archipelago of small islands that had acquired special significance for many Latin American writers. It was an artistic commune founded by Ernesto Cardenal, the Nicaraguan priest/poet/revolutionary whose earlier experience as a Trappist monk in Kentucky had left a clear imprint on the artistic ideals of this beautiful and small island retreat. The story of Cortázar's first visit would eventually become part of an anthology, *Nicaragua, So Violently Sweet*, that gathers various accounts of trips he made to that country over a span of seven years before his death in 1984.

'Apocalypse at Solentiname,' though brief, brilliantly engages the complex relationships among politics, literature, and the representation of otherness from within the realm of artistic form, a pursuit that informs nearly all of Cortázar's later works. But the story's considerable notoriety is due largely to its prophetic value, since it can be said to forecast the apocalyptic end that came to Solentiname at the hands of the Somoza National Guard about a year after its publication. Ernesto Cardenal and his aesthetic/religious collective had allowed training and military expeditions to be launched from their commune as a sign of their solidarity with the Sandinista revolution during the final stages of the insurrectionist struggle. Shortly after the first Sandinista guerrilla attack was launched from Solentiname, the Somoza National Guard wiped out the entire commune. One of the few buildings left standing had housed an exceptional library of unpublished literary and religious manuscripts. It was turned into the National Guard's main barracks.

Barbara Harlow includes a detailed account of the story as prophesy in her *Resistance Literature*, drawing definitive conclusions about its political meaning. This text, she writes, 'presents in its reading of the images of Solentiname the necessary conditions for subsequent resistance to the situation of repression and terror exercised by the hegemonic powers of the First World and its collaborators in the Third World.'[26] Reading it only as a prophesy neatly fulfilled in history, however, fails to account for many significant and problematic aspects of the story, some of which are pertinent to the political conclusion proffered by Harlow. Linking the story to a subsequent and historically verifiable outcome such as the destruction of the commune at the hands of the National Guard is not inapposite, but Cortázar's representation of the massacre at Solentiname turns out to be somewhat more polysemic than Harlow has allowed.

The narrative unfolds from pictures taken by Cortázar during his brief and peaceful stay in Solentiname, pictures developed and viewed in a slide projector after his return to Paris. Suddenly, as he studies them, they begin to show more than the friendly and serene surroundings he had photographed. Government soldiers appear out of the blue. A young man is shot through the head. As Cortázar proceeds with his private screening, images of arrest and torture from his native Argentina also come into focus, and the identity of the young man is revealed: it is Roque Dalton, the renowned Salvadoran poet who had been brutally assassinated in El Salvador one year earlier. When Cortázar's wife Claudine appears, he leaves the room and asks her to view the slides. She, however, does not see any of these unusual revelations.

In Harlow's analysis of this story, we are told that 'Claudine, who comes in only at the end of the showing and repeats the sequence of slides for herself, sees nothing of those events which the shocked narrator had discerned in the photographic images.'[27] In her 'blindness,' adds Harlow, 'Claudine may resemble the naive reader for whom there is only the text . . .'[28] Such a reading understandably attempts to underline the importance of political awareness and contextualization when reading the Other, but in her rush for political metaphors, Harlow appears to leave the text too soon. If Cortázar is the ideally informed reader, then we would need to explore all of what he sees, which includes not only Argentinian and Nicaraguan right-wing soldiers, but also a reflection on left-wing violence, represented by Roque Dalton's execution. Cortázar's clairvoyance, therefore, requires a broader political frame that can only issue from a closer analysis of the text. In that same light, Claudine's blindness or naiveté may also be subject to further textual scrutiny.

Cortázar's mode of fictionalizing lived experience is of particular interest, given that the story's self-awareness as art would seem to challenge from within how texts and revolutions read each other. The author's trip to the Solentiname archipelago in the south of Lake Nicaragua already carries a multitude of signifying elements that are intricately woven together in rather suggestive ways. From Paris, where he lives with his wife who will be left in the dark until the need for that 'innocent' reader arises, we see that he travels to Havana – perhaps a necessary stopover in the contextualization of a political journey to meet the revolution. From there he goes on to San José, Costa Rica, the closest city from which to fly to the lake in a Piper Aztec – a possibly coincidental reference to the world of Native Americans. While in Solentiname, Cortázar attends a Sandinista mass, a mixture of spiritualism, oral tradition and liberationist politics – the truly autochthonous cultural form of that revolution. He then talks to a few campesinos about their application of the gospel to their lives and engages in friendly conversation with Ernesto Cardenal, Sergio Ramírez and other well-known writers. From the outset, the author/ narrator openly assumes the profile of a visiting famous artist who values the revolution but is not about to nullify or camouflage his social bearings. On the contrary, in a fashion worthy of Walter Benjamin, his sense of politics is only defined by his zeal to bring his artistic means to the revolution.

Before he leaves Solentiname, the customary farewell photographs are taken by hosts and guests alike, and just here the story grows a bit more complicated, demanding further review of the political conclusions implicit in the prophesy already discussed. Before Cortázar takes the slides he will later review in Paris, one of the locals uses a Polaroid, a device the narrator claims never to have seen in action before. This becomes a crucial gesture with multiple implications, for it places Cortázar – a cosmopolitan latino-Parisian artist with an international reputation – in a position of less technological sophistication than the campesino community. The scene functions as a cultural equalizer of sorts, analogous to Galeano's nullifying his body before meeting the guerrillas. The nature of this move is political to the extent that it is also textual, since it identifies a mode of artistic reproduction and reception, again in Benjaminian fashion, that Cortázar will take from the campesinos and employ in the development of the story later in Paris.

As Cortázar observes the Polaroid, he describes how this 'celestial piece of paper, slowly and marvelously polaroid, begins to fill itself with images, first disquieting ectoplasms and then, little by little, a nose, a curly hair, Ernesto's smile, doña María and don José, leaning against the veranda.'[29] 'They were all used to this,' he says, 'but I wasn't . . . I remember asking Oscar what would happen if one day after a family picture, this celestial paper were to begin filling itself with Napoleon on horseback, and don José just laughed.'[30] Pondering whether Napoleon could surface in the picture is, however, only a playful distraction from the image of Ernesto standing next to Joseph and Mary that has already been placed before us. The worlds of miracles and photographs have already fused.

The Polaroid photograph is thus transformed, before our very eyes, not into an image of the real, but into a syncretized picture of the Holy Family, perhaps inspired by the Sandinista mass Cortázar had just witnessed. More important, the poetic depictions of Polaroid magic foreground and anticipate the eventual transformations seen by Cortázar in Paris later. This other reading, more textually bound, seems to indicate a particular investment in how technology and peripheral

modernity come together as artwork. Ectoplasm, spiritualism, Sandinista politics and theology of liberation – all come into play right there
in Solentiname, through the Polaroid magic Cortázar has supposedly
never seen before.

The unexpected images of torture Cortázar observes at the end of the
story are undoubtedly meant to bring into focus a Latin American
context of political and military repression, including that which comes
at the hand of left-wing guerrilla groups. Roque Dalton's death had
resulted from a factional fight within the FMLN (Frente Farabundo
Martí de Liberación Nacional). It is therefore important to resist the
rush to enclose this story within a framework that pans out in a
historical interpretation without attending to the broader critique of
violence inscribed in it. Reality effects can overwhelm the reading of a
story like this one, given its almost irresistible prophetic content. The
slippery relationship between reality and literature it indicates reminds
me of one of Tlön's most severe precepts, which holds that 'manuals,
anthologies, summaries, literal versions, authorized re-editions and
pirated editions of the Greatest Work of Man flooded and still flood the
earth. Almost immediately, reality yielded on more than one account.
The truth is that it longed to yield.'[31]

A closer reading of this story, therefore, calls for a different and
much more specific understanding of literature and revolution in
contemporary Latin America than those that derive their impetus from
the too simple category of resistance literature. In contrast to Galeano's
concern with social history, Cortázar's text seems much more fictiona-
lized. It reveals a much greater control over how his writing will
accommodate the few days spent in that special, almost mystical,
Solentiname in 1976, during the insurgency stage of the Nicaraguan
revolution. Indeed, Cortázar's artistic design overwhelms any attempt
to throw himself into the story with some degree of spontaneity, as one
might otherwise expect of a travel narrative. The story's impact thus
depends radically upon its literary form, in its immanent approach to
the notion of revolution as a text that can beget other texts,
crisscrossing from the literary to the non-literary and back. Through
these creative impulses, Cortázar forges a self-reflexive fusion of
technological novelty, Sandinista spiritualism, and his own memory of
politically motivated violence in Latin American liberation movements. In this unusual mix of texts and chronologies, it could be said
that his art and the early phases of the Nicaraguan revolution
transform a snapshot into a disturbing mirror, thereby giving a new
meaning to the idea of revelation.

VI

By the beginning of the eighties, after Nicaragua's revolutionary government took power and the insurrection in El Salvador grew stronger, Central America became a focal point of US foreign policy. Mainstream American television and journalism, perhaps responding to a new post-Vietnam rigor, closely reflected the alarmist discourse of political figures from both parties. In time, writers and filmmakers became more directly acquainted with ongoing events in the area, not only to provide a more balanced or complex panorama than mainstream media, but as a personal and artistic exploration as well. Joan Didion's *Salvador* can be said to respond to this context in the United States. It constitutes yet a different turn of the relationship between textuality and revolution explored in this essay. Didion, well known for combining journalism and fiction, has authored more than ten books since the late sixties, including *Run River, After Henry, Democracy, a Novel, Miami* and *Salvador*.

Before publication in 1983, most of the various vignettes that later became *Salvador* were serialized in the *New York Review of Books*. But the most striking early reception of this book is to be found in the blurbs awaiting the reader on the cover of the first paperback edition. They promise 'a surrealist docudrama,' 'a poetic exploration in fear,' 'a muted outrage that appalls the mind and stiffens the spine,' 'bodies found everywhere – in vacant lots, in garbage, in rest rooms, in bus stations . . . bodies, bodies – and vultures to feed on them wherever they lie . . .'[32] This litany concludes with the observation (suggested by the epigraph Didion supplies for the book): 'El Salvador has truly become the Heart of Darkness.'[33] As with the advent of music videos that superimpose a visual narrative structure upon the listener, the reader must here confront not simply a reading, but a thoroughly constructed cultural reference point, be it Conrad's masterful story, or Francis Ford Coppola's contemporary film, *Apocalypse Now*. Africa and Vietnam are immediately brought to mind, along with images of violence, foreign intervention and misrepresentation of the Other. Readers are being asked to transfer these time-honored Western reference points, entirely uncritically, to a new Latin American setting.

George Yúdice, a Salvadoran-born critic who lives in the United States, has commented on these promotional campaigns in the text's margins, stating: 'One has to trust the "wisdom" of the marketing industry to understand the prurient taste for horror that links desire to read this book with the desire to see the *Texas Chainsaw Massacre*, *The Terminator*, *Angel Heart*, and other displays of mutilation.'[34] He is led to conclude that 'like pornographic representations of violence against women, works such as *Salvador* draw much of their fascination from the violation of "marginal" Others, the oppressed.'[35] As with Harlow's reading of Cortázar, this take on *Salvador* is surely pertinent, but it leaves much of the text behind, including elements that bear on the question of Didion's representation of violence in El Salvador, and whether, like the publisher's blurbs that adorn its cover, the book simply caters to a need to present revolution in a sensationalist light.

Salvador narrates Didion's two-week trip to that war-torn country in 1982, accompanied by her husband John Gregory Dunne, who remains anonymous whenever he appears in the story but is identified in the book's prefatory note acknowledgements. In Cortázar's story, it will be recalled, Claudine only surfaces at the end when her husband, the author/narrator, stereotypes her as a naive reader. In Didion's book, the husband plays no discernable role, yet he frequently appears in her daily references to the ongoing plot. One is led to infer that this anonymous 'husband' character is also a device within the story, standing for the need for trust and security that an investigative reporter requires in a truly dangerous setting, where neither the Salvadoran government nor the American embassy inspires any degree of confidence. Similarly, one also surmises that his cultural and linguistic sameness provides a respite for the author/narrator/protagonist during an exploration of otherness from which she feels a different sort of threat.

Unlike Galeano and Cortázar, Didion never travels to any guerrilla camp, alone or accompanied. Her reportage focuses exclusively on the violent life in the capital city, San Salvador – its sights, sounds and, most particularly, the language that sustains such a world. Her story describes what happens in a first-person account that is not quite ready to inscribe the Other as either a new historical subject, like Galeano's, or as an incursion within artistic form, like Cortázar's. Instead, Didion seems to pursue an experience of otherness as a loss of self, as a bewildering experience for an American journalist lodged in downtown San Salvador, caught in the crossfire of bullets and conflicting claims from the guerrillas, the US embassy and the Salvadoran government. On the very first page, she observes:

> ... in the general absence of tourists these hotels have since been abandoned, ghost resorts on the empty Pacific beaches, and to land at this airport built to service them is to plunge directly into a state in which no ground is solid, no depth of field reliable, no perception so definite that it might not dissolve into its reverse.[36]

One can almost hear echoes of Tlön's main aesthetic precept here, which exhorts one not to 'seek for the truth or even for verisimilitude, but rather for the astounding.'[37] It is important to notice, however, that Didion does examine, sporadically, the concrete elements of power that traverse this uncanny world. By the third page we read about police cars, roadblocks and unidentified bodies of dead men, women and children, as well as how these are reported by the local media, from which, she adds, 'the United States embassy compiles its body counts which are transmitted to Washington in a weekly dispatch referred to by embassy people as "the grimgram," . . . a kind of tortured code that fails to obscure what is taken for granted in El Salvador, that government forces do most of the killing.'[38]

Indeed, *Salvador* does feed on the collusion between the United States and the Salvadoran government, underlining a political concern that is not likely to be advertized in the publisher's blurbs. In this sense, it bears some analogy to Galeano's story, except that its primary interest is not causal, historical or accusatory, but a more ambivalent and synchronic presentation of how it feels to be in a culture that can seem so foreign to the protagonist's sensitivities. What we get, then, is a fairly detailed grammar of terror: the daily grimgram of body counts, how 'to disappear' is often used as a transitive verb in El Salvador, how agrarian reform can be promoted and its desirability precluded at the same time, how asking people for the truth is interpreted as a test of what the government means, in short, how an elaborate code of dissimulation underlies the pretense of democratic rule.

In this strange world Didion begins to question how her writing will respond. This apparent loss of confidence, if not identity, is carefully outlined when she visits an exclusive Americanized shopping mall filled with Sergio Valente jeans, big towels with maps of Manhattan, and all the trappings of US upper-middle-class suburbia. As she gets set to depict the apparent incongruity of such a scene in San Salvador at the time, she turns on herself:

> I wrote it down dutifully, this being the kind of 'color' I know how to interpret, the kind of inductive irony, the detail that was supposed to illuminate the story. As I wrote it down I realized I was no longer much interested in this kind of irony, that this was a story that would not be illuminated by such details, that this was perhaps less a 'story' than a true noche obscura.[39]

Whereas, for their respective entries into the world of the Other, Galeano's text required a self-inscribed nullification and Cortázar's a quasi-religious revelation of Polaroid magic, Didion's predicament is considerably different; her interest lies in that 'noche obscura' itself. By denying herself recourse to irony, she allows her writing to drift about without a clear subject to affirm and, more important, without a familiar textual form. Thus, what the story pursues is a model for writing El Salvador as a loss, one it seeks to discover as it writes it. With that aim in view, we learn one night that Didion has met Victor Barriere, a well-to-do Salvadoran painter who has volunteered to give her a quick, personalized rundown of his country's history. As it turns out this man is history himself, since he is the grandson of the late General Maximiliano Hernández Martínez, whose thirteen-year-long dictatorship in El Salvador was built upon the massacre in 1932 of Farabundo Martí, his followers, and 30,000 other Salvadorans.

As fate would have it, Didion also discovers that this most ruthless of dictators has literary relevance, for he is said to have directly informed Gabriel García Márquez's well-known *Autumn of the Patriarch*, one of the most celebrated of the 'dictator novels' that have become a special Latin American subgenre. Didion's search for a different voice is thus claimed by Central America's own textual traditions, as she discovers the significance of the 1930s in the voice of General Martínez, recalled amidst the echoes of revolutionary wars, the memory of living relatives, and current literary masterpieces. All of them appear as surreal to her as the world she has been trying to describe in 1982. The general was, she says, 'a sinister visionary,' who 'held seances in the Presidential Palace,' and 'conducted the country's affairs along lines dictated by eccentric insights, which he sometimes shared by radio with the remaining citizens.'[40] She goes on to sample two of his most grotesque pronouncements:

> It is good that children go barefoot. That way they can better receive the beneficial effluvia of the planet, the vibrations of the earth. Plants and animals don't use shoes.
>
> Biologists have discovered only five senses. But in reality there are ten. Hunger, thirst, procreation, urination, and bowel movements are the senses not included in the lists of biologists.[41]

At this moment, Didion's willingness to drift without a clue as to the form her writing will finally take comes to a sudden halt under the weight of Latin American fiction. The intertextual relations between García Márquez's *The Autumn of the Patriarch* and General Martínez's eccentric musings from the 1930s suddenly translate the author's search into a direct encounter with magic realism, as if it were the only possible form for representing such a world after all. One could surmise from this conclusion, in a manner inspired by a narrow interpretation of Borgesian principles, that history reveals itself to Didion as literary form, ultimately the only way to rewrite the past, particularly in Latin America. Conversely, one could judge that Didion's attempt to write about a problematic and ongoing revolution ultimately gives way to a contemplative, and somewhat reductive, exercise in literary appreciation. But it could also be argued that Didion's text thwarts such clear-cut enclosures, given that what informs her approach to the language of magic realism is a brush with revolution as a lived, and not just read, threatening experience.

After dining with the general's grandson and suffering through an earthquake at midnight, Didion concludes a most difficult day with an awakening: she now understands García Márquez in a new light, that is, 'as a social realist.'[42] Later, she adds that 'language has always been used a little differently in this part of the world (an apparent statement of fact often expresses something only wished for, or something that might be true, a story, as in García Márquez's *many years later, as he faced the firing squad, Colonel Auareliano Buendía was to remember that distant afternoon when his father took him to discover ice).*'[43]

Like Galeano and Cortázar, Didion delves into the world of revolution through a self-reflective progression that incorporates an initial loss and then a transformation. Her story does not attempt a direct contact with a guerrilla camp and appears to hover on the surface of events, constantly drawing information from readily accessible US embassy contacts and colorful oligarchical figures. A San Salvadoran cityscape filled with violent, demeaning images of the Other is ever-present, as Yúdice suggests. But *Salvador* also permits a different and more complex reading. It flows from Didion's need to reach beyond the language of ironic depictions into a dialog with two other forms of writing, both foreign to her: the grammar of terror and magic realism. The first allows her to move about between episodes of violence in descriptive fashion, drifting along without a sense of structure, other than the ever-present US embassy and its clients, the local generals and their offspring. The second brings her to read García Márquez as many Latin Americans do, as an effect of the real that includes but complicates the practice of reading and writing with ongoing experiential exigencies.

Didion goes to El Salvador to explore the revolution and comes back a better reader of García Márquez. Unquestionably, such a turn constitutes as much of a device as Cortázar's discovery of Polaroids and Galeano's accidental experience as an urban spy. These travel stories conjure up the image of a diary, where living and writing are supposedly closely linked, as if they mirrored each other in some simplified way to bring an experience with 'the real' to a text. But that may be just another literary conceit implicit in the intensive act of editing and rewriting obviously present in these narratives. Some readers of Borges, not to be denied, would probably see them as just literary permutations of one basic story, and perhaps even a further reflection on the *Arabian Nights*, Borges's ultimate model for a sense of historical reality. Yet there is more than an immanent reflection on writing that defines otherness in these texts. A chronologically inscribed community of demographically constitutive others is also present, claiming its place in that sense of loss from within that each writer experiences.

The historical value of the stories discussed here will obviously remain open to debate. This is not to suggest, however, that they are open to just any form of manipulation. Placing them neatly into this or that model of representing or deconstructing Latin America will probably become a transparent imposition for the sake of another text or experience. They respond to a sixty-year-old constellation of texts and revolution, to the grammar of terror supported from within and without, to local generals and the fiction they inspire, and, most important, to a rich cultural experience performed through narratives such as these and through readings complex enough to do them justice.

Hybridity, an image frequently invoked in postmodern aesthetics, is operative in these texts only as a dually inscribed property where both writing and revolution bring otherness into dialog with what Enrique Dussel calls 'the Reason of the Other'.[44] Dussel, an Argentina-born professor of philosophy and theology at the Universidad Autónoma Metropolitana in Mexico, argues that modernity and postmodernity have a different meaning for those who have been historically 'excluded, dominated, or compelled' to an asymmetrical position in history and epistemology. He adds:

> Unlike the postmodernists, we do not propose a critique of reason as such; but we do accept their critique of a violent, coercive, genocidal reason. We do not deny the rational kernel of the universalist rationalism of the Enlightenment, only its irrational moment as sacrificial myth. We do not negate reason in other words, but the irrationality of the violence generated by the myth of modernity. Against postmodernist irrationalism, we affirm the 'reason of the Other.'[45]

Traces of such a reason can perhaps be observed in the current Zapatista revolt, arguably the most recent chapter in the Latin American revolutionary text. To many observers it signals a postmodern conflict. Others have seen it as a classic seventeenth- or eighteenth-century claim for equality justified under Mexican and international law. Zapatista subcommander Marcos has indeed toyed with the question of his 'real identity,' and his group's manifestos subscribe to a local more than a national definition of community. But the Zapatista rebellion has from the outset also laid claim to Article 39 of the Mexican constitution. That reads: 'All public power emanates from the people and is established for the benefit of the people. The people have, at all times, the inalienable right to alter or modify the form of their government.'[46] That provision, derived from John Locke's 1690 *Essay on Government*, can also be traced to the English and American revolutions. Undoubtedly, it is still to be read for more than its literary values.

Notes

1. Kempton's column in *Newsday*, May 19, 1993, p. A101.
2. Ibid.
3. The work of CISPES (Committee in Solidarity with the People of El Salvador) and NACLA (North American Congress on Latin America) are important examples. In the art world, *Cineaste* published a number of very informative surveys of new documentaries on Central America during the eighties.
4. Sheldon Hackney, 'Organizing a National Conversation,' *Chronicle of Higher Education*, April 20, 1994.
5. Jacques Derrida, 'Spectres of Marx,' *New Left Review*, no. 205 (May–June 1994), pp. 37–8; emphasis in the original.
6. Ibid., p. 37.
7. Carlos Rincón provides an original critique of Borges's influence on current European theorists in 'The Peripheral Center of Postmodernism: On Borges, García Márquez and Alterity,' *boundary 2*, vol. 20, no. 3 (Fall 1993); this issue is edited by John Beverley and José Oviedo.
8. The story is recounted in Nestor García Canclini's *Culturas Híbridas: para entrar y salir de la modernidad* (Mexico: Consejo Nacional para la Cultura y las Artes, 1990), p. 105.
9. Jorge Luis Borges, 'Tlön, Uqbar, Orbis Tertius,' in *Labyrinths*, edited by Donald A. Yates and James E. Irby (New York: New Directions Books, 1964), p. 8.
10. This particular reading very much informs two recent paradigmatic examples of Latin American literary deconstructionism. See Alberto Moreiras's 'Pastiche Identity, and Allegory of Allegory,' in Amaryll Chanady, ed., *Latin American Identity and Constructions of Difference* (Minneapolis: University of Minnesota Press, 1994), pp. 204–38; and Roberto González Echevarría's 'The Novel as Myth and Archive: Ruins and Relics of Tlön,' in his *Myth and Archive* (Cambridge: Cambridge University Press, 1990), pp. 142–86. For a more balanced reading of Borges and an assessment of the critical modes his work has inspired in Euro-American institutions, see Beatriz Sarlo, *Jorge Luis Borges: A Writer on the Edge* (London: Verso, 1993); and Jean Franco, 'The Utopia of a Tired Man: Jorge Luis Borges,' *Social Text* (Fall 1981), pp. 52–79.
11. *The Spanish Civil War* (New York: Harper and Row, 1961); and *Cuba: The Pursuit of Freedom* (New York: Harper and Row, 1971).
12. Donald C. Hodges, *Intellectual Foundations of the Nicaraguan Revolution* (Austin: The University of Texas Press, 1986), pp. 167–72.

13. Alberto Bayo Giroud, *150 Questions for a Guerrilla* (Boulder, Colorado: Panther Publications, 1962).

14. In Spanish, *La guerra de guerrillas* (La Habana: Editorial de Ciencias Sociales, 1978).

15. Borges, *Labyrinths*, p. 13.

16. González Echevarría's reading of this story as a Borgesian deconstruction of the ideological and literary projects behind the realist fiction of the time is thorough and imaginative, but, in typical de Manian dogma, it leaves nothing but literary unwriting of social projects to be celebrated from afar. In this account Latin America becomes a triumphant repository of literary monuments that unmask the inherent impossibility of all social projects or any discourse that does not acknowledge itself primarily as fiction, the ultimate and unavoidable character of all historical reflection. This narrow application of deconstructive insights is even more dramatic in Djelal Kadir's *Questing Fictions* (Minneapolis: University of Minnesota Press, 1986); and presented with greater fervor in his more recent *The Other Writing* (West Lafayette: Purdue University Press, 1993).

17. Derrida, p. 56. Needless to say, Derrida does not propose here a dialectical understanding of how such a debt persists, but in this essay he does problematize the relation between deconstruction and the social realm, perhaps in a fashion never seen in his previous work. He looks here at neoliberal hegemony as a contemporary ideological problem embodied in specific political forces, a risk that many literary deconstructionists prefer to eschew.

18. Paul de Man, 'Literary History and Literary Modernity', in *Blindness and Insight: Essays in the Rhetoric of Contemporary Criticism* (New York: Oxford University Press, 1983), p. 165.

19. Arif Dirlik provides a closely argued critique of this tendency in 'The Postcolonial Aura: Third World Criticism in the Age of Global Capitalism,' *Critical Inquiry*, no. 20 (Winter 1994), pp. 312–49.

20. Donald C. Hodges, *Sandino's Communism* (Austin: University of Texas Press, 1992).

21. Quoted by John Beverley and Marc Zimmerman in their *Literature and Politics in the Central American Revolutions* (Austin: University of Texas Press, 1990), p. 53.

22. Eduardo Galeano, *Guatemala, Occupied Country* (New York: Monthly Review Press, 1969). My quotations are taken from the earlier Spanish text, *Guatemala: país ocupado* (Mexico: Editorial Nuestro Tiempo, 1967); my translation. Julio Cortázar, 'Apocalypse at Solentiname', in *Nicaragua, tan violentamente dulce* (Barcelona: Muchnik Editores, 1984); my translation. Joan Didion, *Salvador* (New York: Simon and Schuster, 1983).

23. Eduardo Galeano, *Open Veins of Latin America*, translated by Cedric Belfrage (New York: Monthly Review Press, 1973).

24. Galeano, *Guatemala: país ocupado*, p. 11; my translation.

25. Ibid., p. 56.

26. Barbara Harlow, *Resistance Literature* (New York: Methuen, 1987), p. 79.

27. Ibid., p. 77.

28. Ibid.

29. Cortázar, p. 19.

30. Ibid.

31. Borges, p. 17.

32. Quoted by George Yúdice in his 'Marginality and the Ethics of Survival,' in Andrew Ross, ed., *Universal Abandon? The Politics of Postmodernism* (Minneapolis: University of Minnesota Press, 1988), p. 234. Yúdice is quoting from a different edition of Didion's book than mine: *Salvador* (New York: Washington Square Press, 1983).

33. Ibid.

34. Ibid.

35. Ibid. See also Mary Louise Pratt's incisive reading in her *Imperial Eyes* (London: Routledge, 1992), pp. 225–7.

36. Didion, p. 13.

37. Borges, p. 10.

38. Didion, p. 15.

39. Ibid., p. 36.

40. Ibid., p. 53.

41. Ibid., p. 54.

42. Ibid., p. 59.

43. Ibid., p. 64; emphasis in the original. After many years, Didion has concluded that a 'systematic obfuscation' of massacres in El Salvador has followed in the US media. 'Something Horrible in El Salvador,' *New York Review of Books*, vol. XLI, no. 13 (1994), pp. 8–13.

44. See Dussel's 'Eurocentrism and Modernity (Introduction to the Frankfurt Lectures),' in *boundary* 2, 20:3 (1993), pp. 65–77.

45. Ibid., p. 55.

46. I am indebted to Robert W. Benson for his analysis of the Zapatista revolution's reliance on the Mexican constitution. See his 'Mexican Reform Can't Be Trickle-Down Kind,' *Newsday*, July 28, 1994, p. A40.

7

Refugees and Homecomings: Bessie Head and the End of Exile

Rob Nixon

One morning in Johannesburg a few years back, I was roused early by the dawn chorus of the telephone. In my penumbral, precaffeinated state I found myself listening to an agitated voice inquiring from the far end: 'Hello, excuse me, are you the ANC Repatriation Office?' It took me some little while to awaken to the fact that I was neither in the grip of one of my recurrent bureaucracy nightmares nor being enveloped by yet another variant of the South African dementia. For that week I had moved in to share a house with Mzwai Booi, a guerrilla leader, recently returned from Moscow and Lusaka, who had landed the mind-bending job of chief orchestrator of the exiles' return.

To speak of the culture of exile at this moment in the South African struggle is to speak above all about the culture of return. Or, more precisely, about the culture of reentry. For the word 'return' among the South African, as among the Palestinian, diaspora carries a hugely resonant set of expectations that current conditions have scarcely begun to satisfy. Return has accrued associations of reclamation and restitution. As in all anticolonial struggles, the word summons to mind, above all, emotional and economic claims on the land.

South African repatriation has come not through liberation but through a by now bloodstained amnesty replete with cynical military efforts to foster violence and deepen inter-ethnic rifts. The freedom to pass through customs without fear of arrest surely marks an advance, but it remains an insufficient criterion for return. South Africans have experienced the attenuation of exile without the fullness of return; without, that is, anything approaching liberation, deliverance, or what the Martinican poet Aimé Cesaire once called 'the rendezvous of victory.'[1]

Mzwai Booi reaffirmed my sense that homecoming does not allow for simple restorations. When I met him, Booi would, as a reprieve from his heady week at the Repatriation Office, drive off on a Sunday night and join the tuxedoed ranks attending concerts and operas in the heart of Johannesburg. There he sought to satisfy the classical aesthetic enthusiasms he had acquired through a seven-year stint in Moscow. During fifteen years of enforced absence from the rural hamlet of his birth – a time spent in cities as divergent as Moscow and Lusaka – Booi had become a total *métissage*, someone who, for all his absorption in the South African struggle, had traveled out of range of simple cultural allegiances and reclamations. He had become, in short, what Salman Rushdie calls an irrevocably 'translated person.'[2]

The coming to an end of South African exile should spur us to reassess the literature that that condition inspired – a challenge to be undertaken not simply in a commemorative but in a prospective spirit. The arrival of wave upon wave of 'translated' people reminds us that words such as 'banishment,' 'uprootedness,' 'loss,' and 'yearning' cannot contain the state of exile. It can be a deadening condition but it can be, equally, a cruelly creative one, forcing people to achieve complex, often imaginatively provisional ways of being. This creativity wrought from loss can be an asset during an era when the ground rules of both South African and Palestinian politics are shifting underfoot, an era that has heightened our need for resourceful, even visionary improvisation.

Officially the epoch of South African exile that began in the late 1950s ended in 1990. One of the specific conditions of the African National Congress (ANC) for entering into negotiations with the South African regime was the unconditional return of all exiles. But the returnees have had to face the immense breach between their often apocalyptic sense of anticipation and the abject conditions of contemporary South Africa. The principal revolution has been the revolution in expectations unleashed by the unbannings, the reentries, and the release of prisoners. As in the former Soviet Union and much of Eastern Europe, the rhetoric of endings has produced an upward spiral of political expectations amidst downward-spiralling economic circumstances.

For the liberation movement to have wrested the right of reentry from the South African regime is in itself an achievement. However, while reentry offers promise insofar as it breaks the deadlock of banishment, we should put this promise in perspective: only 10 percent of the South African exiles who have come back have found jobs. The prospects are dim – especially for demobilized guerrillas who, from the perspective of business and industry, are not heroes of the struggle, but underqualified men and women with tatty bush war CVs.

Indeed, in the case of the 'returnees,' this upsurge in expectations has only compounded the often airy hopes that burgeon so freely in exile. Whilst glorious anticipation helps make the years of banishment bearable – providing a bedrock of solidarity and exhortation – such assumptions become an encumbrance when people reenter. To speak of the politics of memory at this juncture, therefore, is to speak very much of memories of wounded expectations.

All this has put the ANC in an acute dilemma. The moment of reentry increased the organization's responsibilities in circumstances where it possessed minimal institutional power. It possessed neither the funds and infrastructure to provide jobs, nor facilities to help people adjust to reentry in a trough of local and global recession. Consequently, while the ANC made repatriation a condition of negotiations, it also, privately, urged exiles who held jobs overseas to remain abroad.

So much South African, like Palestinian, literature of the era following the Second World War has arisen out of the experience of exile that one is inevitably led to ask how this moment of reentry transfigures our perception of that corpus of work. All exiles, whether writers or not, share a certain churning in the stomach as they ride the emotional waves that surge between memory and expectations. What distinguishes writers, however, from most other exiles is the professionalizing of their reliance on that violent passage between past and future that so often becomes the source of their inspiration and reputation. Many such writers become habituated to blanking out the alien present – it becomes the least relevant, most distant, most insubstantial of tenses. Time is lived, instead, in a loop of backward and forward projections, the replay and fast forward buttons moving the tape in the same direction, towards an often desperate jumbling of past and future. This *mélange* serves as an imperfect compensation for their losses while sustaining their hopes. Such a convergent experience of time is particularly rampant among exiles who immerse themselves in anticolonial struggles, where the power of these projections gets intensified by the belief that the impetus of history and justice are on one's side.

With the end of exile, that loaded phrase 'back home' is changed utterly in all its temporal and spatial implications. 'Back home' can no longer serve as a place and a time quarantined from the realm of choice.

With the lifting of the proscriptions on reentry, the exiled writer gains new options but also loses the familiar sense of deferred responsibility. Some South African authors have now elected to return, many others have not. Others still have engineered sabbatical homecomings – taking the precaution of temporary leave from their American and European jobs while they hazard a trial rendezvous with their erstwhile homeland.

The decision to reenter may offer release; it may also provoke, in the same breath, an outpouring of trepidation. On the one hand return, however compromised, presents the prospect of imaginative renewal. This is a priceless resource for writers who have found themselves plumbing an ever shallower pool of recollections, the initial wrong of banishment having been compounded by that secondary injustice, the evaporation of memory. Yet the promise of replenishment has its threatening side, too, for it draws writers away from the imaginative obsessions that sustained them in exile, obsessions that, however melancholy, came over the years to offer a version of security.

The very notion of exile is, of course, susceptible to a lurking theatricality. In its most catholic usage, it can signal little more than a fashionable alienation and attract some dubious claimants. Breyten Breytenbach, who was barred from South Africa after marrying a Vietnamese woman, has shown irritation at the license with which the term 'exile' is invoked. He has given voice to a fatigue not just with the histrionics of imitation exiles, but with those more rightful claimants to the title who have allowed themselves to become immobilized by their condition. Breytenbach excoriates those who

> . . . on auspicious occasions bring forth the relics and sing the cracked songs and end up arguing like parakeets about what 'back home' was really like. They lose the language but refuse to integrate the loss, and accordingly will think less, with fewer words and only morbid references to suspend their thoughts from. They are dead survivors waiting for postcards from the realm of the living. The clock has stopped once and for all, the cuckoo suffocated on some unintelligible Swiss sound . . .[3]

To such moribund exiles, one should add, reentry may offer a second chance, either kickstarting their creativity or forcing them to face their terminal inertia. So, too, the advent of the freedom to reenter – whether in Eastern Europe, the CIS, Palestine, or South Africa – can help to flush out those *ersatz* exiles who wore the title like a literary lapel badge.

Although exile is an affliction, those who refuse to concede ruination may transform it into a cultural resource. That which disfigures may,

with determination and fortune, become transfiguring. This is worth
bearing in mind when we reflect on the amnesias of nationalism, those
conscientious forgettings that help mold a shared sense of memory.[4]
The phrase assumes a fresh force if we bring it to bear on all the shards
of memory that get ferried back with each reentering exile. Such jagged
memories afford us the chance to reconceive the cultural barriers
between the indigenous and the alien, the significant and the inconsequential, indeed, to imagine the nation anew.

The need for such reconceptions is sharpened in contemporary South
Africa by the rigid divides between relevant and irrelevant writing that
arose under the pressures of the apartheid/anti-apartheid agon. It is
surely no coincidence that the fiercest critic of those divides, Njabulo
Ndebele, is himself an erstwhile exile. Arguably South Africa's finest
cultural critic and an accomplished writer of fiction, Ndebele charges
that the range of experience admitted by the main currents of South
African writing has been unhealthily narrowed by the pressure on
writers to display relevance, commitment, and political engagement –
to write, that is, visibly in the service of the struggle.

Ndebele seeks, in his essays, to weigh the literary and political cost of
the anti-apartheid imperative. The predominance of accusatory politics
in much of the literature produces, in Ndebele's words, 'not knowledge
but indictment' and has, paradoxically, a dehumanizing effect. The
familiar panoply of victims, revolutionaries, and sell-outs

> . . . appear as mere ideas to be marshalled this way or that in a moral
> debate. Their *human* anonymity becomes the dialectical equivalent of
> the anonymity to which the oppressive system consigns millions of
> oppressed Africans. Thus, instead of clarifying the tragic human
> experience of oppression, such fiction becomes grounded in the very
> negation it seeks to transcend.[5]

Thus Ndebele has called for alternative forms of writing that are less
Manichean and reactive, that refuse to subordinate the cultural
resources of black communities to the dynamics of racial conflict.

Ndebele has voiced a particular concern that South African anti-
apartheid literature is obsessively urban, that it has driven rural
experience and indigenous styles of storytelling into the forgotten
margins of the country's literature, disregarding them as a source of
cultural renewal. The pattern of exile that predominated among South
Africans assumes a direct relevance to Ndebele's observation. For like
most Palestinians, the majority of South Africans who fled abroad did
not resettle in Europe and North America, but became proximate exiles
who crossed over into neighboring countries where they often

remained vulnerable to the predations of South Africa's regional imperial designs. These people experienced exile principally as a rural plight. However, South Africa's literary exiles proved to be atypical of this broader movement: most headed for those venerable magnets for the bohemian diaspora – London, Paris, New York, Chicago, and Berlin.

Some literary exiles, like Dennis Brutus, played a considerable role in giving the struggle international dimensions, by helping import it into the power centers of world politics and the media. However, such cosmopolitan exiles could not offer the specific kind of regenerative literature that Ndebele has urged, one that reconceives rural life as a neglected resource and refuses to confine black experience to the rhythms of the apartheid/anti-apartheid two-step.

It is in this regard that the life and writings of Bessie Head, who lived as a refugee for most of her adult life, assume a singular value. Head's angular perspectives challenge her readers into reconceiving the barriers between the indigenous and the alien, between the significant and the inconsequential; indeed, into reimagining the amnesias of the culture at large. Head is the only exiled South African writer of note to have avoided the rutted literary routes that led from her native land to Europe and North America; she decided instead to move to the frontline state of Botswana, in her words, just 'one door away from South Africa.'[6] Consequently, her imaginative perspective was one of rural internationalism achieved through neighborhood exile, where the crosscultural differences were offset by regional continuities.

The extremity of Head's estrangements from tradition placed her under relentless pressure to improvise a sense of community and ancestry. Stranded at what one commentator has called the 'crossroads of dispossession,' she compensated for her losses by reconceiving herself through a set of fragile, surrogate allegiances.[7]

Head bore the burden of a doubly illegitimate birth: she was conceived out of wedlock and, in apartheid argot, 'across the color bar.' Thus her entry into the world placed her in a transgressive relationship to the racial and gender dictates of her society, portending the torments of her later life in exile. She was thirteen before her origins were revealed to her:

I was born on the 6th July 1937 in the Pietermaritzburg mental hospital. The reason for my peculiar birthplace was that my mother was white, and she had acquired me from a black man. She was judged insane, and committed to the mental hospital while pregnant.[8]

Head's mother, Bessie Amelia Emery, came from an upper-class white South African family renowned for breeding racehorses. When Emery fell pregnant, her parents had her locked away in a mental asylum on the grounds of 'premature senile dementia.'[9] She gave birth to Head while in the asylum and six years later, in 1943, committed suicide there. Head never met her mother, nor did she ever learn the name of her father, who fled the Emery estate without leaving a trace.

Head was named not by her parents but by the apartheid state: 'My mother's name was Bessie Emery and I consider it the only honor South African officials ever did me – naming me after this unknown, lovely, and unpredictable woman.'[10] Thus at Head's christening the distinction between private and public realms disappeared, foreshadowing her almost lifelong sense of the power that the nation-state wielded over the most intimate facets of her identity – an awareness underscored by her suspicious treatment during exile.

By age thirteen, Head had amassed four sets of parents: her biological parents; the Afrikaans foster parents who adopted her as an infant only to return her a week later complaining that she 'appeared to be black'; the 'mixed race' foster parents into whose care she was then delivered; and finally, the state, which, acting *in loco parentis*, removed the young girl from these second foster parents and placed her in an orphanage as a ward of the state. From an early age, Head came to experience the ideas of home and family not as natural forms of belonging but as unstable artifices, invented and reinvented in racial terms, and conditional upon the administrative designs of the nation-state.

Head's sense of familial and racial estrangement was compounded by the fact that, until the age of forty-two, she was denied the moorings of nationality. Her first twenty-seven years were spent in South Africa as a disenfranchised 'mixed race' woman, and the next fifteen years in Botswana, where she was denied citizenship and forced to live as a stateless refugee. This was partly the result of South African regional imperial designs, which placed pressure on the Botswanans to deny sanctuary to South Africans fleeing apartheid. While in Botswana, Head, like her mother before her, was interned in a mental asylum – though temporarily. She thus lived the uncertainty of the word 'asylum' in both its psychological and political meanings: the etymological roots of the term may promise sanctuary, but it is more often experienced as brutal confinement.

Having been rejected by both her natal land and her adopted country, Head experienced the nation-state first and foremost as a gruelling administrative experience. From 1964 to 1979, her official identity remained sandwiched between two of the world's most risible, immobilizing documents – a South African exit permit (which barred her from returning) and a United Nations Refugee Travel Document. Both effectively denied her a national identity.

When an American literary journal innocently sent Head a question-naire about her writing habits, she responded ruefully: 'I am usually terrorized by various authorities into accounting for my existence; and filling in forms, under such circumstances, acquires a fascination all of its own.'[11] As a result of the perennial, reciprocal suspicion between her and all national authorities, she approached questionnaires with the expectation not that they would ratify her identity, but that they had been devised to invalidate it.

Philip Schlesinger has described the nation as

> . . . a repository, *inter alia*, of classificatory systems. It allows 'us' to define ourselves against 'them' understood as those beyond the boundar-ies of the nation. It may also reproduce distinctions between 'us' and 'them' at the intra-national level, in line with the *internal* structure of social divisions and relations of power and domination.[12]

Schlesinger's remarks are directly pertinent to South Africa, where the classificatory obsessions of British imperialism, inherited and trans-formed by Afrikaans nationalists, insured that most black South Africans lived the nation-state as a brutally administered form of disinheritance. This experience of the nation-state as a set of institu-tions destructively reinventing people by categorizing them is forcefully evoked by Don Mattera, a 'mixed race' author of Head's generation. Writing of the era when apartheid bureaucrats sought to institutiona-lize a revamped version of the category 'colored,' Mattera recalls how 'a twilight people . . . were being conceived on the drawing board of apartheid. A hybrid species, signed, sealed and stamped into synthetic nationhood.'[13]

Head's liminal status as a 'mixed race' South African left her particularly resistant to the synthetic projections of the nation in categorically racial terms. Yet she might have become less resistant to the idea of the nation *per se* had her negative experience of the mutually reinforcing exclusions of nation and race not been repeated, disturb-ingly if less violently, in Botswana after she moved there in 1964. In Serowe, the village where she finally settled, she found that the inhabitants identified themselves strongly in ethnic nationalist terms as Batswana. Like many such communities, they consolidated their identity by defining themselves in opposition to certain outcast groups. The lot of the pariah fell principally, in Serowe, to the lighter-skinned

'Bushmen' or 'San,' for whom the Batswana reserved a special term of disdain: 'Masarwa' (pl. 'Basarwa'). To her mortification, Head found herself cursed as a 'half-caste' and 'low breed' alongside the so-called 'Basarwa.'[14] The familiarity of the insult must have sharpened her agony, for 'Boesman'/'Bushman' was a standard slur spat at 'coloreds' by white South African policemen and farmers. The traumas of adoption had come full circle: the orphan whose foster parents had rejected her for appearing too black was now derided, in her adopted village, for seeming insufficiently so. Having left the racist nationalism of South Africa behind her, Head found herself in a situation where the Botswanan state refused to accept her as a national, and members of her local community vilified her in racial terms.

Reading between the lines, one begins to discern the discriminatory rationale behind the bracketing of Head with the 'Basarwa.' From both a white colonial and a Botswana perspective, the nomadic character of the 'San' or 'Basarwa' militated against their claims to ownership of the land. Indeed, the abusive term 'Masarwa' bears the contradictory meaning of 'a person from the uninhabited country.'[15] This formulation for perpetuating the cycles of dispossession is reminiscent of the catastrophic colonial designation of Palestine as 'a land without a people.' In both instances, the argument begins by designating a people as nomadic, proceeds by claiming that this precludes them from owning land, and thereby concludes that such landless people cannot, by definition, suffer dispossession. The motive for and consequence of this rationale is the accelerated dispossession of the people in question, be they Palestinians or 'San.'

It would thus seem that discrimination against people envisaged as 'wanderers' – Jews, Romani, Palestinians, and 'San' – is not confined to the West. Moreover, a related version of this prejudice is projected onto refugees as 'undesirable' in their errancy. Thus the earmarking of Head as a pariah in Botswana brought together the perceptions of her as a 'tribeless half-caste,' as ethnically similar to the 'landless Basarwa,' and as a refugee. To compound matters, she bore the stigma of the single mother – a 'loose' woman, anchored neither through land nor marriage to the agrarian system of property that determined social value.[16] The certification of Head as insane, and her confinement in Lobatse Mental Institution in 1971, may have further exacerbated the perception of her as 'wandering' and 'loose' – given the mutually confirming projections in some societies of 'madwomen' as 'strays,' and 'stray' women (that is, single ones, especially single mothers) as unhinged. Lynette Jackson's groundbreaking work on the construction of female madness in certain southern African mental institutions is particularly suggestive in this regard.[17]

In short, the circumstances of Head's birth were not the only forms of liminality with which she had to contend: as a first generation so-called 'colored,' an orphan, a changeling, a refugee, an inmate in an insane asylum, and a single mother, she led a profoundly disinherited life on every front. Moreover, as a mixed-race woman writer engaging with rural themes in southern Africa, Head worked without the sustenance of a literary heritage.

Head's prose is peopled largely with two types: characters whose sense of belonging is an unsettled, precarious achievement rather than a birthright, and those who risk or forfeit their inherited privileges by breaking with claustral traditions. Indeed, Head repeatedly projected forms of community and ancestry that could not be premissed on the unexamined authority of inherited tradition. Her own vexed relationship to questions of origins, succession, legacies, heritages, and bloodlines left her with a deep-seated suspicion of traditions, above all national traditions, whose invented authority rests on the assumption that the nation is both natural and born of a continuous historical lineage.

Although the nation is a political and bureaucratic invention, the discourse of nationalism commonly imbues it with the natural authority of blood lineage by representing the nation as a set of familial bonds. Etymologically, the word 'nation' is rooted in the idea of conception, while the pervasive figure of Mother of the Nation has been attached to women as diverse as Winnie Mandela, Eva Perón, and the British 'Queen Mum'. More broadly, the language of nationalism is a language of new nations being born, of motherlands, fatherlands, homelands, adopted lands, and neighboring countries. So, when we speak of the exiles' homecoming, their imagined destination is at once a national and a domestic space.

Feminist theorists of nationalism like Anne McClintock, Elleke Boehmer, Floya Anthias, and Nira Yuval-Davis have analyzed the contradictions between the frequent projection of the idea of the nation through a female idiom and the exclusion of women from the statutory rights available to 'nationals,' whose normative identity has been institutionalized as male.[18] At a rhetorical level, however, as Donald Horowitz argues, ethnic national groups, with their hereditary and hierarchical obsessions, tend to perceive themselves as 'super-families.'[19] The analogies between national and family ties have proved crucial to political efforts to portray the nation as a self-evident category authenticated by historical and biological continuities. This process suppresses the irrational, incoherent, and contingent dimensions of nations whose ancestry and boundaries are not emanations of an organic past but largely the products of repeated bureaucratic interventions.

The administrative labor of presenting the nation as a surrogate work of nature is manifest, for instance, in the title of the American Department of Immigration and Naturalization, the body responsible for transmogrifying so-called resident 'aliens' into 'naturalized' Americans. Anyone who has struggled through that labyrinthine paper tunnel can testify to the perversity of construing the process of nationalization as a form of integrating people into something natural. The discourse of 'undocumented immigrants' depicts much more accurately outsiders' experience of the nation as a bureaucratic, not an organic phenomenon.

Many of the fundamental criteria for social acceptance —notably those of family, race, and nation – frequently assume or invoke the authority of blood lineage. Because Head's relationship to these categories was so radically and traumatically marginal, she could never live the illusion of their naturalness. As such, her best books – *Serowe: Village of the Rain Wind, The Collector of Treasures,* and *Tales of Tenderness and Power* – offer sharp insights into the contingencies underlying efforts to seal group membership or exclusion on grounds of blood, nature, or ancestry. Her books testify, moreover, to her determination to reconceive herself as a writer of 'mixed ancestry' in far more than the narrowly racial sense.

In exile, Head forcibly remade herself outside the pseudo-natural matrix of familial, racial, and national traditions that had formed the very grounds of her ostracism. Bypassed by nationalism, Head reconceived herself as a transnational writer. While her books are set in Botswana, they convey a powerful sense of the incessant border crossings of refugees, migrant workers, prostitutes, school children, missionaries, and armies that score southern Africa as a whole. Head's writing thus helped her convert the sense of crosscultural belonging foisted on her by the state into an allegiance of her own.

Alone among the host of black South African authors who were exiled by apartheid, Head set the bulk of her writings not back in the South Africa of memory, but in her present surroundings. As a result, her writings are full of loss, but scoured of nostalgia. By the mid-seventies, she had decided to immerse herself in local history as a strategy for survival. The act of writing both fiction and an oral history of her adopted village helped this denationalized orphan improvise a genealogy.

Southern Africa's precolonial history and its transition from colonialism to independence form the backdrop to many of Head's exile writings. Yet she was neither a cultural preservationist nor an advocate of modern nationalism as a progressive force. Increasingly, she saw the issues of precolonial, colonial, and postcolonial experience through the optic of women's relation to male authority structures, property, and the land. Her writings suggest, too, that the core colonial issue of land is ineradicably gendered. While passionately supporting the idea of independence, she came to feel firsthand women's and men's unequal access to the fruits of nationhood.

Head's mistrust of the sweeping narratives of national politics was compounded by her very intimate sense of what they routinely bypass, especially women's experience, rural life, and oral traditions. Relatedly, one senses Head's anxiety that racial domination, through its power to provoke antiracism, would continue to preoccupy black forms of self-definition; it would thereby hamper – in much the way that Ndebele feared – efforts to establish more independent imaginative coordinates.

It is hardly surprising that Head grew to be obsessed with memory. Yet as a writer comprehensively orphaned by the familial and national past, she was well placed to recognize the imaginative violence that may accompany selective memory, how it may connive in the creation of brutally exclusive stories of who does and does not belong. The estrangements, the idealism, and the resourceful affiliations of her work all testify to a vision of national community not as a passively transmitted set of birthrights, but as the offspring of active remembrance and zealous amnesias. To compensate for her cavernous past, Head determined to become the agent of her own origins; to this end, she wrested an alternative train of memories from her adopted village and from southern Africa as a region.

Defecting from both colonial and anticolonial standards of what constitutes a significant event, Head declared wryly, 'I have decided to record the irrelevant.'[20] Her faith in the redemptive value of the irrelevant and the mundane is at times most reminiscent of Walter Benjamin. Indeed, her ambushes on the ordinary recall Benjamin's remark that 'to articulate the past historically does not mean to recognize it the way it really was. It means to seize hold of a memory as it flashes up at a moment of danger.'[21] Those whom calamity has left stranded in the present may develop uncommon powers for discerning history in the most fragmentary of things.

Head's exaltation of the ordinary is intertwined with her fascination with everything impure and unsettled. She once portrayed herself as surviving by 'performing a peculiar shuttling movement between two lands.'[22] While most of her fiction is set in Botswana, she felt that the persistent violence of her imagination betrayed her South African beginnings. That is, her subject matter and her sensibility had been shaped on either side of the national divide.

'The circumstances of my birth,' Head once wrote, 'seemed to make it necessary to obliterate all traces of a family history.'[23] Nothing was given to her: she lived her dream of belonging as an ongoing and always unfinished labor. Her investment in this dream hinged on a paradox. As an orphaned, uprooted, and stateless writer, she experienced a profound craving for the certainties of what she called a 'whole community.' Yet at the same time, she felt in the intimacy of her bones, the violence from which wholeness, sameness, origins, shared extraction, and the assurances of rooted community are born.[24]

At a time when she faced ostracism on local and national fronts, Head expressed her resolution to belong in one of her standard familial metaphors: '[T]he best and most enduring love is that of rejection . . . I'm going to bloody well adopt this country as my own, by force. I am going to take it as my own family.'[25] Having lived, as a child, through the shallow, artificial genealogies produced by successive adoptions and rejections, she determined to become with a vengeance the agent of her own origins. She wrested from Serowe a surrogate history, an alternative trail of memories to that other, never wholly obliterated past of familial abandonment, racial rejection, colonial domination, and national disinheritance.

In striving to remake herself, Head came to rely on another, more unsettling trail of memories. Particularly during the buildup to her confinement in a Botswanan mental hospital, she feared that she was destined to recapitulate her mother's life. She was fully aware of the pathological circumstances of her mother's incarceration – they were symptomatic of what she once called 'the permanent madness of reality' under apartheid.[26] None the less, Head found herself haunted by the possibility that her mother had transmitted to her the burden of madness.[27] As the daughter of a 'stray' woman, she feared that she, too, might have to pay the ultimate price for her 'errancy.' Certainly, in her autobiographical writings of the late sixties and early seventies, one senses her lurking anxiety that just as racism had pursued her to Serowe, so, too, congenital madness would find her out and return her to the grip of the past.

However, as she began to cobble together a sense of belonging, she came to reimagine her mother's transgressive bequest; there had been, as she once put it, 'no world as yet' for what Bessie Emery had done.[28] Head observed, similarly, of her own achievements:

> The least I can ever say for myself is that I forcefully created for myself, under extremely hostile conditions, my ideal life. I took an obscure and almost unknown village in the southern African bush and made it my own hallowed ground. Here, in the steadiness and peace of my own world, I could dream dreams a little ahead of the somewhat vicious clamour of revolution and the horrible stench of evil social systems.[29]

Her sense here of the creativity born from isolation implies a quite different perception of 'errancy.' Head came to see her mother's actions increasingly less as a threat, passed down to her, of regression into insanity, than as an exhortation audaciously to invent a world adequate to such visionary error. Through her imaginative insistence that the inconceivable take its place within the orbit of the ordinary, Head was, as she recognized, dreaming in advance of her time.

Head's work was apt to project a degree of social acceptance that, in her own life, she knew only as a wavering prospect. Such determined optimism quieted in her fiction the cadences of desolation that distinguished her letters. If, to the last, Head's integration into Serowe on paper remained somewhat ahead of her integration in daily life, she at least acquired a degree of allegiance and acceptance unimaginable in the sixties and early seventies. Moreover, she had engineered for herself a spread of commitments that spanned writing as a vocation, the village, the southern African region, and those rural women who sought a greater share of Botswana's unevenly distributed state of independence. In the process of forging these ties, Head exposed a cluster of amnesias in southern African writing and yielded a greatly expanded sense of its prospects.

With a few notable exceptions, 'coloreds' have been admitted into white South African literature mainly as shiftless, 'tribeless' people burdened by their 'impurity', in plots staging the relentlessly fateful repercussions of miscegenation. While Head's life and work were wrought from tragedy, neither remained merely tragic. Indeed, together they provide one of the richest anticipations of Salman Rushdie's simple, resonant remark that 'notions of purity are the aberration.'[30] In negotiating her impacted sense of loss and her imposed sense of deviance, Head admitted a whole new range of possibilities to the phrase 'mixed ancestry.' Remote from racially charged determinisms, those words came to celebrate the hard-won if fitful freedom to elect and reject one's affinities and provenance. Head's foreign sojourn may have been thrust upon her, but she turned it to advantage, dreaming a little ahead of her time, not least in her insistence that the inconceivable assume its rightful place within the compass of the ordinary.

Head's determination to redeem the irrelevant gives her writings a distinctive resonance amidst the post-exile turmoil of South African life. One of the most exacting challenges in the current milieu is how to accommodate those vast tracts of culture that have been sidelined, trivialized, or mutilated by the dictates of the apartheid/anti-apartheid agon. In a society facing the monumental difficulty of producing a culture of tolerance from a ruinous culture of violence, the exiles' Janus-faced vision may offer a symbolic challenge to blind and murderous chauvinisms. Reentering exiles should thus be recognized as cross-border creations, incurable cultural misfits who can be claimed as a resource, rather than spurned as alien, suspect, or irrelevant.

Notes

1. Aimé Cesaire, 'Notebook of a Return to Native Land', in *Collected Poetry*, translated by Clayton Eshelman and Annette Smith (Berkeley: University of California Press, 1983), p. 77.

2. Salman Rushdie, quoted in Stuart Hall, 'Our Mongrel Selves,' *New Statesman and Society*, June 19, 1992, p. 8.

3. Breyten Breytenbach, 'The Long March from Hearth to Heart,' *Social Research* vol. 58, no. 1 (Spring 1991), p. 70.

4. On this issue, see especially Benedict Anderson, *Imagined Communities* (London: Verso, 1983).

5. Njabulo Ndebele, 'Turkish Tales: Some Thoughts on South African Fiction,' in his, *The Rediscovery of the Ordinary: Essays on South African Literature and Culture* (Johannesburg: COSAW, 1991), p. 23.

6. Bessie Head, 'Preface to Witchcraft,' in *A Woman Alone*, edited by Craig MacKenzie (Portsmouth, New Hampshire: Heinemann, 1990), p. 27.

7. Caroline Rooney, ' "Dangerous Knowledge" and the Poetics of Survival: A Reading of *Our Sister Killjoy* and *A Question of Power*,' in *Motherlands*, edited by Susheila Nasta (London: Women's Press, 1991), p. 118.

8. Bessie Head, quoted in Susan Gardner, ' "Don't Ask for the True Story": A Memoir of Bessie Head,' *Hecate*, no. 12 (1986), p. 114.

9. Letter dated October 31, 1968, in Randolph Vigne, ed., *A Gesture of Belonging. Letters from Bessie Head, 1965–79* (London: S. A. Writers, 1991), p. 65.

10. Quoted in Gardner, p. 114.

11. Bessie Head, in 'Bessie Head,' in Ann Evory, ed., *Contemporary Authors*, vol. 29–32 (Detroit: Gale Research Co., 1978), p. 288.

12. Philip Schlesinger, *Media, State and Nation* (London: Sage, 1991), p. 174.

13. Don Mattera, *Sophiatown: Coming of Age in South Africa* (Boston: Beacon Press, 1989), p. 150.

14. This terrain is a terminological minefield. There is no indigenous 'San' term covering the many formerly nomadic groups whom other Africans and Europeans have variously gathered together under the umbrella terms 'Masarwa,' 'San,' and 'Bushman.' 'Masarwa' is unacceptable since it is the term of abuse dished out by the Batswana who have historically dispossessed and enslaved the 'San.' Although 'San' has achieved a

certain anthropological respectability (if that is not a contradiction in terms), it, too, is derogatory in origin and has been flatly rejected by the people themselves. A number of commentators have observed that, despite its origins in colonial racism, 'Bushman' is the term most commonly embraced within the culture. (See Megan Biesele and Paul Weinberg, *Shaken Roots: The Bushmen of Namibia* [Marshalltown, South Africa: EDA Publications, 1990, p. 72]; Casey Kelso, 'The Inconvenient Nomads Deep Inside the Deep,' [*Weekly Mail*, July 24 to 30, 1992, p. 12]). Is this endorsement from within a defiant appropriation of a previously abusive term? Or has it been adopted in Botswana as an alternative to 'Masarwa,' which is associated with the people's principal contemporary source of oppression and dispossession, namely, the Botswanan state? Even if the racist connotations of 'Bushman' can be overturned, the problem of the term's gender specificity is insurmountable.

15. Quoted in Rooney, p. 227.

16. A largely autobiographical version of the projection of Head as sexually 'loose' on grounds of ethnicity and marital status is to be found in *A Question of Power* (1974; reprinted London: Heinemann, 1986).

17. In some remarkable research into the discourse of madness in Rhodesian mental hospitals between 1932 and 1957, Jackson observes how African women who appeared single in public spaces were sometimes apprehended by the authorities and institutionalized as mad on the grounds that they were, in the medical argot, found 'stray' at the 'crossroads.' ('Stray Women and the Colonial Asylum,' unpublished paper delivered at the Institute of Commonwealth Studies, London, October 26, 1991). As recently as the first half of this century, certain British women were locked away in mental asylums on the grounds that giving birth out of wedlock was a mark of insanity. (See Steve Humphries, *A Secret World of Sex: Forbidden Fruit, the British Experience 1900–1950*. London: Sidgwick and Jackson, 1988.)

Strictly speaking, Head was not an unmarried but a single mother, since she was estranged from her husband who had remained behind in South Africa. However, this distinction appears not to have made much difference to Botswanan perceptions of her as a woman with a child but no husband in train.

18. See Anne McClintock, 'No Longer in a Future Heaven: Women and Nationalism in South Africa,' *Transition*, no. 51 (1991), pp. 150ff.; Elleke Boehmer, 'Stories of Women and Mothers: Gender and Nationalism in the Early Fiction of Flora Nwapa,' in Susheila Nasta, ed., *Motherlands: Black Women's Writing from Africa, the Caribbean and South Asia* (London: Women's Press, 1991), pp. 3–11; Floya Anthias and Nira Yuval-Davis, 'Introduction,' in Anthias and Yuval-Davis, eds., *Woman–Nation–State* (London: Macmillan, 1989), pp. 1–15; and Andrew Parker et al., 'Introduction,' in their *Nationalisms and Sexualities*, (New York: Routledge, 1992), pp. 1–18.

19. Donald Horowitz, *Ethnic Groups in Conflict* (Berkeley: University of California Press, 1985), p. 35.

20. Head, *A Woman Alone*, p. 99.

21. Walter Benjamin, *Illuminations*, translated by Harry Zohn (1970; reprinted London: Fontana-Collins, 1973), p. 258.

22. Bessie Head, 'Social and Political Pressures That Shape Writing in Southern Africa,' *A Woman Alone*, p. 67.

23. 'Biographical Notes,' in ibid., p. 95.

24. The critiques of Raymond Williams by Paul Gilroy and by Stuart Hall are directly relevant to Head's ambiguous experience of settled community. Gilroy and Hall both point out the racial and ethnic nationalist implications of Williams's unquestioning affirmation of the value of 'rooted settlements.' See Gilroy, *There Ain't No Black in the Union Jack: The Cultural Politics of Race and Nation* (London: Unwin Hyman, 1987), pp. 49–50; Stuart Hall, 'Our Mongrel Selves,' *New Statesman and Society*, June 19, 1992, pp. 6–8.

25. Letter dated April 2, 1968, in *A Gesture of Belonging*, p. 58.

26. Head, 'Preface to Witchcraft,' p. 27.

27. See 'Biographical Notes,' p. 95, and letter dated June 4, 1984, in *A Gesture of Belonging*, p. 164.

28. Letter dated October 31, 1968, in *A Gesture of Belonging*, p. 65.

29. Head, *A Woman Alone*, p. 28.

30. Salman Rushdie, 'Minority Literatures in a Multi-Cultural Society,' in Kirsten Holst Petersen and Anna Rutherford, eds., *Displaced Persons* (Sydney: Dangaroo Press, 1988), p. 35.

8

The Struggle Over Representation: Casting, Coalitions, and the Politics of Identification

Ella Shohat

Many of the political debates over race and gender in the United States have revolved around the question of self-representation, seen in the pressure for more 'minority' representation in political, academic, and artistic institutions. The connotations of the word 'representation' are at once religious, aesthetic, political and semiotic. They are religious, for example, in that the Judeo-Islamic censure of 'graven images' casts theological suspicion on directly figurative representation and thus on the very ontology of the mimetic arts.[1] The word's connotations are aesthetic in that art too is a form of representation, in Platonic or Aristotelian terms a mimesis. Representation is also theatrical, and in many languages 'represent' means 'to enact' or play a role. Representation is also political, in that political rule is not usually direct but representative. The contemporary norm of democracy in the West rests on the notion of 'representative government,' evident in the rallying cry from the American Revolution: 'No taxation without representation.'

What all these instances share is the semiotic principle that something is 'standing for' something else, or that some person or group is speaking on behalf of some other persons or groups. On the symbolic battlegrounds of the mass media, the struggle over representation is homologous with that in the political sphere, where questions of imitation and representation easily slide into issues of delegation and voice. The heated debate around which celebrity photographs, whether of Italian-Americans or of African-Americans, should adorn the wall of Sal's Pizzaria in Spike Lee's *Do the Right Thing* (1989) vividly exemplifies this kind of struggle within representation.

Today's discussion of 'political correctness' takes place in an atmosphere dominated by issues of self-representation and identity politics. These issues are fraught with conflicting arguments over who speaks, when, how, and in whose name. The politics of identity call for the 'self-representation' of marginalized communities, and for 'speaking for oneself.' While poststructuralist feminist, gay/lesbian, and postcolonial theories have often rejected essentialist articulations of identity, along with biologistic and transhistorical determinations of gender, race and sexual orientation, they have at the same time supported 'affirmative action' politics, implicitly premissed on the very categories they themselves reject as essentialist.[2] This leads to a paradoxical situation in which theory deconstructs totalizing myths while activism nourishes them. Theory and practice, then, seem to pull in opposite directions. The 'constructionist' view has been instrumental in combating racism, sexism and homophobia, but when pressed it seems to imply that no one can really speak for anyone (perhaps including even for oneself), or, conversely, that anyone can speak for anyone. Identity politics, on the other hand, suggests that people belong to recognizable social groups, and that only delegated representatives can speak on their behalf.

But is permission to represent a given community limited to card-carrying, epidermically suitable representatives of that community? Does the experience of oppression confer special jurisdiction over the right to speak about oppression? Can only an African-American direct *Malcolm X*, as Spike Lee has argued? Should Paul Simon not have made *Graceland*? Would it have been better had Stevie Wonder made it? When does the fear of 'appropriating' turn into a form of mental segregationism, a refusal to recognize one's co-implication with otherness? How can scholarly, curatorial, artistic and pedagogical work embody multiculturalism without defining it simplistically as a space where only latinos would speak about latinos, African-Americans about African-Americans and so forth, with every group a prisoner of its own reified difference?[3] To what extent can a member of one minoritarian group speak for another? How, finally, can prolonging the colonial legacy of misappropriation and insensitivity toward so-called 'minorities' be avoided without silencing potential allies? Talk of antiessentialism and hybridity does not completely allay the anxiety concerning who speaks, about what, for whom, and to what end.[4]

Gayatri Spivak's celebrated question, 'can the subaltern speak?' might in this sense be altered to ask: 'can the nonsubaltern speak?' To begin to answer it, we may note that these anxieties about speaking are asymmetrical. Those who have been traditionally empowered to speak feel relativized simply by having to compete with other voices. Made aware of their own complicity in the silencing of others, they worry about losing a long-taken-for-granted privilege. The disempowered or newly empowered, on the other hand, seek to affirm a precariously established right. 'Disempowered' and 'empowered,' furthermore, are relational terms; people can occupy diverse positions, being empowered on one axis, say that of class, but not on another, say that of race and gender. Instead of a simple oppressor/oppressed dichotomy we find a wide spectrum of complex relationalities of domination, subordination and collaboration. At the extreme ends of this continuum, certainly, are groups respectively empowered along all the axes, on the one hand, and groups empowered along none of them, on the other. But even here there are no guarantees, for one's ancestral community does not necessarily dictate one's identifications and affiliations. It is not only a question of what one is or where one is coming from, but also of what one desires to be, where one wants to go and with whom one wants to go there.

Cinematic spectatorship, interestingly, offers a privileged space for the examination of these processes of identification and symbolic affiliation (or disaffiliation). Indeed, it is a commonplace to say that the media in the postmodern era play a fundamental role in shaping one's identifications and affiliations. By experiencing their bond to people never actually seen, consumers of electronic media can be affected by traditions to which they have no ancestral connection. Thus the media can play a role not only in exoticizing other cultures but also in normalizing them.

Film theory, in its quasi-exclusive focus on sexual as opposed to other kinds of difference, and in its privileging of the intrapsychic as opposed to the intersubjective, the discursive and the intercultural, has often elided questions of racially and culturally inflected spectatorship. Although recent media theory has productively explored sociologically differentiated modes of spectatorship, it has rarely done so through the grid of multiculturalism. In this sense, one can doubt the existence of any racially or culturally or even ideologically circumscribed essential spectatorial identity – *the* white spectator, *the* black spectator, *the* latino/latina spectator, *the* resistant spectator. That is, it is doubtful that cinema can contain spectatorship within any essentialized racial, cultural or ideological identity that people in the audience might bring to a film. Within a complex *combinatoire* of spectatorial positions, members of an oppressed group might identify with the oppressing group (Native American children being induced to root for the cowboys against the 'Indians,' Africans identifying with Tarzan, Arabs with Indiana Jones), just as members of privileged groups might identify with the struggles of oppressed groups. Spectatorial positioning is relational: communities can identify with one another on the basis of a shared closeness or on the basis of a common antagonist. The spectator, in sum, inhabits a shifting realm of ramifying differences and contradictions.

That the spectator is the scene of proliferating differences and contradictions does not mean that an opposite, agglutinative process of cross-racial identifications and imagined alliances does not also take place. Amending Raymond Williams, one could argue for the existence, in life as in spectatorship, of 'analogical structures of feeling,' that is, for a structuring of filmic identification across social, political and cultural situations, through strongly perceived or dimly felt affinities of social perception or historical experience. Spectatorship is not sociologically compartmentalized; diverse communities can resonate with each other. In a context where one's own community goes unrepresented, analogical identifications become a compensatory outlet. A member of a minority group might look for him/herself on the screen, but failing that, might identify with the next closest category, much as one transfers allegiance to another sports team after one's own team has been eliminated from the competition.

Given the contradictory character of the socially situated psyche, individuals are traversed by dissonance and contradiction, existing within a constantly shifting cultural and psychic field in which the most varied discourses produce evolving, multi-valenced relationships, constituting the subject, like the media, as the site of competing discourses and voices. Thus the individual may identify upward or downward; a person empowered on all the axes may identify with, and more important, affiliate with, the disempowered, just as the disempowered may identify with the powerful and feel that the powerful represent their interests.[5] The self on this account is a matrix of multiple discursive forms and identifications – which is in no way to deny realities of race, class, gender, or nation, but only to complicate them.[6]

The extreme sensitivity about these issues derives partially from what has been called the 'burden of representation.' For artists and cultural critics on the margins, speaking, writing, and performing are a constant negotiation of this burden. Representations tend to be taken as allegorical, that is, every subaltern actor/actress, character, filmmaker, and even scholar is seen, at least partially, as synecdochically summing up a vast and presumably homogenous community. The sensitivity to these issues also operates on a continuum with everyday life, where the 'burden' can indeed become almost unbearable. The media's tendency to present black males as potential delinquents, for example, impacts directly on the lives of black people. In the Stuart case in Boston, the police interrogated and searched all black men in a black neighborhood presuming that the criminal could only be black. This would be unthinkable in white neighborhoods, which are rarely seen as representative sites of crime. The Bush campaign for the US Presidency, similarly, made use of the figure of Willie Horton to trigger the sexual and racial fears and phobias of white voters, dramatically sharpening the burden of representation carried by black men. The very same president 'worried' that 'political correctness' and 'complaints about racism' might be inflaming racial tensions on university campuses. Minority sensitivity also derives from the historical poverty of representations. As Judith Williamson suggests, groups with power over representation need not be unduly concerned with being adequately represented.[7] But representation of an underrepresented group is necessarily, within the hermeneutics of domination, overcharged with allegorical significance.

Film and theater casting, one obvious form of representation, constitutes a kind of delegation of voice with political overtones. Here, too, Europeans and Euro-Americans have occupied a dominant position, relegating non-Europeans to supporting roles and the status of extras. In Hollywood cinema, Euro-Americans have historically enjoyed the unilateral prerogative of acting in 'blackface,' 'redface,' 'brownface' and 'yellowface,' while the reverse has rarely been the case. From the nineteenth-century vaudeville stage through such figures as Al Jolson in *Hi Lo Broadway* (1933), Fred Astaire in *Swing Time* (1936), Mickey Rooney and Judy Garland in *Babes in Arms* (1939), and Bing Crosby in *Dixie* (1943), the tradition of blackface recital furnished one of the most popular of American mass cultural forms. Even black minstrel performers like Bert Williams, as Marlon Riggs's film *Ethnic Notions* points out, were obliged to carry the mark of caricature on their own bodies: burnt cork literalized, as it were, the trope of blackness. Political considerations in racial casting were overt during the silent period. In *The Birth of a Nation*, subservient Negroes were played by blacks, while aggressive, threatening blacks were played by whites in blackface. After prolonged protests by the National Association for the Advancement of Colored People (NAACP), Hollywood cautiously began to cast black actors in small roles. Nevertheless, even in the sound period, white actresses were called on to play the 'tragic mulattas' in such films as *Pinky* (1949), *Imitation of Life* (1959), and even the Cassavetes underground film *Shadows* (1959). Meanwhile, real-life 'mulattas' were cast in black female roles – for example Lena Horne in *Cabin in the Sky* – although they could easily have 'passed' in white roles. In other words, it is not the literal color of the actor that has primarily mattered in casting. Given the 'blood' definition of 'black' versus 'white' in Euro-American racist discourse, one drop of black blood was sufficient to disqualify an actress like Horne from representing white women.

African-Americans have not been the only 'people of color' to be played by Euro-Americans; the same law of unilateral privilege has functioned in relation to other groups. Rock Hudson, Joey Bishop, Boris Karloff, Tom Mix, Elvis Presley, Anne Bancroft, Cyd Charisse, Loretta Young, Mary Pickford, Dame Judith Anderson and Douglas Fairbanks Jr are among the many Euro-American actors who have represented Native Americans in film, while Paul Muni, Charlton Heston, Marlon Brando and Natalie Wood have all played Latino characters. As late as *Windwalker* (1973), the most important Indian roles were not played by Native Americans. Dominant cinema is fond of turning 'dark' or Third World peoples into substitutable others, interchangeable units who can 'stand in' for one another. Thus the Mexican Dolores del Rio played a South Seas Samoan in *The Bird of Paradise*, while the Indian Sabu played a wide range of Arab-Oriental roles. Lupe Velez, of Mexican extraction, portrayed Chinese, 'Eskimos' (Inuit), Japanese, Malayans, and Indian women, and Omar Sharif, an Egyptian, played Che Guevara.[8] This asymmetry in representational power has generated intense resentment among minority communities, for whom the casting of a non-member of the minority group is a triple insult, implying: (a) you are unworthy of self-represention; (b) no one from your group is capable of representing you; and (c) we, the producers of the film, care little about your offended sensibilities, for we have the power and there is nothing you can do about it.

These practices have implications even on the brute material level of literal self-representation. Minority actors need the work just like everyone else. The racist idea that a film, in order to be economically viable, must use a 'universal' (that is, white) star, reveals the imbrication of economics and racism. The fact that people of color have historically been limited to racially designated roles, while whites are ideologically seen as 'beyond ethnicity,' has had disastrous consequences for 'minority' artists. In Hollywood, this situation is changing only now, with star actors such as Larry Fishburne, Wesley Snipes and Denzel Washington winning roles originally earmarked for white actors. At the same time, even 'affirmative action' casting can serve racist purposes, as when the role of the white judge in the novel

Bonfire of the Vanities was given to Morgan Freeman in the Brian de Palma film as a defense mechanism to ward off accusations of racism.

Nor does chromatically literal self-representation guarantee non-Eurocentric representation. The system can simply 'use' the performer to enact the dominant set of codes, at times over the performer's objection. Josephine Baker's star status did not enable her to alter the ending of *Princess Tam* (1935) to have her Berber character marry the French aristocrat instead of the North African servant; nor could she conceivably marry the working-class Frenchman played by Jean Gabin in *Zou* (1934). Instead, Zou ends up alone, performing as a caged bird pining for the Caribbean. Despite her protests, Baker's roles were circumscribed by the codes that forbade her screen access to white men as legitimate marriage partners. Their excessive performance styles allowed actresses like Baker and Carmen Miranda to undercut and parody stereotypical roles, but they could never gain substantive power. Even the expressive performance of the politically aware Paul Robeson was enlisted, despite the actor's protests, in the encomium to European colonialism in Africa that is *Sanders of the River*. In recent years Hollywood has made gestures toward 'correct' casting; African-American, Native American, and Latino/Latina performers have been allowed to 'represent' their communities. But this 'realistic' casting is hardly sufficient if narrative structure and cinematic strategies remain Eurocentric. An epidermically correct face does not guarantee community self-representation, any more than Judge Clarence Thomas's black skin entails his solidarity with the interests of the majority of African-Americans.

A number of film and theater directors have sought alternative approaches to self-representative casting. Orson Welles was fond of staging all-black versions of Shakespeare plays, most notably in his 'Voodoo Macbeth' in Harlem in 1936. Peter Brook, similarly, cast a rainbow of multicultural performers in his filmic adaptation of the Hindu epic *The Mahabharata* (1990). Glauber Rocha deliberately confused linguistic and thespian self-representations in his *Der Leone Have Sept Cabecas* (1970), the title of which already subverts the linguistic positioning of the spectator by mingling five of the languages of Africa's colonizers. Rocha's Brechtian fable animates emblematic figures representing the diverse colonizing nations, suggesting imperial homologies among them by having an Italian-accented speaker play the role of the American, a Frenchman play the German, and so forth. Such anti-literal strategies provoke an irreverent question: what is wrong with non-originary casting? Doesn't acting always involve a ludic play with identity? Should we applaud blacks playing Hamlet but not

Laurence Olivier playing Othello? And have not Euro-American and European performers often ethnically substituted for one another (for example, Greta Garbo and Cyd Charisse as Russians in *Ninotchka* [1939] and *Silk Stockings* [1957], respectively)?

Casting has to be seen in contingent terms, in relation to the role, to the political and aesthetic intention, and to the historical moment. We cannot equate a gigantic charade whereby a whole foreign country is represented by players not from that country, and is imagined as speaking a language not its own (a frequent Hollywood practice) with cases in which non-literal casting forms part of an alternative aesthetic. The casting of blacks to play Hamlet, for example, militates against a traditional discrimination that denied blacks any role, literally and metaphorically, both in the performing arts and in politics, while the casting of Laurence Olivier as Othello prolongs a venerable history of deliberately bypassing black talent. We can see the possibilities of epidermically incorrect casting in *Seeing Double* (1989), a San Francisco Mime Troupe play about the Israeli–Palestinian conflict. In the play, an ethnically diverse cast took on shifting roles in such a way as to posit analogical links between communities. An African-American actor played both a Palestinian-American and a Jewish-American, for example, thereby hinting at a common history of exclusion binding blacks, Jews, and Arabs.

The question of casting, in sum, is multidimensional, involving the individual participants in the collective process of filmic production, their communal and institutional affiliations, the textual operations of representation, the impact on films themselves of systemic and what Stuart Hall calls 'inferential racism,' as well as critical and spectatorial reception. Each filmic or academic utterance must be analyzed not only in terms of who represents but also in terms of who is being represented, for what purpose, at which historical moment, from which location, using which strategies, and in what tone of address. Seeing all the speakers and addressees, present or potential, as socially situated helps formulate a relational, non-originary notion of representation, but one that still respects the identities of distinct historical communities.

The denial of aesthetic representation to the subaltern has historically formed a corollary to the literal denial of economic, legal, and political representation. The struggle to 'speak for oneself' cannot be separated from a history of being spoken for, from the struggle to speak and be heard. Speaking for oneself is not a simple act, however, but rather a complex process. From Fanonian nationalism to Afrocentrism,

Third Worldist anticolonialist identity has been linked to the reassertion of the precolonial past, and the forging of a revitalized community. But Third World peoples, like women, like gays and lesbians, as critics such as Henry Louis Gates and Elizabeth Fox-Genovese have pointed out, must speak today in a theoretical context where the notion of a coherent subject identity, let alone a community identity, is endlessly fragmented and de-centered, even epistemologically suspect.[9] Third Worldist frustration with this articulation of the subject is eloquently summarized by the Kenyan feminist Debra P. Amory:

> Doesn't it seem funny that at the very point when women and people of color are ready to sit down at the bargaining table with the white boys, that the table disappears? That is, suddenly there are no grounds for claims to truth and knowledge anymore and here we are, standing in the conference room making all sorts of claims to knowledge and truth but suddenly without a table upon which to put our papers and coffee cups, let alone to bang our fists.[10]

Should Third Worldist notions of becoming 'subjects' of history, in the era of poststructuralist/postcolonial discourse, be dismissed as totalizing, operating allochronically in another time frame?[11] And when a certain postmodernism declares the 'end of narratives,' one wishes to ask precisely whose narrative is coming to an 'end'? The master narratives of the West have been told and retold, endlessly assembled and reassembled, not only in the cinema but also through the major academic disciplines from geography and history to anthropology and literature. But what about oppositional narratives? Can one grant the force of the poststructuralist critique of the 'unitary' subject, while still recognizing communities as the 'subjects' of history? How is it possible to critique macrocosmic global narratives, while struggling to narrate a global interdependent understanding of difference in the world?

It is crucial to push the postcolonial critique in a politically resisting direction. It is imperative, to be more precise, to negotiate the social mobilization of minority communities as 'imagined,' but also as capable of narrating their histories and their ongoing resistance. At the same time, it is important to interweave the local, the specific, with global oppositional narratives. Identities can be formulated in provisional, non-finalizing terms, as situated in geographical space and 'riding' historical momentum. The fact that identity and experience are narrated, constructed, caught up in the spiral of representation and intertextuality does not mean, as Stuart Hall has maintained, that nothing is at stake, or that the struggle is over. What Spivak calls 'strategic essentialism' and what Hall refers to as 'the fictional necessity of arbitrary closure,' of putting a period to the sentence, are crucial for any multicultural struggle that is to allow for communities of identification, even if they are multiple and discontinuous.

Some contemporary antiessentialist critique comes at times dangerously close to dismissing all search for a communitarian past as an archeological mode of what Spivak dismisses as 'substituting for the lost figure of the colonized.' But is it possible to forge resistance on the basis of amnesia, without reinscribing communal identities prior to colonial dispossession? The current postcolonial discursive privileging of the palimpsestic present in the metropolis carries its own burdens. It ignores the need, particularly pressing for historically brutalized peoples, for what might be called compensatory originarism, the strategic requirement to recover (or construct) a past, even if it is a partially imaginary one. It allows little space, for example, for the indigenous Kayapo in the Amazon forest who, on the one hand, use video cameras, thus demonstrating cultural hybridity and a capacity for mimicry, but who, on the other, use them precisely to stage the urgency of preserving the essential contours of their culture, including their relation to the rainforest and communal possession of land. For communities that have undergone brutal ruptures, now in the process of forging a collective identity, no matter how hybrid that identity has been before, during and after colonialism, the retrieval of even a fragmented past becomes, at least symbolically, crucial for a resistant collective identity. A celebration of syncretism and hybridity *per se* thus always runs the danger of appearing to sanctify the *fait accompli* of colonial violence. While avoiding any nostalgia for a prelapsarian community, for any transparent, unitary identity predating the 'fall,' analysis must incorporate the act of force by which colonialism remapped the globe, along with the consequences of that remapping for the articulation of identities. The imperial process of drawing lines in the sand, as the Persian Gulf War revealed, has hardly ended.

Framing the debate simply around 'essentialism/antiessentialism,' in other words, proves to be theoretically and politically limited. Whether or not to return to essentialist origins isn't the point; the question is what exactly is being mobilized in the articulation of the past, and, further, what should be the different modes of interconnectedness with collective experiences for a politically viable set of identities, identifications, and representations. The postcolonial critique of the notion of the past as static ideal is useful in that some nationalist anticolonial critique tended to give little attention to complex, hybrid identities. But the notion of the past might also be negotiated differently, as overlapping sets of narrated memories and fragmented experiences from which to represent contemporary community mobilizations.

Postcolonial multiculturalism, furthermore, tends to be associated with Western metropolises as the meeting ground for these hybrid and hyphenated identities. Metrocentric discussions need to be challenged through a more globalized multiculturalism. Are not India and Brazil, Iraq and Israel/Palestine, the Middle East and Latin America, also multicultural? How then can we avoid a monoculturalist multiculturalism, that is, a multiculturalism that fails to see that subalternality changes from context to context, forming a mobile global flow of positionalities? Difference alters meaning and valence with changing contexts. The idea of blackness, as Henry Louis Gates suggests, is not without its tropic dimension; it subtly shifts meaning in different situational locations. In Britain, blackness is deployed as a mobilizing category that also embraces Asians. In Israel, a country with few blacks in the conventional sense, the marginalized majority of Arab Jews (Sephardim) serves the social function of blacks in the United States; the Sephardim are seen as, and literally called, 'blacks.' For myself – an Iraqi–Israeli Arab Jew unable to return to my ancestral homeland in Iraq, burdened by British colonialism in both Iraq and Palestine, and a history of anti-Sephardic oppression in Israel – it is comprehensible that in my third country, the United States, my arena of identification should be that of Third World 'minorities,' the theoretical and political locus that provides space for my specific identity and my specific history of displacement and racial marginalization. This identification with Third World peoples has also been important to the Sephardic movement in Israel itself. That is why Sephardim turned the term 'Schwartzes' (blacks) – first used as a slur by European Jews (unofficially referred to as 'whites') against Arab Jews – into a mark of resistance, as manifested in the Sephardi 'Black Panthers' in Israel, pointedly named after the American black liberationist movement. Such instances suggest the existence of fractured, multiply situated, and historically discontinuous identities of the type discussed by postcolonial theory, but they also suggest that the marginalization of communities has to be negotiated in relation to a global network of positional displacements. Any licit approach to questions about representation, in other words, must make available a shifting multifocal and mobile set of grids.

To sum up, 'identities' are not fixed entities expressing a 'natural' difference; they are, rather, changing sets of historically diverse experiences. Identities are articulated in relation to parallel, contradictory, and complementary collectivities, overlapping, decentered circles of identities. It is these overlapping circles that can make possible intercommunal coalitions based on historical oppressions and affinities, which generate analogical structures of feelings. Understanding multiculturalism as a globally interdependent issue and as a question of intercommunal alliances helps us transcend the originary discourse of self-representation. To return to our initial question, rather than ask who can speak, we should ask what are the different modes of speech to explore in our own future work. While it is hazardous to 'speak for someone,' that is, paradigmatically to replace them, it is something different, as Charlotte Bunch points out, to 'speak up for,' that is, to speak on behalf of, a group when that group is blocked from representation, just as it is something else again to 'speak alongside' in the sense of forming coalitions or alliances.

Attempting to avoid either falling into essentialist traps or being politically paralyzed by deconstructionist formulations, I believe it is precisely the overlapping of these circles that makes possible intercommunal coalitions based on historically shaped affinities. Rather than ask who can speak, then, we should ask how we can speak together, and more important, how we can move the dialog forward. How can diverse communities speak in concert? How might we interweave our voices, whether in chorus, in antiphony, in call and response, or in polyphony? What are the modes of collective speech? In this sense, it might be worthwhile to focus less on identity as something one 'has,' than on identification as something one 'does.' The concept of crisscrossing identifications evokes the theoretical possibility, and even the political necessity, of sharing the critique of domination and the burden of representation. It involves, finally, making representation less of a burden and more of a collective pleasure and responsibility.

Notes

1. Religious tensions sometimes inflect cinematic representation. A German film company plan from 1925 to produce *The Prophet*, with Muhammad as the main character, shocked the Islamic University at Al Azhar, since Islam prohibits representation of the Prophet. Protests prevented the film from being made. Moustapha Akkad's *The Message* (Kuwait–Morocco–Libya, 1976), in contrast, tells the story within Islamic norms, respecting the prohibition against graven images of the Prophet, God and holy figures. The film traces the life of the Prophet from his first revelations in 610 to his death in 632, in a style that rivals Hollywood biblical epics. Yet the Prophet is never seen on the screen; when other characters speak to him they address the camera. The script was approved by scholars from Al Azhar University in Cairo.

2. The concern of the Society for Cinema Studies Task Force on Race, established in 1988, was not only to engage in minoritarian discourse but also to promote 'minority' participation in the discipline.

3. Trinh T. Minh-Ha makes a similar point in 'Outside In Inside Out,' included in her *When the Moon Waxes Red: Representation, Gender and Cultural Politics* (New York: Routledge, 1991).

4. In art, it is not always clear who is speaking. Countless cases of artistic reception contradict the view of literary texts as transparently conveying the unmediated experience of an originary identity. The best-seller *Education of Little Tree*, the 'true' story of a Native American orphaned at the age of ten, who learns Indian ways from his Cherokee grandparents, was hailed by critics as 'deeply felt' and 'one of the finest American autobiographies ever written.' Yet the book was written under a pseudonym by Asa Ear Carter, a Ku Klux Klan terrorist and anti-Semite who also penned Governor George Wallace's notorious 1963 'Segregation Forever' speech. But *Little Tree* was just the latest in a long chain of ventriloqual racial narratives (for example, *Confessions of Nat Turner*), racial impersonations and *ersatz* slave narratives. Readers of Frank Yerby's historical romances or Samuel R. Delaney's science fictions, in contrast, rarely imagine that both authors are black.

5. The white male Jewish lawyer William Kunstler, for example, is affiliated with disenfranchised communities and strives to empower them, whereas the black male judge Clarence Thomas often seems to work against the interests of his own people.

6. That is why the recent academic fashion of identifying all speakers by their ethnicity – 'Hopi artist . . ., white critic . . .' – is so dubious. While on one level correcting the unilateral inscription of ethnicity and the surreptitious encoding of whiteness as norm, on another it does not go far enough because it encodes only the most superficial indices of ethnicity – color, origins – while eliding issues of ideology, discourse, identification, affiliation. Thus if one were really to pursue such labeling to its logical conclusion, one might produce hybrids such as 'white-identified, neoconservative, homophobic black critic . . .,' or 'black-identified, neo-Marxist, anti-feminist white critic . . .,' and so forth.

7. See Judith Williamson, 'Two Kinds of Otherness – Black Film and the Avant-Garde,' *Screen*, vol. 29, no. 4 (Autumn 1988).

8. Clear social hierarchies also inform the practice of substitutional casting. The evolution of casting in Israeli cinema, for example, reflects changing strategies of representation. The heroic nationalist films of the 1950s and 1960s, which focused on the Israeli–Arab conflict, typically featured Euro-Israeli Sabras, played by European Jews (Ashkenazis), fighting villainous Arabs, while Sephardi Arab-Jewish actors and characters were limited to the 'degraded' roles of Muslim Arabs. In most recent political films, in contrast, Israeli-Palestinian actors and nonprofessionals play the Palestinian roles. Such casting allows for a modicum of 'self-representation.' And at times the Palestinian actors have forced radicalization of certain scenes. In some films Palestinian actors have even been cast as Israeli military officers, as was the case with Makram Houri in *The Smile of the Lamb* and in the Palestinian–Belgian film *Wedding in Galilee*. For more on casting in Israeli cinema, see Ella Shohat, *Israeli Cinema: East/West and the Politics of Representation* (Austin: University of Texas Press, 1989).

9. See Henry Louis Gates Jr, 'Canon Formation and African-American Tradition,' in Dominick LaCapra, ed., *The Bounds of Race* (Ithaca, NY: Cornell University Press, 1991), and Elizabeth Fox-Genovese, 'The Claims of a Common Culture: Gender, Race, Class, and the Canon,' *Salmagundi*, no. 72 (Fall 1986).

10. Debra P. Amory, 'Watching the Table Disappear: Identity and Politics in Africa and the Academy,' unpublished paper delivered at the African Studies Association (1990).

11. Johannes Fabian, in *Time and the Other: How Anthropology Makes its Object* (New York: Columbia University Press, 1980), accuses classical anthropology of making its colonized objects of study 'allochronic,' that is, as if living in another, former time unconnected to the present of colonialism or neocolonialism.

9

Performing in the Postcolony: The Plays of Mustapha Matura

May Joseph

Unhinging British Theater Historiography

Postcolonialism is a manifestation of the confluence of colonialism and its legacies. The presence of colonized peoples from Africa, the Caribbean, and Asia in the country of their former colonizers leads to collisions of cultures, histories, and languages, which in turn destabilize simple notions of the 'post' in postcolonial, and other paradigms such as First World/Third World, and the West/non-West. This, in turn, transforms and ruptures the existing cultural codes of both host countries and ex-colonies, raising questions related to Eurocentric constructions of racial categories and the denial of class, gender, and cultural differences. These debates have become crucial to understanding the performative aspects of cultural encounter. Whilst they have been a subject of interest in the theater over the last three decades because of a growing presence of immigrants from former colonies, there has been little effort to date to synthesize or articulate the resulting transformations with any degree of complexity. For the purposes of this essay, I shall address the question of how immigrant playwrighting of African, Caribbean and Asian peoples has contributed to postcolonial debates through a brief critique of British theater historiography and analysis of the work of the black British playwright Mustapha Matura. I argue that black British representations in Matura's writing go beyond oppositional discourse to emerge with more ambivalent and complex representations of the postcolonial subject.

179

Because of its history of colonialism, British culture is now a site where many peoples from Africa, the Caribbean, Asia, Europe, and the Middle East jostle each other for recognition and respect. The British stage has become the strategic arena for the representation of these cultural collisions. Postcolonial discourse in the context of the black British theater provides a means of decoding and reconstructing the tensions inherent in the Third World immigrant who, straddled between his 'native' country and adopted home, lives this experience of conflict.

In the context of Western theater historiography, and specifically in the British context, a cursory appraisal of British theater since the Second World War discloses the exclusions that traditional narratives of British theater since the 1950s conceal. While mainstream British theater and the fringe, or non-conventional theater, remain crucial points of reference for the developments of other non-white theater groups, the elision of the new, non-anglo, British theater constituencies points to the need for new work in contemporary theater historiography. This essay is part of that attempt to recontextualize the narrative of British theater within an international, postcolonial, and 'Third World' framework within the First World. Acknowledging the simultaneous and contingent coexistence of different theatrical traditions and forms within the specific geographical location of Britain makes it possible – indeed unavoidable – to address the decisive impact of imperialism, colonialism, and Eurocentric ethnography on performance.

The postcolonial theater text of the 1970s in Britain is peculiarly positioned in the sense that its very presence was an act of resistance. No structures of commodification were set in motion during the early 1970s to encourage the production and consumption of these texts in the international theater market. To produce 'black' theater was a requirement for gaining access to representation and entering into dialog with the white as well as the black communities. But the material reality of black cultural production contained and restricted these artistic forays on the peripheries of British life.

Black British theater history of the sixties and the early seventies is primarily an oral mosaic of sporadic and dispersed trajectories. As black people in the British theater scene, the black British occupied a transitory position as oddities, a peripheral presence to enact the occasional stereotypical 'colored.' Inadequate funding, institutional racism, and a lack of access to drama schools kept the number of black theater professionals in the seventies to a minimum. Virtually living on the fringes of British life, black actors, for instance, constantly had to make crossovers into film and television in order to survive, while only a handful of black British playwrights gained visibility. As texts from the margins of British society, black plays in the seventies had to contend with limited support from the mainstream theater community. Consequently, these plays were positioned as border texts portraying border cultures in Britain.

Performing in the Interstices

The shifting paradigm of borders is an effective means of accounting for the slippage or excess of what is framed as British theater. It delineates the parameters of postcolonial British theater in a more complicated geography of the vanished empire. Notions of borders and memory perpetuate visual territories of the past and the present. In order to understand the question of borders, we have to account for memory that cannot be contained, that overruns its limits. Such memory complicates the ways in which generations of immigrants contest and/or assimilate into the dominant culture. Exemplary of the dynamics of borders and memories in the black British theater, Matura's work displaces any monolithic argument around culture such as 'the dominant versus the marginal' or 'the colonizer versus the colonized'.

Mustapha Matura's work is the first body of dramatic texts to emerge out of Britain and challenge British theater culture on racial and ethnic grounds. Matura is particularly interesting because his voice is one of the most widely accessible from this first generation of black British playwrights. Born in Trinidad, he arrived in England in 1960. Positioned by the dominant culture as merely 'black,' Matura had to create a space to articulate the complex politics of difference and the wide and disparate histories of blackness among Britain's black communities. His hybrid genealogy crosses over into his experiments with the theater as his plays explore the in-between and transitory spaces of postcolonial culture and the conflicts of identity and tradition in both Trinidad and Britain.

Beginning in 1971, when his first full-length play *as time goes by* was produced at the Traverse Theatre Club, Edinburgh, and the Royal Court, London, winning both the George Devine and the John Whiting Awards that year, Matura's work emerged as an intervention on the British fringe. He was the first prominent black voice to emerge in the British theater of the seventies. *Black Pieces* (1970), *Bakerloo Line* (1972), *Nice* (1973), *Play Mas* (1974) [which won the

London *Evening Standard*'s Most Promising Playwright Award and
was transferred to the West End], *Black Slaves White Chains* (1975),
Rum 'N Coca Cola (1976), *Bread* (1976), *Another Tuesday* (1978),
More (1978), *Independence* (1979), *Welcome Home Jacko* (1979),
A Dying Business (1980), *One Rule* (1981), and *Meetings* (1982)
brought Matura recognition as a major playwright. His further
visibility in the United States would make him a crucial voice in the
development and practice of black theater in the transatlantic context
as well.

Matura's work is a collective of multivoiced narratives that explore
the precolonial, colonial, and postindependence moments of Trinidadian culture. It raises questions about decolonization and cultural
identity by constantly juxtaposing the past and the present, Trinidad
and England. Every one of Matura's pieces can be read as part of a
larger voyage of recovery and confrontation of both personal and
public history. From *as time goes by*, which deals with the ideological
and personal implications for the first generation of black immigrants
to Britain from the Caribbean, to *Play Mas*, *Meetings* and *Independence*, which critique colonialism and its aftermath in Trinidad,
Matura's work unfolds as an oral map of remembering personal stories
of the subaltern in the postcolonial moment.[1]

Border cultures/border writing

By positioning his writing at the borders of both Trinidad (by his
emigrating) and England (by being an immigrant), Matura through his
work constructs an alternative dialog to the dominant discourse of the
British theater of the seventies. Not just class, but race and ethnicity
(black nationalism in particular) problematize the contemporary
British experience. His texts continually cross the lines of the familiar
constructions of Englishness, exploring the borders of cultural transition in British culture. They are simultaneously British and more than
British because they occupy the interstices of cultural interchange, as
they shift and alter the paradigms of British and, by extension, urban
Western cultural norms through a privileging of Afro-Caribbean and
Asian cultural codes. Matura coerces into discussion the rhetorics of
empire and what comprises the postcolonial British identity by
constructing the black British presence as the dominant force in his
texts.

Matura's plays foreground the blind spots of British theater culture
and crowd the blanks of mainstream drama with the bodies of other
territories from the edges of British society (such as black skinheads,

black bus conductors from the London Transport Underground Guards, or black council dustmen), and from other cultures (Afro-Caribbean, Indian, 'Trini,' Pakistani, black working class). They centralize the margins in this unmapping space and construct 'England' within the periphery of these blurring borders. His work is a marking of the 'disorderly' centers of Britain's 'borders.' For example, *as time goes by* explores the following urban locales: Brixton, Southall, Shepherd's Bush, East London, Notting Hill, the Portobello Road, and the London Underground. By extension, the former colonies and postcolonial history are reframed as a complex, heterogeneous series of imagined boundaries and maps outside as well as inside Britain's borders, interrupting and altering the very terrain of contemporary British culture.

Matura complicates this mapping further by highlighting the syncretic nature of the cultures involved as the various hybrid ethnicities of the Afro-Asian communities insert themselves into British culture through gestures and linguistic variations to mark their specificities. Patois, Gujurati and British working-class accents deliberately interrupt and inscribe the language of Englishness in *as time goes by* and *Party*.

The notion of borders, their construction and dismantling, their presence or lack, superimposed or imaginary, is central to these texts. Emerging from the periphery of British cultural life and having to negotiate the parameters of the various constituencies that such a positioning involves, they contain and alter Britain's received cultural norms. In Matura's representations, England becomes a colony on the edges of a globally dispersed center. The geography of this dispersed center is imagined through the discursive spaces of its nations: several characters being 'Trini' or being 'English'; being a woman from the Asian or African diaspora, located within the frames of patriarchy, immigration policies, and class politics; being from the imaginary homelands of 'Africa,' 'India,' or 'Trinidad' itself. The borders of empire are revealed as a construct that is at once fixed and mutable, shifting the centered Afro-Caribbean households and neighborhoods in Britain where the hegemonic culture becomes peripheral. This in turn positions the Caribbean as a border in *as time goes by*, while elsewhere centering independent Trinidad within whose borders the multinational, neocolonial and ex-colonial influences impinge, as in *Independence*.

The implications of occupying the borders shifts in these texts from one of economic necessity to one of cultural and political strategy. Initially in the fifties and sixties, constructed and positioned as other, as 'black,' as 'them,' the postcolonial immigrant in the seventies appropriates the term 'black,' transforming it into a political force. The term alters from being a colonial and racial construction to being a positive political identification. The cultural constructions of these border cultures also shift as a consequence of their political engagement with life in Britain, becoming more complex in their ethnic specificity and differences. No longer merely 'black,' the ethnicities of this 'blackness' soon blur the distinction between border and core. The composite nature of Britain's 'black' cultures redefines notions of identity and national culture.

Spatial borders/travel stories

As the notion of borders and of crossings, departures and arrivals manifests cultural dislocation throughout these plays about passage, their contingent moments enable the unpredictable and the unwritten to emerge. Travel becomes a theoretically enabling idea in this discourse of and about borders. It implies the construction of borders, involves spatial displacement, and positions the body in various moments of transition that challenge, alter, alienate, distort, and confront the individual. It implies a refraction of time – both historical and local time. Within this shifting, transitional space of the traveler, the borders have to be constantly redrawn. The territory of the familiar is immediately restructured as the traveler occupies and displaces this space.

Travel in Matura's writing is woven into the narrative through tales of arrival and departure told from the transitory spaces that his characters occupy. Matura's characters tend to come from the ex-colonies and occupy very tenuous positions within the structures of the new culture. What interests me about these intermediary spaces that his characters occupy in the case of *as time goes by*, for instance, is the fact that almost all are junctions between points of travel in the British transport system, be it bus, train or garbage disposal. In effect, these new immigrants become sites of passage while being in passage themselves. They own little in material terms and function merely as checkpoints of arrival and departure. In a sense, they are literal manifestations of the term *'en route.'*

In these intermediary traveling spaces of London's subaltern existence, the telling of the tale becomes the moment of recovery. Fiction and memory improvised and transformed to create a return and a celebration through the oral narrative is Ram's medicine for the subalterns who seek him out for help in *as time goes by*. As an eclectic shaman of various gods his invocation cum welcoming salutation announces: 'Ram, Ram, salam, wale com, shalom, peace, hi, hello, good evening, welcome to the house of truth and reality, come in.' Ram occupies a liminal space in this city of travelers and displaced people, London.[2] His home becomes an important transit point for all the characters in the play as they converge on this location at the fringes of the city, where the working-class, immigrant colored communities live. Here, in an imagined space of ritual, fiction, and memory, Ram's front room, 'lavishly decorated with religious objects and pictures,' a subaltern such as Arnold can humanize his invisibility, dressed in the dehumanizing London Transport Underground Guards' uniform. As Arnold says: 'Well brother Ram . . . if a could only no why she left me a would feel good but anyhow ita good talking to you a start to feel good already.'[3] Within the fantastical space of Ram's living room, *as time goes by* becomes a series of vignettes narrated about black British experiences.

The oral narrative is populated by travelers and nomads. It has a long genealogy in oral cultures and becomes crucial to historicizing the dialogs of migrants, refugees, immigrants, and the displaced from the borders of society in Matura's writing.[4] As a form of textuality it occupies the most elusive, precarious position, that of transitional utterance. It can be made to carry the burden of a culture, can create the elasticity of fiction for fashioning subjectivity, as Ram in *as time goes by* suggests in his gesture of welcome: 'What you need I provide. What you provide I need. What you desire I recommend. What you recommend I desire. My thoughts are at your service. Come in.'[5] Any word spoken must alter itself in transition from one speaker to another, from one moment to another. Its minimal material condition, that of being able to speak and to be spoken to, constructs the oral narrative as an archetype of dispersed cultures. It takes up space but cannot be owned or bought. Always in transit, it can become the charged though irretrievable location of coming into consciousness, into voice, through speech. To utter is to act and engage. To speak locates the speaker in time and history.

Orality has a special place in the creation and dissemination of culture in colonial and postcolonial societies. Through orality, Western configurations of non-Western cultures have been redressed by indigenous cultures. The oral emerges as a powerful weapon of subversion and force, one that is immensely malleable, tensile, with a thousand heads, making it impossible for the colonizing presence to seize it in its entirety. Oral narratives under colonialism become the means of cultural survival, of retaining otherwise unrecorded events.

as time goes by stages the ways orality marks the unwriting of 'Englishness' in a predominantly literate culture where access to narrative power is linked to the magic of print. By foregrounding certain kinds of stories in his plays, Matura raises the question of whose oral narratives are privileged in the official spaces of British culture that lie outside his texts. Through the heteroglossia of oral traditions that Matura inscribes onto the British stage, he performs the rewriting of England through diaspora English, buttressed with Hindi, patois, pidgin, creole Tamil, butchered Arabic, and working-class dialects.

The oral narrative in postcolonial British culture delineates the complex intersections of gender, race, and class. To elaborate: in order to have the power to represent, one must have access to the means of representation. For those with little opportunity for education, the primary mode of exchange is the oral mode. This implies that immigrant black communities who comprise a section of the working class are considerably limited by their minimal access to representation; hence Matura's foregrounding of the oral over the written. This is particularly true in the case of the wave of postcolonial immigrants from the Caribbean, Africa (particularly the petty-bourgeois Asian entrepreneurs from East Africa), and India during the seventies. For these groups in particular, whose oral traditions are very strong, the oral narrative comprises the predominant mode of cultural exchange. Black British representations up to the mid-eighties were dominated by men, whilst the emergence of the collective project in 1988 of *Charting the Journey: Writings by Black and Third World Women* marks the first major break in representation through writing of postcolonial women's subjectivities.[6]

Independence illustrates how Matura allows voices from the fringes of both black British culture (through the use of black British actors) and Trinidadian society (through the *mise-en-scène*) to speak for themselves, to achieve a voice in a way that repositions the colonized in a position of agency rather than as subjects overdetermined by circumstance, passive in their participation in the colonial machine. It demystifies both the colonial and postcolonial moments by juxtaposing two characters located firmly in different generations (Drakes, part of the colonial legacy, and Allen, the future of independent Trinidad) with different political vectors. Written eight years after *as time goes by*, *Independence* unfolds as a series of parables about colonialism and the decompressing economic effects in a newly independent country.

In *Independence*, the narrated story becomes the only way for the indigenous people to preserve and transfer unofficial history from the colonial to the postindependent phase. Both Drakes and Allen were pool barmen in the Grand Hotel in independent Trinidad, but while Drakes's storytelling is firmly fixed in the colonial past, which he glorifies, Allen's stories are dreams about the future of independent Trinidad based on a critique of imperialism and slavery, struggling to find a place in the economic and cultural decolonization of his newly independent country. In Act II of *Independence*, the site of the former pool bar, now in ruins, becomes the link between the colonial and the postcolonial moment for Allen. As he says: 'I en' romantising dis place, a tell yer wat it was like wit me, an I was here at de end but I hear stories wen I was here about how worse it was.'[7]

Storytelling is the primary mode of communication in colonial and postindependent Trinidad for Drakes's generation with restricted access to literacy.[8] Through anecdotes, stories, riddles, banter and jokes, Drakes slowly unfolds to Allen the unwritten and quickly receding history of the material relations between the colonial subaltern and the colonizing presence. The poolside bar becomes the *mise-en-scène* of Drakes's narrations and a crucial mark for Allen's mapping of his own history later on:

> . . . I do' love dis place, but dis is where I saw – we here – we come from, dis place, yes, I needed dis place ter show we where we come from an where we going yes, we need places like dis dat is one a de jokes about it, we need de horror ter show we or else we could never know, my eyes open in dis place, ter wat we was, wat we used ter be an I value it fer dat ter push off, push off from it, yes I need it, I need dis place, an anodder one a de jokes about it is dat de more dis place treat yer like a boy is de more I felt like a man, de more I wanted ter be a man, I felt alive here, I saw tings clear here fer de fist time in my life how de system operated how it killed people, dere used ter be a fellar here working wid me call Drakes. I en' know wat happen ter him, but he was one, he was somebody who dis place enslave, because he couldn't see how it worked, but he help me, he is a man. I would never forget him an fer men like him it was too late fer dem, dey was born into it, but we lucky we had a chance ter look at tings an see dem clear fer de first time, but fer dem who give us dat chance, all de Drakes a dis world.[9]

The oral narrative functions as 'informal' knowledge, local knowledge, which in turn is shaped against the dominant form of information, the written word. Gossip, storytelling, and anecdotes occupy the borders of information. They carry the charge of the unwritten and unnameable. The fragility of this mode of communication makes the oral narrative a powerful unmapping space, as people like Drakes give the mapped their own configuration. For instance, the subject of cocktails becomes a rich site of colonial power relations. For Drakes, 'it was happiness in dose days' when 'everbody had dey own territory,' referring to 'de old days wen it was a pleasure ter serve drinks, ter see de pleasure on people's faces wen yer place de drink in front a dem an dey start ter run.' The colonial moment is evoked by Drakes as the moment of excess and plenty without critique of the systemic enslavement of the native populations by the colonial presence. For Drakes, the ambivalence of the colonized is deeply mixed with the feeling of power over the art of cocktail shaking:

> Wat you know bout sparkle, yer do' know dey have Black cocktail, dull cocktail, cocktail you could see through, cocktail yer car' see through . . . I could make any kinda cocktail. I could make drinks change color right before yer eyes an yer car' remember wat it was before . . . If a had me ingredients I'd show yer wat cocktail was all about. I'd hit yer wid so much cocktail . . . dat yer would feel like yer was de Prince of Wales.[10]

Cocktails signify Englishness for Drakes, as his description of 'Rapid Rage' suggests: 'Dat is white rum, wid brown rum, wid Coca Cola separating de sides, like de United Kingdom, an wen dey hit yer belly, is war yer see.'[11] Englishness and colonialism become synonymous for Drakes as he describes the 'Planters Punch' to Allen: 'You en' know wat a Planters Punch is an you want ter be a farmer. Dat is wat after yer ride all day over yer plantation yer man servant come an put before yer after he stable yer horse, man.' Englishness inscribes the system within which Drakes has found a function under the old order of colonialism; it becomes the mark of his redundancy within the contemporary context as the ironic moment at the end of Act 1 reveals:

> Harper: Brother Drakes, today is the eighteenth of September,
>   Nineteen Seventy-Eight, you agree.
> Drakes: Yes, Brother Harper.
> Harper: Good. Champagne. Bollinger RD. 69.
> Drakes: None.
> Harper: Roederer Cristal Brut. 73.
> Drakes: None . . .
> Harper: Veuve Clicquot Gold Label 73.
> (Lights begin slow fade.)
> Drakes: No.[12]

Drakes accepts Harper's dismissal as someone whose 'special skill is not one dat is easy to use in a Developing Progressive Society.' Says Drakes: 'It mean a might en' get another job, dat's wat, or one a know how ter do. A might end up sweeping Frederick Street, or de market.' As a member of the generation that came into middle age during colonialism, Drakes finds himself in the tragic position of being relegated even further to the borders of the new society by the likes of Harper: 'An he also drop a hint bout a man of my age, how difficult it is, everyting difficult.' Neither 'here' in the sense that Allen is, engaged in the contemporary struggle for power, agency and visibility in independent Trinidad, nor able to use the past in a marketable way, Drakes in his position is symptomatic of the chaos that unfolds on the borders of a postcolonial society. His inability to qualify for even a pension because 'it came in after independence' and he 'didn't make anough units, I started too late' foregrounds the unaccountable history of the subalterns who occupy the interstices of society and get ejected during the transition phase.[13]

Oral speech becomes the primary mode of anti-colonial resistance in Matura's *Independence*, as both Drakes and Allen demonstrate. What is interesting about the unmapping space of the oral narrative is that it marks itself as the originating site for thoughts on anti-imperialism and decolonization. For Allen, the Molotov cocktail is the only type of cocktail he is interested in. His conversations with Drakes lead him to see the past in all its contradictions as embodied by Drakes. They force Allen to formulate the mode of action for the future, initially as a response to Drakes's storytelling, but later as a coherent line of action by active participation in the economic life of the country. What Allen puts into practice from the borders of Trinidadian society as a subsistence farmer, eventually to sell in the market, instances the ways in which power gets redistributed and redefined within the new social space of independent Trinidad.

Whilst Allen and Drakes are positioned in the contradictory spaces of an independent nation, Matura suggests in no uncertain terms that the only way out of the old dispensation is a radical erasure of the former structures by the same means that created them, namely violence. Matura projects Fanon's problematic notion of therapeutic violence onto the postcolonial space through Drakes's violent suicide, which demolishes the oppressive presence of the Grand Hotel, as one means of psychological and cultural retrieval. According to Matura's play, the only way to shift effectively from the colonial to the postcolonial phase for the colonized is through violence, which in Drakes's case involves self-immolation, death. Only out of the ashes of violence can a culture begin to search and reconstruct new subjectivities. Such an absolute choice of engagement with history contrasts with the character of Harper, who carries on the project of exploitation in postcolonial Trinidad without a rupture in his existence. For Allen, however, Drakes's gesture is both nihilistic and necessary. Allen comprehends why Drakes chooses violence as the only means out of an irreversible situation. He realizes that for Drakes, only by annihilating the source of oppression, however symbolic it may be (the Grand Hotel), can the ghosts of colonialism be banished. Returning to the remains of the burned-down hotel a year later, Allen normalizes the moment of violence as inevitable as he narrates his colonial experience to his companion Yvonne:

It used ter be bad it was everthing a told yer about it wid Black people spending dey whole life running about ter seve white people, till dey dead but look at it now, look at it, it dead now it harmless, I wouldn't a bring you wen it was still standing because in dem days just ter come near it, yer had ter change, yer had ter, yer manner had ter be different, ter come in, dat's de kinda effect it had on people an dat went on fer whole generations a people dis place affect.[14]

Independence constructs the oral narrative as a safety valve for the logic of violence that structures life under colonialism and during the transition phase that follows. Through narration and storytelling, through a recounting of experience and coming to terms with it, the anger and violence of history begin to be channeled into productive means. Allen insists upon this fact throughout the text. While taking into account Drakes's absolute act of confrontation in death, Allen believes in an alternative way of dealing with history's horror. Committed engagement with the land and learning to be self-reliant become Allen's way out of the vicious circle of colonial and postcolonial structures within which he finds himself.

By foregrounding violence as the most effective means of recovery, Matura reinscribes the Manichean logic of binarisms onto the postcolonial space at the same moment that he points to alternative ways of salvaging a decimated culture. The play in that sense coexists in tension between binarisms and multiplicity in the way the narratives are structured. The demarcation between the old dispensation and the new is simultaneously abrupt, as between Drakes and Allen, and blurred, as projected by Harper. Harper breaks the binary structure constructed between Drakes and Allen by configuring yet another model of the postcolonial condition. As Drakes describes Harper: 'People like you just take over wey de English leave off . . . you an people like you spoil it, all, yer jump in de water like fish an carry on de same ting, power, power in yer mind.'[15] Harper embodies one end of the spectrum of ambivalence of the colonized toward the colonial machine, as he seriously plans on carrying on where the colonial bureaucracy left off, but in the name of independence. For Harper, Drakes represents 'everyting dat is bad wit de past and wat de Republic is trying to eradicate . . . yer car' change and changes is in de air, if yer car' change, yer go get run over, dat is a promise.'[16]

Between Harper, Allen and Drakes, the oral narrative becomes a conjuncture of different locations. It is the only link between these people as they converge and then are catapulted into separate orbits. For all three, the systems of power are translated primarily in oral terms. This is why Drakes must act in perhaps the only way he knows how when language fails to make sense of power anymore. Drakes destroys in material terms what language fails entirely to account for, including his own body. As Drakes says in his last speech:

> I have ter stay here I have ter watch dis place . . . ter see dat notting ever move in dis place, ter see it never rise up again . . . Nobody must touch it, I is de only one, because I build it, wat man build man could pull down, an I en' only I could pull it down, an I do dat every day . . . in a hundred years time people go come here an say wat was dis place wat did it stand fer wat did it do, who did it benefit, wat BC was dat or wat AD was dat. Yes an interesting period dat was yer see . . . On a graph or a chart . . . a date, a date on a map . . . But we go be still here, so go . . . do' come back . . . you have notting ter look back here for . . . I is de watchman.[17]

Through the mode of storytelling, the border becomes an unmapping space, a link in Matura's writing, as the territories of various ethnicities cross and reposition constantly within their changing material relations. In these texts, social and political forces alter the power relations between the various cultural and class divisions. In *Independence* we see this in the context of two moments of transformation in Trinidadian history and culture, while in *as time goes by* we saw these shifts in the context of the working lives, as opposed to the private experiences, of subaltern communities in London. In all these texts, dominant British culture and the diasporic black British culture collide, producing the characteristic tensions of British race relations during the seventies and the eighties.

What is Black?

The dispelling of essentialist ideas of blackness as singular and homogeneous comes into play in all of Matura's plays. In *Party*, for instance, the various black characters emerge with different political positions from indifference (characters A and B) to the moderate (character C) to the left (V) and the radical militancy of Malcolm X and the Black Power movement (as preached by Z). *Party* demonstrates how power roles alter visibly as whites enter Black territory. Within the space of the party, the white middle class and working class and the black working class play out the frictions of race politics, exposing the limitations of both white liberalism and black nationalism within the context of Britain. Sue and P are positioned as committed liberals, supporters of the Anti-Apartheid Movement whose tolerance and solidarity with black people are challenged by Z's violent repudiation of their lip-serving political correctness. Z's oversimplified indictment of hegemonic culture suggests the impasse to be reached on either side of a binary political configuration:

> Well I say their turn has come, because your white God is either a racist or he color blind, or he is just a nice, little excuse for your white liberal conscience. First it was fear of the unknown so you killed, then you killed to convert us to your God of Love, then you killed us because we didn't want to be slaves, now it's God's will, so the poor Black man have to wait until you run out of reasons to kill him. Well my Black god say it is his will that we kill . . . and stop givin' you our blood while you act out your fantasies on us . . . My Black god say you are a savage and a devil and you should be destroyed, chopped up in little pieces and eaten . . . So, you take your nice convenient little white God, and ask to help yer, and you tell him you don't think it's right that all these Black people should suffer and see what he says, and come and tell me if you find me.[18]

This diatribe drives Sue to betray her own deep prejudices concealed beneath the façade of her liberal politics by calling Z a 'Black beast.' By juxtaposing white liberalism against a range of political positions under the rubric 'Black,' *Party* attempts to complicate the idea of blackness, albeit in a somewhat reductive manner.

In *Party*, Miles Davis, Nelson Mandela, Malcolm X and the Black Power movement become the key points of reference for white British culture to negotiate. Islam and Z's 'Black God' are the worldviews against which Sue's feeble liberalism contends. The 'holy waters of the Thames' is repositioned according to Z's mapping of London as 'Holy what it full a shit and dead people, that's what it full a.' In this unmapping space what gets foregrounded are the other narratives of the black struggle invoked through the signifying dashiki Z wears. Z says:

> Yer ever see that film report on the Black people starving and dying, their ribs sticking out, their veins bursting, their eyes staring and dead, their legs shot off, their limbs dangling, young babies turn grey with hunger, Black people being clubbed and shot, herded like animals?

South Africa, Biafra, and Guinea become the extended centers in Z's life within the borders of Britain, where 'Blackness' signifies resistance and revolution, alongside the contradictions of daily existence. As Z's narrative suggests, the borders too are multiple and dispersed, incorporating both essentialized and hybridized constructions of 'Blackness.' Z's rhetoric of black nationalism constructs a totalizing view of both struggle and resistance, while his own position and affiliations are constantly shifting within his narrative as he vacillates between vulgar Marxist stances, radical black politics, sexist overtures, and the disempowering utopia of hashish. Likewise, in Matura's other texts, imagined centers and borders collide and alter each other, as the imagined communities of ex-colonial African and Asian peoples are further framed within their political, class, and cultural locations, in the manner that *Party* demonstrates.[19]

As noted earlier, borders are tenuous locations in Matura's plays, as they blur the distinctions between here and 'back home' at one level, while demarcating very clear boundaries at other levels, such as gender politics. They become the site of hybridity, the *bricolage* of colliding codes. In a sense they occupy the imagined space of being, as they construct within the confines of their neighborhood the projections of home, self, nation, family, and culture, always 'quite but not quite' English or Trinidadian in the case of the first-generation immigrant characters in *Party* and *as time goes by*.[20] The syncreticism of these borders is simultaneously fractured by contradictions. Postcolonial black British subjectivities play out the ambivalences of living in England while retaining aspects of their culture, though in a radically altered form. They multiply their politics depending on their class and gender locations, and in turn construct independent notions of what nation or 'home' means.

To elaborate: the three texts discussed above all raise issues of dislocation, identity, nationality, and the problem of belonging, but in gender-specific ways. The characters with power in these texts are predominantly heterosexual men; therefore, their projections of self, culture, and 'home' are constructed along lines that are parallel to rather than conjoining with gender. Let me return to *as time goes by* to expand upon what becomes symptomatic of Matura's and, by extension, of black British, playwriting of the seventies.

Immigrant postcolonial culture in *as time goes by* is primarily articulated through the voice of black men, while the black women in the text are relegated to the background as mere appendages to the men's lives. A reading of the projections of England in *as time goes by* reveals rifts along gender lines. For Ram, the Trinidadian of Asian descent, England is the site of masquerade where anonymity has earned him the freedom to transform himself from what Trinidadian society expected of him to what he enjoys doing: being a self-appointed counselor and holy man. Masquerade allows Ram entry into white culture, but only as a commodity, the shaman who can sell a quick fix, be it spirituality or drugs, for 'de hippies,' 'dem long hair people who does wear den funny kinda clothes.' For Batee, on the other hand, who is a Trinidadian Hindu, England means the four walls of her kitchen, while home, family, and the feeling of belonging are firmly rooted in the island she has emigrated from: 'I dying ter go back home, it too cold de people don't like me, dey tink we is dirt an' de treat we like dirt . . . how yer could like a place like dat?' Further on Batee says, 'A don't have ter go nowhere ter know dey don't like we . . . but one place dey carn't touch me is in my kitchen. Dat's de only place I safe because is mine.'[21] Batee is rendered powerless by being entirely dependent on her husband. By contrast, the Trinidadian women of Afro-Caribbean descent, Thelma and Una, are constructed as dependent and subordinate but with more social leverage. Batee is simultaneously constructed as Asian and 'black' within British culture. Finally, for 'Auntie Ruby' back in Trinidad, England has all the classic colonial associations, as she sends word that she still waits for Ram to send her 'de picture a Buckingham Palace . . . an' one a de Queen.' England, India, and Trinidad are constructed differently by different individuals, depending on the fictions or partial facts they want to perpetuate. Culture, in that sense, emerges as the crucial marker of distinct affiliations; the differences within border cultures demarcate the ways in which alliances are or might be made.

The excess of mimicry and the contradictions of such a position in the construction of nation or home become more explicit in the instance of the black skinhead boy in *as time goes by*. Skinhead, a second generation black British, exemplifies the generational gap and the problems of British identity. While Skinhead's father Albert is a Trinidadian immigrant working in Britain who remains very much on the periphery of British culture, Skinhead is more working-class than black in the way he initially positions himself. His preference for reggae, his refusal to join the British Army, and rejection of all his father's working-class aspirations put him into a new category of what it means to be British in postcolonial Britain. For Skinhead, home is neither in Trinidad, which he has neither seen nor in which he has any immediate interest, nor white Britain, which offers him no clear place in the new emerging post-empire society of the seventies. Skinhead's own politics are ambivalent as he adopts the codes of the very sections

of society that are known to be racist and xenophobic. Such contradictions serve to problematize further the notions of identity and
nationhood, for Skinhead clearly falls outside the dominant discourses
of cultural and racial homogeneity of the nation-state in Britain.[22]

With such a proliferation of identities and cultures, Matura's
depiction of border cultures in effect constructs these spaces through a
series of centers, where the Sikh's Gurudwara, the Muslim's mosque,
the Jew's synagogue and the Christian's church may all be located.[23]
The idea of the border is continually redefined within what informally
separates 'us,' the 'authentic British,' from 'them,' the changing faces of
Britain, as communities create multiple focal points of interest and
exchange. Borders deterritorialize the city and reconfigure space into
new relationships in the housing estates, the suburbs, and the Afro-
Caribbean and Asian areas of Britain.

Positioned as outsiders from the inside, charting the arrivals and
departures of expatriate life, the storytellers in these texts inevitably
have to come to terms with the limits of their own self-conceptions, as
Ram and Batee in *as time goes by* demonstrate. England is inscribed
within these narratives as the border that has to be crossed, coming
from or going 'back home.' In *as time goes by*, the title itself implies the
inherent state of flux which for Ram becomes a useful phrase to
describe the condition of things to his ex-colonial, working-class
clients, as well as to his flower-power clients. As time goes by, the
borders become centered, acquiring roots, as occurs with Albert and
his son Skinhead. As time goes by, the expatriates will become
immigrants, and in turn will alter the culture around them.

While dispersed in their narrative strategies, these plays both
transform and are inflected by mainstream British culture of the
seventies. In Matura's plays, the legacies of colonialism, neocolonialism and the projects of cultural imperialism are the knowns that are
given materiality in the writing, contextualized within the local and
global politics of living on an island, be it colonial or independent,
Trinidad or Britain. The visible military presence of US and British
forces in postindependence Trinidad in *Play Mas*, the exploitation of
'Third World' countries as fodder for multinational corporations in
Meetings, and the struggle for power and legal rights by the black
communities in Britain in *My enemy* instance the multiple ways in
which this dynamic is enacted. The hybrid spaces in this writing from
the borders suggest the variety of these cultures and their impact upon a
hitherto uncontested British identity. Matura's texts explore this
syncretic culture to propose a heterogenous concept of Englishness by
disclosing those people and locations inside metropolitan Britain and

its former colonies who had remained largely hidden from mainstream representations. Their project is to infuse a measure of 'blackness' into the infamously lily-white (and red and blue) Union Jack.

Notes

1. References to Mustapha Matura's plays are to the following editions: *as time goes by & Black Pieces* (London: Calder and Boyars, 1972); *Play Mas, Independence & Meetings* (London: Methuen, 1982).

2. Mustapha Matura, *as time goes by*, p. 9.

3. Ibid., p. 12.

4. See Manthia Diawara, 'Popular Culture and Oral Traditions in African Film,' *Film Quarterly*, vol. 41, no.3 (Spring 1988), pp. 6–7. Diawara discusses the oral tradition in the context of African cinema. This cultural tradition emerged in syncretic forms within the Afro-Caribbean and Black British spaces.

5. 'Matura, *as time goes by*, p. 59.

6. Shabnam Grewal, Jackie Kay, Liliane Landor, Gail Lewis and Pratibha Parmar, *Charting the Journey: Writings by Black and Third World Women* (London: Sheba Feminist Publishers, 1988), pp. 1–6.

7. Mustapha Matura, *Independence*, p. 70.

8. For primarily oral cultures, the spoken was still an important link in the exchange of information during colonial occupation, especially with literacy being available only to privileged natives. Recognizing this, the women of the Sistren Theater Collective in Jamaica have done extensive work in exploring their oral history by speaking for themselves through informal and oral modes of communication; see Sistren, with Honor Ford Smith, *Lionheart Gal* (London: Sister Vision, 1987). The collective is composed of women primarily from working-class communities. Similarly, I view Matura's technique of dialog from the borders as having both a contemporary and an archival importance.

9. Matura, *Independence*, pp. 70–71.

10. Ibid., p. 46.

11. Ibid., p. 46.

12. Ibid., p. 55.

13. Ibid., p. 57.

14. Ibid., p. 69.

15. Ibid., p. 67.

16. Ibid., p. 67.

17. Ibid., p. 72.

18. Matura, *as time goes by & Black pieces*, p. 105.

19. Ibid., pp. 93–110.

20. Homi Bhabha, 'Of Mimicry and Men: The Ambivalence of Colonial Discourse,' *October* no. 28 (Spring 1984), p. 126. Bhabha argues that the discourse of mimicry is constructed around an ambivalence and that in order to be effective, 'mimicry must continually produce its slippage, its excess, its difference.' Bhabha states that colonial mimicry is 'the desire for a reformed, recognizable Other, as a subject of a difference that is almost the same, but not quite.'

21. Matura, *as time goes by*, pp. 82–3.

22. Paul Gilroy, *There Ain't No Black In the Union Jack* (London: Century Hutchinson, 1987). Gilroy's work contextualizes British race politics of the seventies and the eighties.

23. See Salman Rushdie, 'Handsworth Songs,' in *Imaginary Homelands* (New York: Penguin, 1991), p. 117.

10

Piercings
Marianna Torgovnick

The Video

Performance artist Monte Cazazza has made a video of his own genital piercing. There are no titles or credits. We go right to a close-up of a circumcised penis, totally flaccid, lying amid a tangle of pubic hair against a white thigh. Electronic music erupts, punctuated by the word 'surgeon,' repeated over and over in a robotic, heavily synthesized voice. The music increases in sound level and pace, but ceases to be noticed about twenty seconds into the five-minute video.

A hand holding a metallic, needlelike device enters the frame, wielded by an unseen operator. The needle pierces the head of the penis, leaving behind a single, small gold stud, a rounded ball identical to those used to pierce ears in malls all over the United States. The head of the penis, now adorned by the ball, is displayed to the camera for perhaps five seconds, then the penis is flipped over and an identical procedure is performed two to three times more, at the head and along the shaft, still to the rhythmic chant 'surgeon.'

Then, in a sequence that prompts a collective gasp from the audience, a tweezerlike device descends upon the head of the penis, pulling it out like cotton candy further than anyone would have imagined the glans penis could be extended. The organ is pretty much a visual object by now, except that the perception of it as penis is what prompts the deep collective gasp.

Now a broader needle, almost a lance, enters the taffy-shaped, stretched and narrowed head of the penis; it makes a hole clear through, into which a metal bolt is inserted and secured at each end by a gleaming metal hemisphere. For reasons I can't explain there is no blood, even though the video is in a grainy-textured color.

The procedure completed, the penis is once again arranged on the thigh, as at the beginning of the video. For a few seconds, we are asked to admire the new adornments, the difference from the beginning. Then the camera pans up, to the performance artist's face. He is grinning and mouthing some words at us that are inaudible since the sound track consists only of music. But he seems to be saying 'It was great, man. Unbelievable.' I'm inclined to believe him, even as I feel a distinct sense of repulsion.

The Background

The video was shown at a conference at which I was one of the speakers, a conference organized by jewelry-makers and craftspeople at the University of the Arts in Philadelphia. It is part of a quasi-underground phenomenon known as 'piercing,' which was on every-body's mind at this conference, whose subject was modern primitivism in the crafts, and especially in jewelry-making. Many of the particip-ants, students and artists alike, had multiple ear or nose piercings and (I now suspect), sometimes more.

After my lecture, the night before, on primitivism and covert sadistic images in Man Ray's photographs, I was swamped by private questions. Perhaps thirty people came up after the public question period and waited their turn – an unusual post-lecture turnout. Several of the students at the university (both undergraduate and graduate) said my talk raised questions for them about piercing – a practice for which their amply decorated ears and (in some cases) noses testified at least a qualified support. One member of the audience later presented me with a special issue of Re-Search called Modern Primitives and devoted to the contemporary arts of piercing and tattooing, especially on or around the genitals: a full regalia of penis and testicle piercing, labia and clitoris piercing, and nipple piercing for both sexes.

I answered the question of whether piercing was a form of primitivism with a qualified 'yes.' Yes, it alluded to certain practices in parts of Africa, the South Pacific and Indian Ocean regions, and the Americas. But it also had a heavy overlay of Western associations: with pirates and buccaneers, with motorcycle gangs, with gays and lesbians, and with adolescent 'gang' piercings of ears with needles, popular at girls' sleepovers. I pointed out as well that, so far as I knew, no African group pierced the genitals for decorative purposes, and relatively few groups elsewhere were known to have decorated them with tattoos, or scarification – subjects also treated in the *Modern Primitives* volume. That volume claims that both piercing and tattooing were common in the past and are still widespread among certain groups around the Indian Ocean. These claims appear to be at least partially true.

I have found, for example, passing references to genital tattooing of women in Malinowski's ethnographies, and selected scholarly references to piercing practices, especially in societies in the Indian Ocean.[1] James Boon describes the exotic Balinese custom of inserting bells in the penis.[2] *The Blood of Kings* documents instances of ritual bloodletting from ancient Mayan culture that include bloodletting from the penis. Anthropologists have studied Hindu rituals in Sri Lanka that entail various forms of bodily mutilation.[3] In archaic societies, initiation rituals frequently include bodily mutilation (sometimes of the genitals) that is intended (scholars say) to imitate death and confirm the mature being's awareness and acceptance of it.[4] These initiation rituals seem to me closest in spirit to postmodern piercing and I will return later to them. The best-documented instances among the Maya, the Hindus, and archaic peoples function, however, in specific and organized religious systems that make them quite different from examples in contemporary primitivism.

It is difficult both to uncover and to assess information on a touchy subject like this one. The motivations of those who discuss these topics, and those who do not, are often suspect. The basic fact remains: in traditional societies, piercing for decorative or ritual purposes, or both, while common, is usually confined to ears and noses; scarification and tattooing are usually limited to faces, chests, backs, and (in some cases) navels. The current vogue for genital piercing is a postmodern phenomenon, with affinities to, but not completely traceable from, primitive peoples. Its motivations are often more narcissistic than religious and, even when religious, generally operate outside any traditional or organized religious systems.

I knew that the next speaker, Lonette Stinich, an editor, clothing designer, and artist, planned to speak critically about piercing in ways she anticipated that her student audience would not want to hear. Her lecture turned out to be more complicated than that brief description indicated. This woman, brilliant but highly eccentric, provided some startling insights into piercing as a phenomenon. Since I heard her talk, I have read several accounts of piercing in the popular press, where the phenomenon is usually sanitized (omitting, for example, genital piercing) or treated as an amusing fad.[5] Stinich's approach is both more unflinching and more profound than anything I have seen on the subject in the popular press, and so I summarize it here.

Stinich's Lecture

Lonette Stinich, at the time an editor at *New Art Examiner*, supports herself mostly by her paintings, for which she has a waiting list of commissions. She sells her work according to her patrons' needs and ability to pay. Yuppies get charged around $5,000 and told that she might sell a similar painting to a student or street person for as little as $50. All her patrons agree to a price range and then decide what they will actually pay after the work is completed. This method tallies with her political past, in which she established a communal crafts store based on the same principle of bartered prices, and issued political manifestos in handouts distributed at parks and train stations. Lonette has been into piercing, but in this talk (reaching back to her degrees in ethics from the University of Chicago and Harvard) she was interested in the question of when piercing ceases to be an acceptable form of private expression and becomes a troubling public phenomenon. She clearly feels that the line – which she is unable to draw absolutely – has been crossed.

My notes from her lecture turn up the following arresting thoughts or phrases, which I give in the order she gave them, with no more attempt to order them than she did:

- Piercing is a 'modern ritual acted out in seclusion from the modern world and yet conditioned by it.'

- 'Committed' piercers mean to represent the ugliness or decline of the modern world and are connected to surrealism, expressionism, and dada – earlier movements anchored in a protest against cultural decay.

- Piercing is a withdrawal into being 'a magical person' but also into a 'blank wall of subjectivity.'

- Piercing also represents a form of 'compulsive transgression' and 'alternative culture provincialism.'

- Piercing wants a return to mystery, to the body, and to sensations; it evokes initiatory moments.

- Piercing seeks a crossing of the mineral with the living.

- Piercing sanctifies blood and marks; the body is the 'woof' for such practices as scarification and piercing.

- Piercing contains the danger of morbidity or selfish isolation.

- Modern primitives turn the body into a boutique item.

The Ethics of Piercing

What would motivate a man in the United States today to pierce his penis? A woman her clitoris? Or either the highly sensitive tissue of the nipple? The impulse might be decorative, but the hidden location immediately suggests that something more, something deeper, is involved. The decorative value of the piercing could only be experienced in a setting (a beach or nudist gathering, or certain clubs) in which the chest or genitals could be freely displayed. It could also exist as a highly charged erotic moment at an initial undressing. But here the mind reels with further questions.

What is the ethics of lovemaking in a pierced relationship? Are the studs, rings, and bolts removed – like rings in adulterous lovemaking? Or would the removal defeat the point, the purpose, the motivation for the piercing? For pain is what the piercing evokes, although pain in no simple form. For the piercer the pain would be momentary, as fleeting as that involved in ear piercing, though perhaps more fraught with concerns of infection. Is the pain reactivated during sexual contact? Or is the sensation then transferred to the sexual partner, especially when it is the penis that has been pierced and adorned at the head with studs and bolts? Is heightened sensation for the partner the motivation – and if so, is it heightened pain or heightened pleasure? Or are pain and pleasure pretty much the same for everyone involved? I learned after writing this paragraph that the piercers in the *Modern Primitives* volume unequivocally attribute heightened sexual pleasure for the pierced person and lovers as a motivation for piercing.

Is the piercer motivated by hatred – self-hatred or hatred of the culture – as some people suggest? Or is love the motivation – self-love unto narcissism or love for minerals and metals unto love of the flesh or cosmos? Is the piercing a desire to test and transcend the flesh – as in the Native American rituals enacted by Modern Primitives that also form part of the piercing phenomenon: long hours without water in the sun, suspended by the chest tendons, as some Native Americans used to be for initiation? Is piercing related to Christian images of crucifixion or martyrdom: Saint Sebastian riddled by arrows, the Mexican Saint Julian crisscrossed by lances, Saint Theresa receiving the power of divinity, kneeling at the feet of Bernini's spear-bearing, leering angel?

Are these parables of decay or of transcendence – counter-cultural, religious, or both?

What of the element of performance? Cazazza being pierced without the camera is different from Cazazza being pierced for the video. The video preserves the 'ing' in 'piercing': it repeats the moment of pain that would otherwise be lost once the wound is healed, the ring or bolt installed. The video solves what must be a common problem for the piercer: the desire to have the marks seen competes with taboos against genital display in our culture.

All these questions lead back to the ethics of piercing evoked in Stinich's often brilliant observations – with the term 'ethics' meaning for her and for me the principles (whether stated or not) that govern individual or group actions. The term 'ethics' is, admittedly, a term open to 'moral' considerations and standards of reaction and evalua-tion. Yet Stinich was not narrowly or prescriptively moralistic in her approach – and I would like to avoid being moralistic as well.

The first issue raised is precisely the decorative, display element of piercing, the disjunction between the private and the public. In modern American culture, piercing serves private needs. There is no imperative, except within a few small subcultures – a point to which I will return – to pierce or be pierced. Indeed, the piercing marks a difference from the majority culture: one earring per ear – sure – or even one nose stud, plus earrings. Even two or three earrings per ear function within the limits of what is considered normal. But five or six earrings, plus nose ring, make some statement of difference, mark some allegiance to what is now mostly a youthful or outsider experience. And when we suspect genital piercing, an important line has been crossed between decoration for private purposes and an action designed to make some kind of statement.

In its extreme, especially its public, forms, like Cazazza's video, piercing functions inevitably as ritual, by which I mean a stylized, repeatable action with a public dimension, an action designed to give order and meaning to the flux of experience. Cazazza's video and the testimony in the *Modern Primitives* volume make this point quite clear. The video repeats the word 'surgeon,' but it sounds like 'searching,' a word that immediately prompts the question 'searching for what?' Searching to be sure for the right spot for the piercing. But searching perhaps for the ritual itself, for the things that will get to the essential – the difference between living flesh and mineral or, perhaps, the alliance between both. These are rituals in a Dionysiac mode, not the routinized rituals of so many contemporary churches. Like certain art movements, they attract people who think of themselves as anti-bourgeois, as outsiders in contemporary culture.

Decay as art; the body as found object: one sees, immediately as Stinich says the words, the connection between piercing and surrealism and dada (including writers affiliated at times with the surrealists, such as Bataille) – though also a difference. The surrealists and dadaists mostly wrought upon canvas, or in print, or upon objects: they knew the difference between flesh and matter, and rarely asserted the body itself as art, although (as in Man Ray's photographs) the body could become art's constitutive formal elements. In related avant-garde movements, such as futurism, the reduction of bodies to inanimate matter or physical forces occurs in theory, but not in a fully realized way in the art.[6] In recent decades we have been more open to body art, more obsessed with the body. So perhaps, for performance artists, piercing was an inevitable next step – the logical conclusion of trends under way at least since the sixties.

Naked Charlotte Moorman playing her cello in darkened spaces once sent me into spasms of uncontrollable laughter when a moose call pierced the concert hall along with the strokes of a strobe lamp. I have never been able to explain or forget that moment – very late sixties, very surreal. Something similar is involved in piercing when it becomes public display, but it is not the subconscious that is moved, nor is one affected in quite so inexplicable a way. We know that what is being touched is the alliance of pain and the erotic. We know that what is being evoked are rituals of pain that aim at the transcendent.

The term 'Modern Primitives' for advanced piercers is both unfortunate and apt. What is evoked in stringing people up by their chest tendons is Native American rituals. The actions are the same, whether performed by Native Americans, now or in the past, or by men who are not Indians. But there is, and must be, gaps between the meanings of such acts when performed in different contexts: the Plains in the early nineteenth century; a Native American reservation in the late twentieth century; a late twentieth-century white man's city apartment or wilderness campsite.

Practices of genital piercing are not as widely publicized in anthropological literature as the African rituals they evoke – specifically the village rituals of adolescent male circumcision and (for some groups) adolescent female clitorectomy. These practices have held a special fascination for Western ethnographers and have been well documented.[7]

In African villages, circumcision was usually a collective rite, at a specified point in a man's life, a form of bonding with his cohort and also a sign that he would be leaving the cohort to establish new alliances, in marriage for example. The same was true of female clitorectomy, a subject that I, as a female, find harder to contemplate since it limits sexual pleasure, as circumcision does not. Moreover, circumcision is common in our culture (though for infants, not youths), while clitorectomy is exceptional. What is being sought in contemporary piercing is a new form of community – based on holes and jewelry inserted in various parts of the body. We who are pierced are one. We are one as tribal villagers are one. We recognize each other and are recognized as different from the mass. We establish our difference from the norm – hint at it with the multiple pieces we wear in our ears and noses, confirm it with the pieces we wear in 'private' zones we have willed into public speech. Modern Primitive piercing privatizes what was once communal in an attempt to regain the communal. It eroticizes what was never simply erotic. And that eroticization bespeaks one ethical dilemma raised by contemporary forms of piercing. So does the incommensurability between the public and approved quality of the traditional ritual (adults, after all, orchestrating the event and proud of their young passing into adulthood) and the furtive quality of current piercing (its arbitrary timing, its separation from adult and, almost certainly, parental approval).

'Compulsive transgression,' Lonette Stinich said. It is the nature of the 'compulsion' that makes contemporary piercing ethically problematic. That, and the way a social form of entrance (such as African circumcision) is converted into a ritual of exit, 'transgression.' What does it say when one culture (our own) borrows so freely and loosely from others? What does it say when rituals affirming overall communal continuity become something else – the establishment of fringe communities? Does this promote decay or forestall it? Create meaning or deny it? Or is piercing all more trivial than that – is it merely what Stinich called 'alternative culture provincialism,' a fad and a fashion similar to wearing Indian clothing or African jewelry?

Among people who teach the students practicing piercing, one view commonly recurs, always to be dismissed a little uneasily: the extensive body piercing is like long hair and beards in the sixties; it's just the kids' way of protesting, of marking themselves as different. Often the people advancing the view then trail off into a sense that something *is* different – that the kids are filled with self-hatred, not self-love, that they shave their hair and wildly color it and pierce their genitals in a rage of despair, over drugs, over their parents' divorces, over their lives. So the comforting argument that it's just the sixties all over again, but in different terms, does not work. It is not just kids' rebellion. Nor is it just peer pressure that makes people get pierced – though when peer pressure does operate, that is surely a factor making contemporary piercing ethically problematic. But peer pressure is not the major issue – it is a red herring.

Mineral and flesh. Life force or death force. The matter-of-fact acquaintance with death that is at stake in archaic initiation rituals. That is the real issue. Piercing gets to us because it gets to these issues, and we suspect that contemporary piercing favors the death force, something repressed and feared in our culture. It is not just kids, and, even if it were, the kids might not be all right, but they *would* be right in picking this way to get under *our* skin.

Prince Alberts

In the month after the crafts conference, during which I began work on this essay, I found myself repeatedly telling people about what I had learned – a contemporary Ancient Mariner with a postmodern tale. My auditors did not disappoint. Like the wedding guest in Coleridge's poem, they were fascinated despite themselves. They had a universal interest and, sometimes, bits and pieces of information, often gleaned from troublesome teenagers or young adults. For my auditors as for me, and between them and their children, genital piercing was a taboo subject and a transgressive one – that was part of the conversations' zest.

In the *Modern Primitives* volume, published in 1989 as a collection of interviews with people heavily involved in tattooing and piercing practices, the subject plays out quite differently. Though only spotty information is available elsewhere, the volume claims a detailed history for these practices. It matter-of-factly provides names, facts, and distinctions: the Prince Albert is a small hoop on the underside of the head of a penis, named after Victoria's spouse, who reportedly had one; the horizontal penis bolt installled in Cazazza's video is an ampellang similar to those used in areas surrounding the Indian Ocean. A guiche is a ring through the perineum. Mayans, Hindus, French legionnaires, and Europeans during the Middle Ages all practiced forms of genital piercing; which kinds and why they were used are discussed in a cool, historical tone in one section of the volume. This is a world with names, addresses, famous people, and idols. Each section of *Modern Primitives* provides an address for further information to which any reader is welcomed to write.

By the middle of the volume, I found myself, almost against my will, losing the distaste with which I had begun reading it. This effect comes from the reading experience itself; it does not mean that the pictures and text failed to shock me on later viewings. But after spending some time with *Modern Primitives*, I found myself actually admiring the work of tattooer Ed Hardy beyond that of the other tattooers, and believing contributors who described him as inspirational in their lives. I was entering a text where my usual tastes and judgments were temporarily suspended.

To my surprise, all the people represented in *Modern Primitives* have histories and philosophies that are fully coherent and intersect in complicated ways with philosophies in mainstream culture. Several have traveled extensively in New Guinea or Polynesia, living in villages, learning and studying much as ethnographers might. Many have done extensive research and claim ancient precedents for their practices. If these are fringe groups, they are not as nutty as they might at first appear.

Here, for example, is Wes Christensen (described as a painter and scholar of Mayan history) on what piercing means to the male piercer: through genital piercing 'the Male expresses the desire to own the magically fertile menstrual flow by mimicking it, the symbol seems less important than its function of linking the opposing forces of mother/father, sky/earth in one ritual practitioner.'[8] Male piercer and performance artist Genesis P-Orridge invokes a similar mélange of Jung and contemporary desires for androgyny: 'my nipples were a dead zone before they got pierced. Then they became a whole new discovery. It was nice – like being female as well' (p. 176).

The idea of connection to or willful separation from universal images or the images of a culture comes up frequently in these interviews. Tattooer Ed Hardy's interest in tattooing began at age twelve, when he was attracted to the way that tattooers 'were like the Keepers of the Images. They'd have displayed the whole emotional gamut: love and hate and sex and death – all on codified designs that were bright and bold' (p. 52). He sees tattooing as a tribute to the universal and the individual, as 'an affirmation: that this body is yours to have and enjoy' (p. 53). Satanic cultist Anton Lavey agrees that control over the body is the point of such practices, though his accent is less upbeat than Hardy's, stressing separation, not connection, as the point of tattooing: 'if a person feels alienated . . . [and] they didn't happen to be born looking freaky or strange, then activities like getting a tattoo [or piercing] are a way of stigmatizing one's self' (p. 92).

Jewelry-maker Raelyn Gallina sees piercing as a way to move from the alienation stressed by Lavey to the affirmation stressed by Hardy: 'Piercing started at a time in my life when I was experiencing a lot of death, and grief, and transformation. For a lot of people it's a rite of transformation, when they go from one state to the next' (p. 101).[9] Gallina emphasizes that the emotions surrounding the experience must be devoid of violence and filled with trust and support; when that happens, she says, 'A lot of times being cut is a very strengthening and powerful experience' (p. 101). Gallina's statement and others like it were important for me. If there had been no women involved in this phenomenon, or if there had been a sense of violence, especially violence towards women, I would have found it impossible to read the *Modern Primitives* volume at all sympathetically.

The worlds of tattooing and piercing are, then, full and complete, but they are not homogeneous. The tattooers, for example, often regard piercers as adventurers and freaks. Tattooers divide themselves into those who favor single 'Mom'-type tattoos and those (seen as more artistic) who favor overall tribal designs. The tribal design group splits further into those who wear curvilinear patterns and those who wear solid black geometrical patterns. The piercers include those who identify themselves as performance artists and those who identify themselves by their sexual tastes: heterosexual, lesbian, and gay; SM and not SM; in marriages or other long-term partnerships, and not; and various combinations of these. Educational levels and ways of making a living vary. Although some claim them especially for gay male culture, tattooing and piercing belong in fact not to any one group but to a variety of self-defined groups within contemporary culture. They are authentic countercultures, composed of multiple communities. The communities share sets of values and conducts that are understood without necessarily being articulated by their members.

The art students I encountered at the Philadelphia jewelry-makers' conference were mostly kids fascinated by piercing. They do not have the years of study and worked-out philosophies common to the people in *Modern Primitives*. And few seemed to identify absolutely with any of the specific groups mentioned in that volume. Their interest seemed to be more general, based more on a sense that this phenomenon was becoming a part of youth culture. But the students probably sense at some level the appeal of the philosophies behind 'committed' piercing. It is a level at which Prince Alberts and ampellangs exist somewhere between artistic instruments – like acrylics and oils for artists – and sacred ritual – like confession and communion for practicing Catholics.

Art and Life

One could say that piercing and its performative aspect – so vividly expressed in the Cazazza video – test the limits of art and representation, especially what we have come to recognize as body and performance art, by pressing the boundaries of what can and cannot be displayed in museums or other cultural institutions.[10] Most saliently, piercing questions the difference between process and product, action and finished work, permanence, transience, and absence. It reveals how the finished work, the thing reproduced in textbooks and hung in museums –represents an action or process that has occurred in the past and remains a trace or residual element in the finished piece. The artistic process is 'the real thing'; but it can only achieve permanence when embodied in a formal object. The permanent art object memorializes the primary process of creation and thus inevitably announces its own secondariness. In this typically postmodern aesthetic, the objects we fetishize as art always represent but do not coincide with the creative impulse, person, or act.[11]

In this sense, it is tempting to regard piercing as one of a series of postmodern practices that challenge traditional notions of creator and created object, art and thing, museum and memorial. Piercing is art *in* the body, remaining the same even as the body that surrounds it changes and ages. It has a biographical, life-history dimension, like a series of self-portraits from youth to middle age, but it is not separable from the artist's body in the way that Rembrandt's or Van Gogh's self-portraits were. The body becomes not just the subject for the art but its medium and condition; the 'art' or 'mark' travels with the body and is part of it. It dies when the artist dies; it cannot survive the artist except in photographs or narrative accounts. Money may change hands when a piercing or tattooing takes place, but no secondary markets for resale and purchase exist. Only a video or photograph of the piercing or tattooing can have a secondary market or be permanently 'hung' in a museum. Piercing and tattooing resist becoming part of the institutionalized world of high culture. They expose the processing of art as commodity that usually obtains in our culture.

Piercing presses and erodes the boundary between body and thing – an observation that returns us to the most disturbing of Stinich's remarks about the practice. Piercing explores the crossing between mineral and flesh, the contemplation of both on the same plane of being, with equal valuation. This crossing of mineral and flesh has long cultural histories that have always been fraught with double potentialities, some spirit- or life-affirming, some not: Buddhist enlightenment and Freudian death wish.

I find it tempting to assimilate piercing to at least some of these intellectual contexts about the relationship of art and life – tempting, but perhaps not quite right. For that intellectualization evades certain distinctions and questions that I feel to be important – for example, the distinction between 'committed' piercers and faddists or hangers-on. Or the question of what it is legitimate to borrow from other cultures and transform through reenactment. I also sense a 'can you top this?' mentality behind many of these practices that disturbs me and raises further questions. Would, for example, a video of a person's voluntary sterilization be susceptible to analysis as performance art? How about a video of a person's embalming? These prospects return to the morbidity that I sense in these practices and that provoked initial repulsion.

A phenomenon like piercing may not belong in intellectual contexts for other reasons as well. At the moment when piercing enters museums or classrooms, or even an essay like this one, something of its essential motivation is betrayed. We may not want this subject in the official portrait of our culture. But it may reject us more fully than we reject it. And so while I have posed the question of piercings as a question about representation – and represented it, deliberately, in a series of expanding circles – I do not see it as 'simply' or 'merely' about representation in the abstract. I feel it to be – and have wanted you to feel it as – a gut issue.

Notes

1. See Bronislaw Malinowski, *The Sexual Life of Savages* (1929; reprinted Boston: Beacon, 1988), p. 257. For more extensive bibliographic information, see Donald E. Brown, James W. Edwards, and Ruth P. Moore, *The Penis Inserts of Southeast Asia: An Annotated Bibliography with an Overview and Comparative Perspectives*, Occasional Paper Series no. 15 (Berkeley: Center for South and Southeast Asia Studies, 1988).

2. James Boon, *Affinities and Extremes: Crisscrossing the Bittersweet Ethnology of East Indies History, Hindu-Balinese Culture, and Indo-European Allure* (Chicago: University of Chicago Press, 1990).

3. Linda Schele and Mary Ellen Miller, *The Blood of Kings: Dynasty and Ritual in Maya Art* (New York: George Braziller, in association with Kimball Art Museum, Fort Worth, 1986). A sequel to this volume, *The Forest of Kings*, was a Quality Paperback Book Club first-choice selection in March 1991, testifying to the widespread appeal of the topic.

On Hindu ritual in Sri Lanka, see Gananath Obeyeskere, *Medusa's Hair: An Essay on Personal Symbols and Religious Experience* (Chicago: University of Chicago Press, 1981).

4. See, for example, Mircea Eliade, *Myths, Dreams, and Mysteries: The Encounter between Contemporary Faith and Archaic Realities*, translated by Philip Mairet (New York: Harper, 1975); originally published in French in 1957. Eliade sees terror and death imagery as typical of initiations; he reports the flaying of the penis in one group. Although Eliade's structuralist, religious-studies approach to archaic societies overstates similarities and reduces archaic cultures to a single model, I nevertheless find portions of his work locally useful.

5. For a fully sanitized account, see 'Piercing Fad is Turning Convention on its Ear,' *New York Times*, May 19, 1991, Y15. For an account that suppresses ethical issues, see Stanley Miess, 'The Cutting Edge,' *Newsday*, August 21, 1991, pp. 50–51, 70.

6. See, for example, Tommaso Filippo Marinetti, 'The Founding and Manifesto of Futurism,' reprinted in *Marinetti: Selected Writings*, edited by R.W. Flint and translated by R.W. Flint and Arthur A. Coppotelli (New York: Farrar, Straus, and Giroux, 1971).

7. See, for example, Michel Leiris with Jacqueline Delange, *African Art*, translated by Michael Ross, Arts of Mankind series (1967; reprinted London: Thames and Hudson, 1968).

8. V. Vale and Andrea June, eds., *Modern Primitives*, special issue of *Re-Search* (San Francisco: Re-Search publications, 1989), p. 88; hereafter cited parenthetically in the text by page number.

9. The stories of the Hindu mystics in *Medusa's Hair* often reveal a point of personal crisis (a parent's death or a marital crisis) as the point of initiation into trance experiences and body piercing.

10. Piercing resembles the phenomena discussed by Henri Sayre in *The Object of Performance* (Chicago: University of Chicago Press, 1989). The terms in which I discuss it in this section are indebted to his book. Sayre writes about performance arts such as modern dance, landscape art, and (for him, conceptually, the parent of them all) photography. See also Hal Foster, ed., *The Anti-Aesthetic: Essays on Postmodern Culture* (Port Townsend, Washington: Bay Press, 1983).

11. This typically postmodern aesthetic underscores problems and paradoxes that have always resided in art objects and their acquisition of status, value, and the right to permanent display. But these problems and paradoxes have now acquired conscious, conceptual interest.

Index

Printed in the United States
by Baker & Taylor Publisher Services